Joshua Whittaker was born in the West Midlands, England. He is an avid reader of fiction and non-fiction books, but he also enjoys the odd comic book and graphic novel every now and then. From a young age, he was a big fan of sci-fi and fantasy books, not to mention movies, then later in his life, he also developed an interest in horror. He also enjoys anime and true-life stories. His family and friends are an important part of, his life. He enjoys spending time with them, attending the cinema, going to restaurants, and going on days out. Some of his favourite authors include but are not limited to people such as H.P. Lovecraft, Edgar Allan Poe, J.K. Rowling, and Frank Herbert. Other books written by Joshua Whittaker include *The Menagerie*. The author identifies himself as bisexual.

Dedicated to my loving and caring sister, Alice Whittaker.

Joshua Whittaker

SOMETHING IN THE SKY

UFO Sightings and Reports from
Across the UK

AUSTIN MACAULEY PUBLISHERS™

LONDON * CAMBRIDGE * NEW YORK * SHARJAH

A CIP catalogue record for this title is available from the British Library.

ISBN 9781035836079 (Paperback)
ISBN 9781035836086 (Hardback)
ISBN 9781035836109 (ePub e-book)
ISBN 9781035836093 (Audiobook)

www.austinmacauley.com

First Published 2024
Austin Macauley Publishers Ltd®
1 Canada Square
Canary Wharf
London
E14 5AA

I want to thank my publishers Austin Macauley Publishers, and everybody who contributed to making this book what it is now. By doing this, they have helped turn my dream into a reality. I also want to thank you, the reader, for purchasing this book.

Introduction

I thought it would be interesting to write this book as I live in the UK and you don't really hear that much about UFOs in the UK, so when I began writing this book, I was shocked to find many more UFO sightings and reports than I imagined there would be.

My goal with this book was to gather as much information as I could find about UFO sightings and reports from all across the UK and compile these sightings from all around the UK into this book but I wanted to make this book easy to understand and read so that anyone at almost any reading level would be able to understand and get a grasp on the information held within these pages so don't expect a meaty in-depth analysis on the UFO phenomenon this is just a quick and easy to read a book that is laid out in a bullet-point format but not only this by writing this book I wanted to bring more attention to the UFO subject as I feel that it is not being talked about as much as it should be and by writing this book I also wanted to highlight the fact that the UK does indeed have many documented reports and sightings of UFOs not just America.

When writing this book, I did not have access to The National Archives and the information they have on UFOs.

Nearly all the UFO sightings and reports contained within this book are documented cases that were taken by the MOD (Ministry of Defence).

I have been obsessed with UFOs for as long as I can remember the earliest memory I have of UFOs is when I was in primary school me and my brother would go into the back garden and lay down on sun loungers my brother owned a book that had many pictures of UFOs in it and in the book beneath each picture it explained what the UFO looked like and what the UFO could do as well as were the UFO was most sited I remember one time me and my brother went out to the garden one time with binoculars and the UFO book I thought I saw one but as I looked closer it was just a plastic bag floating very high in the clouds but as I grew up I became more enamoured with UFOs which lead me to write this book I have since had two encounters with UFOs the first one was when I was writing this book I had just finished the final chapter when I went downstairs into the kitchen and as I looked outside the window I saw a very bright white flashing and pulsating circular light then the next morning a black helicopter was circling the area where I saw the UFO the next encounter I had was on bonfire night and all my family was with me and saw them we looked while waiting for a firework to go off and saw several bright white star dot shaped objects whizzing and speeding in all directions at very fast speeds.

12th Century

- 1113: Religious pilgrims in the south west of England reported seeing a glowing, fire-belching "dragon" emerge from the sea, fly into the air, and disappear into the sky.

13th Century

- January 1254: In St Albans, England, a scribe wrote of a glowing floating light. This is some of what the scribe wrote: "In the serene sky and clear air, with stars shining and the moon eight days old, there suddenly appeared in the sky a kind of large ship elegantly shaped, well equipped, and of marvellous colour."

- 1290: The Friars of Byland Abbey described seeing "a flat, round, shining silvery object" flying overhead of them.

20th Century

1940s

- February 1942: A woman named Eileen Arnold was walking down Cheltenham High Street in the UK when she suddenly experienced an altered state of consciousness as she became "tuned into another reality." She became aware of a large oval shape moving slowly above the rooftops. She stated that it radiated light from holes in its side and had quills which detached one by one, also emitting light. Following this encounter, Eileen believed she had had numerous psychic experiences.

- September 1942: A man named Albert Lancaster believed he was abducted by aliens while working as a guard at a radar site near Newbiggin-by-the-Sea in Northumberland in the UK. He claimed to have had a sudden urge to go outside, followed by a "strange impulse to look at the sky." He claims he saw a glowing light surrounded by dark mist and, assuming it to be a German weapon, went to raise the alarm before being struck by a beam of light from the cloud, followed by a floating sensation, and then becoming aware he was back at his post. After this experience, he believed he had psychic powers for a period of time.

- 5 August 1944: Newly released reports suggest that Winston Churchill banned the reporting of this incident out of fear that it could or would create mass panic. Reports given to Winston Churchill claimed the incident involved a Royal Air Force (RAF) reconnaissance plane returning from a mission in France or Germany. Allegedly, when flying over or near the English coastline, the aircraft was suddenly intercepted by a strange metallic object that matched its course and speed for a time before accelerating away and disappearing. The plane's crew was reported to have photographed the object, which they said had "hovered noiselessly" near the aircraft before moving off. According to the documents, details of the cover-up emerged when a man wrote to the government in 1999, seeking to find out more about the incident. He described how his grandfather, who served with the RAF in the Second World War, was present when Churchill and U.S. General Dwight Eisenhower discussed how to deal with the UFO encounter.

1950s

- 1 June 1950: A Gloster Meteor at RAF Tangmere passes a flying saucer lit up with lights, described as "Britain's first flying saucer." The object was reported to be "shining, revolving, and disc-like" at 20,000ft at 14:30, flying eastwards over the Portsmouth area. RAF Tangmere asked the radar station at RAF Wartling in Sussex if it had seen the object, and it had on its PPI (Plan Position Indicator) screen. It led to the setting up of the Flying Saucer Working Party.

- 14 August 1950: A 50 ft-diameter disc UFO is seen over the Royal Aircraft Establishment (RAE) at 11:27 by an experienced pilot, Flight Lieutenant (Flt Lt) Hubbard. He claimed to have seen another object on the 5th of September, 1950 at 16:09.

- 26 August 1950: In the early hours of the morning, a 20-year-old woman was walking back to her home in the village of Stanton Drew in Somerset from a party when she decided to take a shortcut through a field near the stone circles, she heard a buzzing sound, she turned to her left, and noticed a bright saucer-shaped object hovering over the next field. A door on the craft began to open, and she screamed, started to run, and did not stop until she got home.

- 14–25 September 1952: On the 19th of September at 10:53, a silver disc-shaped object followed a Gloster Meteor returning to RAF Topcliffe and was seen by observers on the ground. It rotated whilst hovering. It then travelled towards the west at high speed. On the 21st of September, Six RAF planes followed a spherical object over the North Sea. It followed one of the planes back to the base. It was the front-page headline on the 20th of September 1952 in the Yorkshire Evening Press.

- 21 October 1952: Two RAF pilots in a Gloster Meteor saw three disc-shaped objects at 35,000ft.

- 9 October 1953: Two British European Airways (BEA) pilots flying from London to Paris saw a saucer object over the English Channel for thirty minutes in an Airspeed Ambassador, Former RAF pilot Captain Peter Fletcher, of Putney, had taken off at 9:00 from London Airport.

- 3 November 1953: Terry Johnson and Geoffery Smythe, in an RAF de Havilland Vampire, saw a UFO over RAF West Malling.

- 29 June 1954: A BOAC (British Overseas Airways Corporation) pilot in a Boeing 377 Strat cruiser sees seven UFOs when travelling back from New York to London over the North Atlantic at 17:03 on Flight 510-196 heading for refuelling at CFB Goose Bay, where the pilot saw seven UFOs four hours later near Newfoundland for eighteen minutes at 19,000ft from 01:05 GMT to 01:23 GMT Captain James Howard, aged 33, from Bristol, was a former RAF Bomber Command Squadron Leader on his 265th crossing of the Atlantic, and he was interviewed on July 3, 1954, for the BBC.

- 14 October 1954: Flt Lt James Salandin of the Royal Auxiliary Air Force, flying in a No. 604 Squadron RAF Gloster Meteor F8 from RAF North Weald, narrowly missed two UFOs over Southend-on-Sea at around 16:30 at 16,000ft. The objects were circular, with one being coloured silver and the other gold. He narrowly avoided having a head-on collision with the silver object.

- 17 July 1955 at noon: On King Harold's Way in Bexleyheath in the London Borough of Bexley, a 30-foot-wide saucer-shaped object was seen to hover a few feet above a street in broad daylight by Margaret Fry and her doctor on a very hot, cloudless day. Car engines near the object stalled. It was seen by around thirty people, made a humming noise and landed at the junction of Ashbourne Road and Whitfield Road. It hovered over Bedonwell Primary School for around one minute. It finally shot off into the sky. Another UFO had landed a few streets away at the same time. A similar object had been seen in Bexleyheath in 1952.

- 13 August 1956: 12 to 15 objects were picked up by USAF radar over East Anglia at 12:00. One object was tracked at more than 4,000mph by USAF (United States Air Force) GCA (Ground-Controlled Approach) radar at RAF Bentwaters. The object sometimes travelled in formation, then converged to form a larger object and performed sharp turns. One object was tracked for 26 miles (41.8 kilometres) which then hovered for five minutes, then flew off. One object at 22:00 was tracked at 12,000mph. RAF de Havilland Venoms from RAF Waterbeach had sightings of the objects.

- 22 September 1956: A large, spherical, glass-like, 80-foot-diameter object was seen over the Cleethorpes coast for over an hour and also seen on radar from RAF Manby at 15:00. RAF planes approached the object, and it flew away.

- 4 April 1957: A large object was seen on radar at RAF West Freugh near Stranraer at 50,000ft which was stationary for 10 minutes over the Irish Sea. It moved vertically to 70,000ft and was also tracked by radar at Ardwell. The object made an "impossible" sharp turn and was described as being as large as a ship, bigger than a normal aircraft.

- 20 May 1957: A USAF F-86D Sabre based at RAF Manston intercepted an object over East Anglia.

1960s

- From late spring (19 May) to early summer 1965: Many sightings of UFOs were seen in the Warminster area. Cley Hill, near the town, has since been a place of frequent sightings.

- 28 April 1967: For approximately one hour around 12:00, a dome-shaped object was sighted at about 1,600ft above Brixham in Devon. A door was seen in the side of the object, and it had been spotted by the HM Coastguard station at Berry Head.

- 1967: Clapham Wood in West Sussex experienced a rash of UFO sightings and unexplained events during the 1960s.

- 24 October 1967: At 4:00, PCs (Police Constable) Roger Willey and Clifford Waycott were driving from Holsworthy to Hatherleigh along the A3072. They saw a bright object in the shape of a cross at a tree-top height about 40 metres away. They followed the "pulsating" object for about fifteen minutes along the road at speeds of up to 80mph. The object was described as being star-spangled, like "looking through wet glass." It was joined by a second object at 4:23. A motorist, Mr Christopher Garner of Hatherleigh, had also seen it and thought he was having a nightmare. The object disappeared at around 5:00, having been pursued for fifteen miles. It was attributed to the planet Venus, as were other similar sightings that same month.

- 25 October 1967: Policemen in five cars across East Sussex reported a bright flying cross in the early hours, with the first sighting at 4:45 at Halland. The other sightings were a few minutes later and were also seen in Wales.

- 26 October 1967: 54-year-old Mr Angus Brooks, a former BOAC (British Overseas Airways Corporation) administrator from Owermoigne in Dorset, was walking at 11:25 on Moigns Down near Holworth, close to the Dorset coast, with his two dogs in a force 8 gale and took shelter in a hollow. He then saw a circular translucent craft with a "girder" at the front and three pointing to the rear. The "girders" rearranged to form a cross shape around the central 25 ft-diameter disc and then began to spin. Twenty-two minutes later, the "girders" returned to their original position, and the craft sped off in a northeast direction.

1970s

- September 8, 1970: Captain William Schaffner intercepted an unknown object over the North Sea. His BAC (British Aircraft Corporation) Lightning aircraft was later retrieved from the sea. The pilot, Captain William Schaffner, had disappeared and was presumed dead.

- 1971: It is claimed that unidentified silent crafts were regularly seen by two school children near the coastal village of Muchalls, Scotland (but not in the village itself) from 1971 onwards. These events are alleged to have recurred night after night for many years and are reputed to have continued until at least 1991, when some aspects of the apparitions were also filmed in the area.

- 16 October 1973: It is alleged that Gabriella Versacci was taken on board an alien spaceship near a small village in Somerset, England. She was physically inspected after being strapped to an examination table.

- 23 January 1974: A UFO allegedly crashed in the Berwyn Mountains in Wales. The event coincided with an earthquake.

- June 1976: An official British Airways film taken during one of Concorde's flights over southern England depicts a white light moving around the fuselage of the aircraft.

- 4 February 1977: A cigar-shaped craft is alleged to have landed next to Broad Haven Primary School and witnessed by 14 schoolchildren who saw a silver creature. The head teacher, Ralph Llewellyn, interviewed fifteen children on Monday, February 7, 1977, who all made similar drawings.

- Wednesday, February 16, 1977: At Rhosybol in Anglesey, North Wales, nine children at the Primary School see a mysterious object, and make similar drawings.

- 22 November 1978: At 17:15, Elsie Oakensen of Church Stowe, Northamptonshire, was driving southwards down the A5 from Weedon Bec towards her home. She saw two bright lights, one green and one red, and could make out a dumbbell-shaped object. Turning off the A5 to her village, her recently serviced care cut out twice. She then noticed the sky was black and a brilliant white beam of light was shining on the road ahead, then the sky returned to its normal colour. After the experience, Elsie could not account for 15 minutes of her time.

- 9 November 1979: Bob Taylor, a forestry worker, had an alleged encounter with a UFO in a clearing on Dechmont Law in Livingston, West Lothian. He claimed that the UFO had dragged him along the ground. This is considered to be one of the most significant close encounters in Scotland.

1980s

- 29 November 1980 at 5:00: Police officer Alan Godfrey claims to have been abducted by an alien spacecraft in Todmorden in West Yorkshire. A strange luminescent object had been spotted by other local police officers at the same time.

- 26 December 1980: A series of reported sightings of unexplained lights and objects in the sky and the alleged landing of an extra-terrestrial spacecraft occurred at Rendlesham Forest, Suffolk, in England. It is perhaps the most famous UFO event to have happened in Britain, ranking amongst the best-known UFO events worldwide.

- 12 August 1983: 77-year-old Alfred Burtoo was quietly fishing on the Basingstoke Canal when a UFO landed nearby. Two humanoid beings beckoned him onto their dis-shaped vehicle, and he was medically examined by English-speaking creatures. He was "rejected" by the creatures because he was "too old".

- 26 April 1984: Several people reported a UFO over Stanmore in north-west London, and was seen by two police officers.

- 13 October 1984: Several people see a flying saucer over Waterloo Bridge in London.

- 19 November 1987: At 19:00, a large UFO was seen at close quarters hovering over houses in Brierley Hill.

- 1 December 1987: Philp Spencer (pseudonym), a retired policeman, took a picture on Ilkley Moor, which is claimed to be an alien creature, and then saw a white-coloured craft leaving the area. Under hypnosis, he claimed to have been abducted and medically examined.

1990–2000s

- 4 August 1990 at around 21:00: A diamond object estimated to be 100 feet wide was seen and photographed by two men near Calvine, Perth, and Kinkross, Scotland. It was reported as hovering silently in place for 10 minutes before rising rapidly into the sky.

- 21 April 1991: Airline pilot Achille Zaghetti from Grosseto, Tuscany, in an Alitalia McDonnell Douglas MD-80 on a flight from Milan to Heathrow saw a three-metre-long, khaki-coloured object over Lydd in Kent at 22,000ft about 300m away. It was seen on the radar.

- 1992: James Walker noticed unidentified lights in the sky over Bonny bridge, and the town became the scene of numerous UFO sightings. It forms part of the "Falkirk Triangle", an area stretching from Stirling to Fife and the outskirts of Edinburgh. Ufologists claim that Bonny bridge is the world's number one UFO location, with an average of around 300 sightings a year.

- March 1992: Isabella Sloggett and her daughter Carol were walking towards Bonny bridge and saw a blue light hovering above the road in front of them. A UFO landed, and a door on the craft opened.

- 31 March 1993: Multiple witnesses across the southwest and west England saw a large triangular-shaped UFO speeding across the sky, leaving a luminous wake.

- 26 September 1993: A large black triangle is seen over Bakewell in the Derbyshire Dales at 21:30.

- 19 February 1994: A metallic disc-shaped object was filmed over Craigluscar Reservoir near Dunfermline in Scotland by Ian McPherson.
- 6 January 1995: Pilots aboard a Boeing 737 on British Airways Flight BA5061 from Milan saw an object on their descent to Manchester at 4,000ft when over the southern Pennines. The reports describe a bright fireball.

- 5 October 1996: In the early morning, a rotating UFO was seen over Wash by Skegness and Boston police officers. The visual sightings were explained as celestial objects.

- 2 January 1997 at 20:58: In the town of Immingham in Lincolnshire, a large UFO was seen with all different colours of lights around it. It was stationary for some time, then started moving, making small erratic movements.

- 2 January 1997 at 23:35: In the town of Scunthorpe in North Lincolnshire, an object was seen that continually changed colour; it was described to be a "normal star shape".

- 3 January 1997 at 07:45: In the town of Formby/Liverpool in Merseyside, an oval, cigar-shaped object was seen, and when the object speeded up, the witness could see red and white lights around and underneath it.

- 4 January 1997 at 23:20: In the town of Beith in Ayrshire, witnesses saw circular lights that were indistinct; the object was continually orbiting and tilting.

- 13 January 1997 at 21:00: In the town of Brockton in Staffordshire, someone witnessed one, North Star-sized object with red and green colours; it was brighter than a star and was moving from west to north.

- 13 January at 19:35: In the town of Peacehaven in East Sussex, there was one star-shaped object. It had white, red, and green flickering lights. It was very high and moved very slowly.

- 13 January 1997 at 19:40: In the town of Eynsham in Oxfordshire, one object was seen. It was larger than a plane; it was circular and a greenish colour. It moved faster than a plane and then appeared to fall to the ground.

- 13 January 1997, 19:00: In the town of Watling/Kings Lynn in Norfolk, a witness reported seeing two bright white lights and three green lights in a row, with a red light beneath, these were seen hovering above a field.

- 13 January 1997 at 22:30: In the town of Kessingland/Nr. Lowestoft in Suffolk, someone reported seeing huge lights like a child's sparkler. The object was round and as big as a house, but it emitted no sound.

- 14 January 1997 at 20:00: In the town of Selby in North Yorkshire, someone reported seeing one star-shaped object in the sky. It was multi-coloured, and the object stayed stationary for over two hours.

- 20 January 1997 at 08:00: In the town of Rock/Nr. Kidderminster in Worcestershire, five lights were seen in the sky; these lights then formed into two dashes, one moved off, and then they all disappeared.

- 20 January 1997 at 07:00: In the town of Rochdale in Lancashire, two white lights were seen that were oblong-shaped and very bright. They were heading in every direction.

- 20 January 1997 at 6:55: In the town of Coppull/Nr. Chorley in Lancashire, three lights were seen in a triangular formation; the lights split up and then proceeded in three separate directions at the speed of their car.

- 20 January 1997 at 07:00: In the town of Henley-in-Arden in Warwickshire, a triangle of three stars was seen; one was stationary and the other two were moving at the speed of a plane. They were brilliant white.

- 20 January 1997 at 19:15: In the town of Bradford in West Yorkshire, five round-shaped flashing lights were seen. They were red and white in colour; they separated and went in different directions.

- 20 January 1997 at 19:01: In the town of Invergary in Invernesshire, two flying objects were seen. It was an intermittent light that was flashing red.

- 20 January 1997 at 06:50: In the town of Dartmoor in Devon, two objects that were parallel were seen; they were stationary for about 10 seconds, they moved away at speed, and then became brighter.

- 20 January 1997 at 16:45: In the town of Norwich in Norfolk, a green light was seen in the sky. It moved in a curve, falling silent as it went.

- 20 January 1997 at 01:00: In the town of Woodford Green in Essex, three triangular objects were seen in the sky. They were bright white but also turned red, green, and orange. They moved on the spot and then zoomed off.

- 20 January 1997 at 19:45: In the town of Caernarfon Bay in Caernarfonshire, a huge blue fast object was seen in the sky. There was a cloud of smoke in the sky, and it made the ground shake.

- 24 January 1997 at 03:10: In the town of Hainault in Essex, a round glowing object was seen with a dome on top, and underneath it, it had portholes and glowed white and yellow. After a few seconds, it disappeared.

- 24 January 1997 at 19:05: In the town of Spey Bay Beach/Moray in Morayshire, one large, semi-circular-shaped object was seen. It was a very vivid blood-red-orange colour similar to a street light. The object was stationary and then began to move.

- 24 January 1997 at 20:07: In the town of Longfield in Kent, three very bright objects were seen pulsating; they were white, green, and yellow. These objects sometimes moved in a triangular formation.

- 24 January 1997 at 19:00: In the town of Spey Bay in Morayshire, one object was seen. It was a bright red/orange colour with a bright light emanating from it as the object was moving downward.

- 25 January 1997 at 21:00: In the town of Huddersfield in West Yorkshire, one object was seen, and it got larger as it came closer. It was starlight-shaped with a blue light pulsating, and the light was extremely bright.

- 25 January 1997 at 20:30: In the town of Marske By The Sea in North Yorkshire, one bright object was seen; it was a collection of red, green, and blue-coloured lights.

- 26 January 1997 at 00:30: In the town of Edinburgh in Fife, one object was seen in the shape of three dots. It was flashing red, purple, blue, and yellow lights. The witness said they looked like disco lights.

- 26 January 1997 at 20:40: In the town of Chelford/Nr. Macclesfield, in Cheshire, one object was seen. It was 50 metres wide. It was round and dark, with white incandescent lights around it with two very bright red lights beneath it.

- 27 January 1997 at 10:55: In the town of Droylsden in Greater Manchester, one silver/white metallic object was seen. It was a cylinder shape and had stubby wings towards the back; it also emitted a low growling hum. Two more objects were there for 2–3 minutes.

- 27 January 1997 at 20:23: In the town of Flamborough in East Yorkshire, two blue lights were seen in the sky; the shapes were described as being "flint sparking continuously"; both lights varied from being 30 to 100 yards apart.

- 27 January 1997 at 22:40: In the town of Newport in South Glamorgan, a "tube of light" was seen coming down from the sky; the witnesses stated that it first looked like a star moving towards their car. The object left dust covering the car.

- 28 January 1997 at 20:00: In the town of Swansea in Glamorgan, three white lights were seen in the sky, accompanied by a red light. They seemed to be many miles away.

- 30 January 1997 at 17:55: In the town of Marlow in Buckinghamshire one sphere-shaped object was seen emitting a bright white light. The object descended slowly to eye level and slowed, then appeared to spin and accelerate at high speed, and then it disappeared.

- 31 January 1997 at 20:00: In the town of York in North Yorkshire, two to three UFOs were seen circling the area. They were described as looking like fast-moving cloud-shaped objects.

- 2 February 1997 at 20:10: In the town of Chester in Cheshire, an orange round object was seen in the sky. The object was very bright and was very high, and people claimed it made rapid downward descents.

- 2 February 1997 at 14:25: In the town of Selkirk in Selkirkshire, people reported seeing a mirror-shaped object in the sky. People said the object was flickering.

- 2 February 1997 at 07:30: In the town of Caerphilly in Mid-Glamorgan, a cigar-shaped object was seen in the sky people reported that the object had wings but no tail and was a jade green colour, that lights were shining out through the object's windows, and that it moved slowly in a straight line.

- 3 February 1997 at 21:35: In the town of Coventry in the West Midlands, one large triangular-shaped object was seen. It was reported that this object was a very bright white colour and had green on the top of it. It was moving North.

- 3 February 1997 at 10:52: In the town of Farringdon in Oxfordshire an oval-shaped object was seen moving at very high speeds.

- 5 February 1997 at 08:30: In the town of Beeston/Nr. Leeds, in West Yorkshire, one spherical-shaped object was seen. It was reported that the object was silver in colour and very shiny and bright. It remained steady for a few minutes, then disappeared.

- 6 February 1997 at 23:30: In the town of Manchester in Greater Manchester, lots of disc-shaped objects were seen in the sky. They were reported to have been surrounded by lights. As people saw these objects, they could hear a droning noise. One of the objects shot off and disappeared into the sky, but then returned moments later with another identical object.

- 7 February 1997 at 08:05: In the town of Bathgate/Falkirk in Central, one object was seen. It was described by the witness to be like a vapour trail (but too low down). It was white in colour but not very bright and not very fast.

- 8 February 1997 at 18:37: In the town of Southend to London in Essex two strange white lights surrounded by coloured lights were seen, and then not moments later, two more lots of lights appeared. They were moving slowly towards London.

- 8 February 1997 at 19:30: In the town of Cross Green/Leeds in West Yorkshire, one round-shaped object was seen. The object was very bright. It was moving from East to West.

- 9 February 1997 at 19:00: In the town of Mons Mill/Todmorden in West Yorkshire, a spherical-shaped object was seen. The object was a solid blue colour in the centre. It was moving in a Westerly direction.

- 10 February 1997 at 23:00: In the town of Near Plymouth in Devon, a round, deep red object was seen. It was not lit up and didn't have any lights. It was moving from West to East and was very high; it was 4–5 times faster than an airliner.

- 10 February 1997 at 09:35: In the town of Barry in Glamorgan, one oblong object was seen; it was red in the centre and had up to fifteen lights. The object moved constantly.

- 13 February 1997 at 17:30: In the town of Croydon in Surrey, two objects that had one blue and one orange light were seen. They were very bright. They were stationary, then made erratic and high-speed movements.

- 14 February 1997 at 15:10: In the town of Maidstone in Kent, two small triangular-shaped objects were seen; they were said to be black in colour. The objects were seen heading North but then disappeared into the clouds.

- 14 February 1997, 07:45: In the town of Stretham in London, one black, airship-shaped object was seen drifting smoothly.

- 14 February 1997 at 08:15: In the town of Roath/Cardiff in Glamorgan one triangular-shaped object was seen. It was a shiny golden colour and was reported to be moving in a straight line at very high speeds.

- 15 February 1997 at 23:00: In the town of Westbury in Wiltshire, an object was seen landing on top of the Westbury White Horse Beauty Spot in Wiltshire.

- 18 February 1997 at 22:06: In the town of Llanwern/Newport in Monmouthshire, a witness reported seeing a very bright cream-coloured light in the sky.

- 27 February 1997 at 21:00: In the town of Gloucester in Gloucestershire, five round glowing objects were seen moving up and down and side to side at high speeds.

- 23 February 1997 at 19:20: In the town of Chelsea in London, one very large, oblong-shaped object was seen. It was reported that the object was a yellow/blue colour and stayed stationary for a long period of time.

- 26 February 1997 at 21:45: In the town of Marlborough in Wiltshire, one object was seen. It was reported to be green in colour and about 200 feet in the air. It also had a very long tail behind it.

- 5 March 1997 at 02:30: In the town of East Winch/King's Lynn in Norfolk, a bright white light was seen leaving a faint beam/trail behind it until it became stationary, then after a while it showed a little movement.

- 5 March 1997, 21:00: In the town of Edale/Lake District in Derbyshire, a triangular-shaped object was seen. It was reported to be a green/yellow colour and had pulsating lights. It made rapid, jerky movements and moved position.

- 5 March 1997 at 23:00: In the town of East Woodford in London, one object was seen. It was reported to be a similar size to an aircraft but triangular shaped; it had light in the centre and the rest was a dim white colour. It moved left, then right, then stayed stationary until it disappeared into the sky at a very high speed.
- 5 March 1997 at 22:35: In the town of Enfield in Middlesex, a pink/red round object was seen. The person reported seeing a bit come off the craft and fall down. The object was flying in a NorthWesterly direction.

- 6 March 1997 at 18:30: In the town of Crondall in Surrey, a round dome was seen. The person reported seeing the object hovering stationary in the sky at an angle; it had lights all around and internal lights.

- 8 March 1997 at 07:10: In the town of Childwall/Liverpool in Merseyside, one object was reported to be seen. It was the size of a car headlight and was a very bright white colour.

- 8 March 1997 at 19:05: In the town of Ayr in Ayrshire, one object was seen. The object was like a star with a tail. There was a glow all around it. It was stationary.

- 8 March 1997 at 05:30: In the town of Salford in Greater Manchester, two objects were seen: one was solid and a charcoal grey colour, and the other was a bright white light. They zig-zagged and then moved away vertically.

- 9 March 1997 at 03:45: In the town of Southend Beach in Essex, a metallic blue object was seen it hovered above the sea and then crashed into it.

- 10 March 1997 at 03:45: In the town of Llanfair Caereinion in Powys, one object was seen. It was a round ball with a tail. It was like a torch with a flare. There was no movement.

- 11 March 1997 at 20:26: In the town of Lynas-Wal/Llaneilian on the Isle of Anglesey, one object was seen. It was white with red lights.

- 12 March 1997 at 19:30: In the town of Montrose in Tayside, one round, very bright object was seen. The person reported that static beams shone down from the object.

- 12 March 1997 at 20:45: In the town of Gaydon in Warwickshire, five pure white lights were seen; they were reported to be very fast and went from horizon to horizon in two–three seconds.

- 13 March 1997 at 20:50: In the town of Warwick in Warwickshire, one huge circle of bright white light was seen. It was reported that the object was very high in the sky and was circling around.

- 15 March 1997 at 20:30: In the town of Wrexham-Newtown in Denbighshire, one large oval object was seen. It was white and very bright. The object was straight and level and was moving parallel with the witness's car.

- 18 March 1997 at 23:30: In the town of Elgin in Morayshire, three lights were seen, and then about 500ft up in the sky, there was a bright blue flash.

- 18 March 1997 at 04:00: In the town of Kingstanding/Birmingham, in West Midlands, one large triangular-shaped object was seen. It was reported that the object lit up blue and was 200 ft in length. The object also had a very bright light in each corner. The object hovered and then disappeared at high speed.

- 19 March 1997 at 08:40: At Birmingham Airport, in the West Midlands someone reported seeing a small object that was moving very strangely and erratic.

- 19 March 1997 at 21:50: In the town of Kidderminster in Worcestershire one large cigar-shaped object was seen. It was reported that it had four individual red/green lights that were very bright. The object was moving very slowly from left to right.

- 19 March 1997 at 21:15: In the town of Stoke-on-Trent in Staffordshire, one large round white object was seen. It was reported that the object was larger than aircraft lights.

- 20 March 1997 at 06:00: At Coventry Airport in the West Midlands, a saucer-shaped object was seen. It was reported that the object looked like a dull grey cloud. The object was moving slowly but faster than a cloud.

- 21 March 1997 at 22:31: In the town of Crawley in West Sussex, a peculiar object that looked like a flock of birds with a hole in the middle was seen, and it was reported that the object left a vapour trail across the sky. The object also had orange lights around it.

- 24 March 1997: At 22:00 on the Dark Peak, Howden Moor, two sonic booms were heard over the area and recorded at this time, although the RAF denied having supersonic aircraft in the area. They later helped in the night-long search for a crashed aircraft, using helicopters and sniffer dogs from the police along with 150 Mountain Rescue volunteers. No wreckage was found. A triangle-shaped UFO had been seen an hour before the sonic booms in the local area.

- 27 March 1997 at 20:40: In the town of Bedworth in Warwickshire, two objects were seen side by side. It was reported that these objects were a very bright white colour. During this incident, the witness's car radio was producing nothing but static.

- 28 March 1997 at 20:00: In the town of Edinburgh in Fife, two very large round objects were seen. It was reported that these objects were larger than any normal aircraft. The objects were a very bright white colour. The objects were in line with each other and were moving northward.

- 28 March 1997 at 19:43: In the town of Manchester in Greater Manchester, one dark black triangular-shaped object was seen. It was reported that it had a small red light on its nose and two white lights on the edges that were flashing.

- 29 March 1997, time unknown: In the town of Southport in Lancashire, a triangular-shaped object was hovering off the coast.

- 29 March 1997, time unknown: In the town of Burslem/Stoke-on-Trent in Staffordshire, three objects that were orange/red in colour and 500 yards apart from each other began to move from left to right.

- 30 March 1997 at 22:30: In the town of Wigan in Greater Manchester, one object was seen; the object was reported as being of similar size and shape as a star. The object was blue and white in colour, and it occasionally changed to red.

- 31 March 1997 at 22:00: In the town of Didcot/Oxford in Oxfordshire, multiple lights were spotted in the sky. It was reported that the lights changed colour from white then to green, then to red, then to blue. The object was stationary for a short time and then moved from left to right.

- 31 March 1997 at 18:50: In the town of Wythall/Nr. Birmingham, in the West Midlands, one very long, jumbo-sized missile-shaped object was seen. It was reported that the object had fins at its rear and was a white and amber colour.

- 31 March 1997 at 23:45: In the town of Hemel Hempstead in Hertfordshire, one object was seen. It was reported that the object was on fire and pieces were coming off of it. The object was moving at extremely high speeds through the sky.

- 1 April 1997 at 20:05: In the town of Hanwell in London, one very bright round object was seen. It was recorded that the object was moving slowly.

- 1 April 1997 at 20:00: In the town of Notting Hill Gate in London, one object was seen. It was recorded that the object looked like an orange blob with a long, fiery tail from the top and was twenty times longer than wide. The witness compared it to a hot air balloon.

- 7 April 1997 at 20:50: In the town of East Grinstead in West Sussex, one star-shaped object was seen. It was recorded that the object was a bright white colour. The object was travelling in a direct line and was exceptionally fast.

- 8 April 1997 at 09:01: In the town of Penycae in Denbighshire, one object was seen. It was recorded that this object was moving at 90-degree angles. The object then sped up then slowed down.

- 8 April 1997 at 21:00: In the town of Wallington in Surrey, an object was seen. It was recorded that the object was like a dot of like. The object was white in colour and very bright. The object was moving vertically very fast.

- 8 April 1997 at 21:30: Over the Isle of Arran, one object was seen. It was recorded that the object was a circular ball of light which changed from green to red in colours. The object travelled horizontally across the sky.

- 9 April 1997 at 09:15: In the town of Lowestoft in Suffolk, a bright white light which had a circle of lights and a triangle in the middle and also three mauve/blue spots were seen and recorded. This object hovered, then moments later shot off at a high speed to the West.

- 9 April 1997 at 20:30: In the town of Elland in West Yorkshire, three objects of green in colour were seen moving horizontally. The objects were the size of traffic lights and were moving steadily from West to East.

- 10 April 1997 at 18:24: In the town of Aylesbury in Buckinghamshire, there was a sequence of flashing lights seen in the sky which changed colour from red to blue to green to white.

- 10 April 1997 at 04:30: In the town of Brighton in East Sussex, a bright green light with a purple haze was seen. The object moved in a straight line, was low in the sky, and slow making no noise.

- 11 April 1997 at 21:45: In the town of West Parley/Ferndown in Dorset, one saucer-shaped object was seen. The object had red and blue lights on it and was hovering silently for a few minutes before disappearing behind some trees.

- 12 April 1997 at 16:25: In the town of Seaford Head in East Sussex, two small disc-shaped, bright silver objects are seen and recorded. The objects have steady movement and a level elevation.

- 12 April 1997 at 15:45: In the town of Warminster in Wilstshire, a very shiny metallic disc shape is seen and recorded. The object is 15–20 meters in diameter and 5–6 meters deep. The object moved slowly, then sped off.

- 13 April 1997 at 21:30: In the town of Erith in Kent, one very bright, round-shaped object is seen. The object is white in colour but then turns into a red dot. After this, the object speeds off.

- 13 April 1997 at 22:00: In the town of Penarth Marina in South Glamorgan, there were two identically sized crafts. The crafts were extremely bright and both had obscured shapes. The crafts oscillated in an elliptical pattern.

- 14 April 1997 at 00:45: In the town of Thornley Bank in County Durham, a bell-shaped object was seen. The object had one red light and one bright white light. The object was moving across the sky from West to East.

- 15 April 1997 at 21:15: In the town of Chichester, Hampshire, one triangular-shaped object was seen. The object was a light yellow colour at the front, and the rest was black. The object moved sideways then stopped then disappeared at speed.

- 15 April 1997 at 20:00: In the town of Lower Morden/Wimbledon in Surrey, one saucer-shaped object was seen. The object was white/orange in colour and very bright.

- 16 April 1997 at 21:30: In the town of Paignton in Devon, one star-shaped object was seen. The object was star coloured and very bright, and it was moving very fast.

- 17 April 1997 at 00:08: In the town of Datchet/Slough in Surrey, two round white lights were seen performing circular motions in the sky.

- 17 April 1997 at 21:30: In the town of Ramsey in Cambridgeshire, red, white, and blue lights in the shape of a triangle were seen flying across the sky.

- 18 April 1997, time unknown: In the town of Dublin/Amsterdam in an unknown County an Airline pilot reported seeing a UFO (Unidentified Flying Object).

- 22 April 1997 at 19:50: In the town of Bristol in Somerset, two-five disc-like objects were seen. The object on the left was green colour, and the object on the right was yellow colour. The objects were very bright and were moving and fast speeds; the objects would drop down and then reappear in the sky.

- 22 April 1997 at 21:55: In the town of Andover in Hampshire, a very large grey object with red, blue, and green lights was seen. The object made a humming noise and started to descend closer to the witness.

- 30 April 1997 at 12:45: In the town of Liverpool in Merseyside, two objects were seen: one object was a disc shape, and the other object was a cigar shape. Both objects were black in colour. The objects were moving slowly.

- 30 April 1997 at 12:40: At Birmingham Airport in Merseyside, a bright object rose from a rooftop vertically to a great height. The object had a flat, elongated shape and appeared to be grey inside.

- 1 May 1997 at 03:56: In the town of Cathays/Cardiff in South Glamorgan, one round object was seen. The object had many lights on it, but with one medium and constant light. The object also made an unusual noise. The object made erratic and jerky movements.

- 4 May 1997 at 04:00: In the town of Epping in Essex, one round object was seen. The object was 15 ft in diameter. The object was emitting seven or eight bright green lights downward. The object was moving at a steady pace.

- 4 May 1997 at 22:00: In the town of Worcester in Worcestershire, one round, star-shaped object was seen. The object was a very bright orange and yellow colour and was stationary but then began to make steady movements.

- 5 May 1997 at 09:40: In the town of Maidstone in Kent, one round-shaped object was seen. The object was green in colour and was very bright. The object was reported to be moving very fast.

- 7 May 1997 at 03:00: In the town of Edinburgh in Fife, one diamond-shaped object was seen. The object was yellow and white in colour and was flashing. The object was darting around the sky.

- 7 May 1997 at 00:00: In the town of Calne in Wiltshire, one triangular-shaped object was seen. The object was described to be the size of a small aircraft and to be a very bright colour. The object made a buzzing noise as it followed the witness.

- 11 May 1997 at 20:05: In the town of Looe in Cornwall, one cube-shaped object was seen. The object was described to be the size of a microlight aircraft and to be black in colour. The object moved straight across the sky.

- 14 May 1997 at 23:30: In the town of Witney in Oxfordshire, one very large star-shaped object was seen. The object was reported to have a beam coming down from it that twinkled in a range of different colours. The object hovered back and forth for about one and a half hours.

- 15 May 1997 at 01:40: In the town of Bathgate in West Lothian, a cylinder-shaped object was seen moving slowly in the sky.

- 15 May 1997 at 23:59: In the town of Runcorn in Cheshire, 15–20 tail shaped objects were seen. The objects were reported to be making snake-like movements. The objects were a very bright orange colour.

- 19 May 1997 at 23:17: In the town of Bromley in Kent, one round-shaped object that was double the size of a star was seen. The object waspale white in colour but very bright. The object was stationary for a while but then began to travel straight and level.

- 21 May 1997 at 00:45: In the town of Bradford-on-Avon in Wiltshire, blue flashing lights that had no shape were seen. These objects emitted a strange noise that woke the witness. The objects flew in a straight line and were moving North.

- 22 May 1997 at 23:10: In the town of Abergavenny in Monmouthshire, one large triangular-shaped object was seen. The object was black in colour and was moving West.

- 23 May 1997 at 23:30: In the town of Zennor in Cornwall, a brilliant white light was seen travelling at alternating speeds the object disappeared but then minutes later the same light appeared from an egg-shaped object that was hovering in the sky.

- 27 May 1997 at 04:20: In the town of Gorseinon/Nr. Swansea in West Glamorgan, one round object was seen the object was yellow in colour. The object was very bright and shimmered. The object was moving from left to right.

- 29 May 1997 at 23:55: Town unknown in Suffolk: 10–20 lights in the sky were seen. The objects were reported to be flashing red, orange, and green like traffic lights. The objects were stationary and made no noise.

- 29 May 1997 at 20:58: In the town of Harpenden in Hertfordshire, one short object was seen. The object was a very bright white colour. The object was stationary and then began to move to the North from the South. The object disappeared instantly.

- 30 May 1997 at 00:20: In the town of Hatfield Woodhouse in South Yorkshire, one large helmet-shaped object was seen. The object was bright and had lights on its underside. The object was completely silent and was moving slowly then sped off.

- 30 May 1997 at 10:57: In the town of Wrexham in Denbighshire, one object was seen. The object had one light on the front and was about 450ft up in the air and as the object moved west, it began to pick up speed.

- 31 May 1997, time unknown: In the town of Wandsworth in London, one large star-shaped object was seen. The object was white in colour and was moving slowly from North to South.

- 31 May 1997 at 22:55: In the town of Barton/Torquay in Devon, a ball of white light was seen slowly moving across the sky through a pair of binoculars. The object was described as a white globe of light.

- 31 May 1997 at 12:05: In the town of Workingham in Berkshire, an intense white flashing light was seen drifting slowly overhead towards the West.

- 2 June 1997 at 03:00: In the town of Arran on The Isle of Arran, a bright star-shaped object was seen. The object was described as changing into an elliptical shape and rising slowly.

- 2 June 1997 at 02:20: In the town of Scunthorpe in Lincolnshire, one object was seen. The object was described to be a big red dome with a bright red light surrounding it, then after a few minutes, lots of white lights appeared. The object moved in a straight line.

- 2 June 1997 at 06:00: In the town of Bognor Regis in West Sussex, one object was seen. The object was described to be a solid round ball approximately 100 ft in diameter. The object changed colour from dark red to black, and the witness also saw a beam of light come down from the object. The beam of light covered the witness.

- 3 June 1997 at 22:18: In the town of Kilmarnock in East Ayrshire, a small, intense, bright white ball of light was seen. The object was travelling in a straight line but then began to make erratic movements. The object was moving East.

- 4 June 1997 at 02:07: In the town of Kettley/Telford in Shropshire, a circular object was seen. The object was described to have five lights around its perimeter. The object travelled slowly North.

- 6 June 1997 at 16:18: In the town of Gwernaffield/Nr. Mold in Flintshire, a round black object was seen travelling across the sky at high speed. The witness saw something draping from the bottom of the object.

- 6 June 1997 at 11:25: In the town of Woodley/Reading in Berkshire, numerous ball-shaped objects were seen. The objects were a very bright white colour. They were high in the sky and made rapid movements. The objects moved horizontally up and down, round and round.

- 8 June 1997 at 00:20: In the town of Sandown in Berkshire, two round-shaped objects were seen. One object was a white, very bright steady light, and the other object was a flashing, very bright white light. Both objects moved southeast.

- 9 June 1997 at 01:22: In the town of Canvey Island in Essex, a solid, bright white line was seen.

- 9 June 1997 at 22:35: In the town of Calne in Wiltshire, one cylinder/cigar-shaped object was seen. The object was bright white colour. It made a rocket noise and was very loud. The object was very close to the witness and was moving horizontally at high speeds.

- 9 June 1997 at 22:25: In the town of Tore in Rossshire, one object was seen. The object was described as looking like a saucer shape and then a comet with a tail. The object was a very bright orange colour and was shiny.

- 9 June 1997 at 10:50: In the town of Nr. Ilkley in West Yorkshire a cigar-shaped object was seen. The object was about 20,000 ft up in the air and was a silver/blue colour. The object was travelling from North to South.

- 9 June 1997, time unknown: In the town of Otley in West Yorkshire, a long, cylinder-shaped object was seen. The object was a silvery white colour and extremely bright.

- 9 June 1997 at 11:00: In the town of Otley in West Yorkshire, a long cigar/oval-shaped object was seen. The object was a dark grey/silver colour, but when the object was moving, the silver colour became brighter.

- 9 June 1997 at 21:10: In the town of Neath in West Glamorgan, one large house size rugby ball-shaped object was seen. The object was grey and black in colour, and there were lights on it in the shape of a triangle.

- 9 June 1997 at 00:30: In the town of Chesterfield in Derbyshire, there were five star-shaped objects seen. The objects were at an angle of 20 degrees; the objects were rotating and changing colour, the lights also appeared to pulsate.

- 10 June 1997 at 00:04: In the town of Newhaven in East Sussex, a big ball of white light was seen moving in a south-westerly direction, then the object suddenly disappeared into nothing.

- 11 June at 12:22: Town unknown in a county unknown, a man/alien walked in and laid on the witness quilt, then whooshed through the window.

- 11 June 1997 at 11:30: In the town of Isle of Wight, Hampshire, bright lights were seen over the Isle of Wight.

- 12 June 1997 at 14:00: Town unknown in West Sussex, a UFO was seen. It was 100 ft high in the sky and was described as being a circular shape and had three lights on it. The UFO moved slowly and made no noise.

- 14 June 1997 at 09:30: In the town of Luton in Bedfordshire, one small, round-shaped object was seen that was described as being the size of a plane. The object was black in colour. The object was stationary for a moment, then shot directly upward in the sky.

- 15 June 1997 at 21:00: In the town of Brierly Hill in the West Midlands, a group of about 12 lights were seen. The objects were moving West at high speeds.

- 15 June 1997 at 01:30: In the town of Bishops Waltham in Hampshire, many elongated objects were seen. The objects were very bright, brighter than a normal star, and had flashing white lights.

- 16 June 1997 at 01:45: In the town of Hartley in Kent, one balloon-shaped object was seen. The object was an orange colour and was moving low in the sky.

- 16 June 1997 at 02:36: Town unknown in the West Midlands, solid silver objects were seen below cloud level.

- 16 June 1997, time unknown: In the town of Dumfries in Dumfrieshire, a metallic object was seen. The object had blue, green, and yellow lights coming from it that were very bright.

- 17 June 1997 at 22:30: In the town of Clitheroe in Lancashire, one round, very bright object was seen. The object was moving from east to west and going at very high speeds.

- 18 June 1997 at 21:35: In the town of Northallerton in North Yorkshire, one object was seen. The object was described to be the same size as a small civil airliner. The object was moving to the East. As the witness described the object taking a "sidestep" to the right.

- 21 June 1997, time unknown: In the town of Penrith in Cumbria, one object with the shape and brightness of a star was seen. The object moved very fast then stopped abruptly then sped off.

- 22 June 1997 at 22:10: In the town of Malmesbury in Wiltshire, one very large object was seen. The object was orange and yellow in colour and was very bright. The object shot up into the sky.

- 22 June 1997 at 01:00: In the town of Carlisle in Cumbria, three extremely bright lights were seen. The objects moved to form a huge triangle. The objects were of similar brightness to a welding torch.

- 23 June 1997 at 22:35: In the town of Hythe/Southampton in Hampshire, an oblong-shaped object was seen. The object had lights and moved too fast for an aircraft.

- 25 June 1997 at 02:20: Town unknown in West Lothian, one barbeque-shaped object was seen. The object had green and white lights on it and was very low to the ground.

- 28 June 1997 at 01:00: In the town of Troon in South Ayrshire, segments of pale blue lights in a circle were seen. The object was stationary, then the lights vanished and reappeared again within seconds.

- 30 June 1997 at 23:20: In the town of Norwich in Norfolk, one triangular/diamond-shaped object was seen. The object was a very dull orange colour and was circling the sky then began to move away quickly until it disappeared.

- 30 June 1997 at 21:00: In the town of Roydon in Essex, a vague shape of an aircraft that looked like a light was seen. The object began to get bigger as it approached the witness. It got closer then stopped for a moment, then started to move again.

- 1 July 1997 at 01:00: In the town of Exeter, Devon, two triangular-shaped lights were seen.

- 1 July 1997 at 06:48: In the town of Haughmond/Shrewsbury in Shropshire, there were two UFOs travelling at high speed; they looked like two bright discs.

- 1 July 1997 at 08:30: In the town of Oakengates/Telford in Shropshire, two bright lights were seen at 5000 ft in the air; they were stationary for a short time and then disappeared.

- 3 July 1997 at 12:30: In the town of Swindon in Wiltshire, green balloon-shaped objects were seen. The objects were very bright and were travelling East.

- 3 July 1997, time unknown: Near North Weald Airfield in Essex a large oval-shaped object was seen. The object had 12 very bright white lights surrounding it and was moving very fast.

- 4 July 1997 at 18:30: In the town of Bracknell, Berkshire, seven orange lights were seen in the sky. These objects moved very fast in a zigzag formation up into the clouds.

- 5 July 1997 at 21:00: In the town of Fratton/Portsmouth in Hampshire, fourteen objects were seen. Some of these objects were red and some were white at different stages. Nine more objects appeared, but these appeared to be shaped like a triangle. There were different and unexplainable sounds coming from the objects.

- 5 July 1997 at 22:15: In the town of Maesycoed/Pontypridd in Mid Glamorgan, a triangular-shaped object was seen. The object had multi-coloured flashing lights. The object hovered for a few moments, then shot off in an easterly direction at a high speed.

- 5 July 1997 at 20:30: In the town of Ipswich, Suffolk, one small black balloon-shaped object was seen. The object was high up in the sky and was climbing higher towards the sky as it travelled at a very fast speed in a northwest direction.

- 5 July 1997 at 01:00: In the town of Wrexham in Denbighshire, a large round object was seen. The object was described to be as big as a house; it had a cluster of lights coming from inside it. The object was pulsating left and right as if on a pivot.

- 5 July 1997 at 11:30: In the town of Ducklington Village/Oxford in Oxfordshire, one round-shaped object was seen. The object appeared static and was black in colour, and there were no lights visible.

- 5 July 1997 at 22:08: In the town of Mexborough in West Yorkshire, one triangular-shaped object was seen 2000 ft in the sky. The object was travelling slowly, stopped for a moment, then changed direction sharply.

- 6 July 1997 at 23:00: In the town of Skegness in Lincolnshire, a bright star-shaped object was seen. The object sparkled with red, green, blue, and white lights. The object made erratic movements and slowly moved towards the south.

- 6 July 1997 at 17:30: In the town of Mossley in Lancashire, a long silver rod-shaped object was seen. The object was very bright and had a red box at its rear.

- 7 July 1997 at 23:05: In the town of Skegness in Lincolnshire, a bright light was seen not to be moving.

- 8 July 1997 at 22:10: In the town of Llay/Wrexham in Denbighshire, one object was seen with four lights coming from it: all the lights were a yellow/orange colour. The object began to move to the north, then turned to its original position, then disappeared.

- 8 July 1997 at 21:15: In the town of Worthing in West Sussex, a bright orange ball with a tail was seen high in the sky. It was stationary.

- 8 July 1997 at 23:45: In the town of Lerwick, the Shetland Islands, a round light the size of a five-pence piece was seen through binoculars.

- 8 July 1997 at 03:15: In the town of Waltham Abbey in Essex, one object was seen; it had one light underneath and three flashing lights on the side. The object moved around erratically.

- 9 July 1997 at 09:10: In the town of Haverhill in Cambridgeshire, an orange disc-shaped object was seen. The object disappeared at a high speed.

- 9 July 1997 at 09:30: Near Great Dunmow in Essex, a bright white light that was comet shaped was seen. The object was described to have a forked tail and a red glow.

- 9 July 1997 at 23:40: In the town of Stamford in Cambridgeshire, one object in the shape of a balloon was seen. The object was a dark colour but had an orange glow behind it. The object was stationary for a short while until it began to climb vertically.

- 9 July 1997 at 23:15: In the town of Lichfield in Staffordshire, 5–6 flashing white lights were seen. These objects changed shape. The objects were round and very bright; they disappeared and reappeared.

- 9 July 1997 at 22:45: In the town of Okehampton in Devon, there was a vertical orange ball-shaped object that varied in thickness.

- 9 July 1997 at 01:20: In the town of Longhamborugh in Oxfordshire, there were two orange objects; two red lights were also seen, and directly behind them was a cigar-shaped object.

- 10 July 1997 at 20:00: In the town of New Romney in Kent, two objects were seen. The objects were orange, green, and red in colour. The object was static and flashing.

- 10 July 1997 at 21:45: In the town of Broadstone in Dorset, one object was seen. The object was described as having two wings but no fuselage; it was black in colour and was heading in a north-easterly direction.

- 11 July 1997 at 00:10: In the town of Swindon in Wiltshire, three bright lights were seen that were star-shaped. The lights were going around in tiny circles.

- 12 July 1997 at 19:30: In the town of Lye Green/Chesham in Buckinghamshire, one disc-shaped object was seen. The object was silver in colour and was moving smoothly in a south-easterly direction.

- 13 July 1997 at 12:48: In the town of Ingleton in North Yorkshire, an enormous tube-shaped object was seen in the sky. The object was half a mile long and a quarter of a mile wide. The object's shape was made up of a mass of small dots.

- 13 July 1997 at 23:55: In the town of Forfar in Angus, a small spherical object was seen. The object changed colour from yellow to white. The object was fast-moving and made a fizzing sound.

- 16 July 1997 at 02:30: In the town of Burton-on-Trent in Staffordshire, two large triangular-shaped objects were seen. The objects emitted a multitude of lights and changing patterns. One object came vertically down and hovered.

- 17 July 1997 at 10:20: In the town of Brighton in East Sussex, two objects were seen. The objects were white and green in colour and made a booming noise. The objects were moving from west to east faster than a plane.

- 18 July 1997 at 02:00: In the town of Falkirk in Stirlingshire, two white lights were seen. The lights were stationary.

- 18 July 1997 at 19:40: In the town of Preston in Lancashire, one circular-shaped object was seen. The top of the object was shiny, but the bottom of the object was dark.

- 19 July 1997 at 21:30: In the town of Bayston Hill/Shrewsbury in Shropshire, one object was seen. The object was very high in the sky and was a bright white colour.

- 19 July 1997 at 04:15: Town unknown in London, one cigar-shaped object was seen. The object had one bright light on it and was moving south.

- 19 July 1997 at 15:00: In the town of Crawfoot/Glasgow in Lanarkshire, one disc-shaped object was seen. The object was slow-moving and wavering. The object disappeared into the clouds.

- 19 July 1997 at 21:30: In the town of Redditch in Worcestershire, one large cigar-shaped object was seen. The object had three lights at the front. The object moved up and across and was slow.

- 20 July 1997 at 23:00: In the town of Marlborough in Wiltshire, two orange circular-shaped objects were seen. The objects were described as looking like if you held a tennis ball at arm's length. The objects were at a low angle and were stationary.

- 21 July 1997 at 15:45: In the town of Beith in North Ayrshire, a rectangular-shaped object was seen. The object was described as being shiny metal and a bright white colour too. The object appeared to drop and then disappear below the horizon, out of sight.

- 21 July 1997 at 21:50: In the town of Surrey/Nr. Canterbury in Kent, an orange-diffused light was seen slowly moving.

- 21 July 1997 at 02:35: In the town of Bolton on Dearne in South Yorkshire, a semi-circular object made up of 4–5 circular lights was seen. The object was constantly illuminated. A red light seemed to revolve around the semi-circular shape.

- 22 July 1997 at 22:00: In the town of Sandhurst in Berkshire, one circular-shaped object was seen. The object was described to be smaller than the moon and very bright orange colour.

- 22 July 1997 at 23:00: In the town of Queensferry on Fife, one object larger than an aircraft was seen. The object gave off a very bright light in the shape of a V.

- 22 July 1997 at 20:45: In the town of Langley Mill in Derbyshire, one object was seen. The object had green, blue, red, and silver lights; the lights were not flashing. The lights went off, and a large gold-coloured light came on for a few seconds.

- 22 July 1997 at 14:00: In the town of Kilwinning in Ayrshire, a misty silvery-grey sphere was seen with four or five stars linked to it; it looked stationary at first and then started to hover.

- 23 July 1997 at 23:30: In the town of Holland Park in London, a small, well-defined light was seen moving from west to east.

- 25 July 1997 at 00:45: In the town of Rochester, Kent, 9–12 round white lights were seen moving rapidly; some of them appeared to collide.

- 25 July 1997 at 19:30: In the town of Humber Bridge/Hessle in East Yorkshire, a silver cigar-shaped object was seen. The object had sharply pointed wings with a red on one side and a green light on the other. The object hovered at first, then sped quickly away.

- 25 July 1997 at 21:40: In the town of Huddersfield in West Yorkshire, one round-shaped object was seen. The object was bright white and red in colour.

- 25 July 1997 at 22:30: In the town of Great Driffield in Humberside, one round-shaped object was seen. The object was flashing green, blue, and yellow.

- 26 July 1997 at 23:30: In the town of Farnham in Surrey, one very bright white object was seen. The object moved due north and then became stationary.

- 26 July 1997 at 01:00: In the town of Croydon in Surrey, one blue, white, and grey object was seen. The object was described as being like a big swirl, like a dust storm, then it changed and looked like a circle within a circle, like a gas ring. The centre of the object was transparent and changed shape from a circle into a straight line.

- 26 July 1997 at 23:59: On the A14 in Cambridgeshire, one object was seen that looked like a laser beam in the sky. The witness followed the object for 10 miles in the car.

- 27 July 1997 at 00:30: In the town of Shelsley Beauchamp in Worcestershire, one square-shaped object was seen. The object had fifty very bright lights on/surrounding it. The object flashed.

- 28 July 1997 at 19:25: In the town of Monkston/Milton Keynes in Buckinghamshire, a round disc-shaped object about the size of a fighter jet was seen. The object was travelling at 300 mph at approximately 1000 ft. The object had no wings and made no sound.

- 29 July 1997 at 23:00: In the town of Box Hill/Tadworth in Surrey, one circle-shaped object was seen. The object had two prongs coming off of it. The object was a very bright white colour.

- 29 July at 01:45: In the town of Bradford in west Yorkshire, one cottage loaf-shaped object was seen. The object had a mass of red lights and one large light in the middle that was pulsating.

- 29 July 1997 at 05:30: In the town of Holborn in London, one object was seen. It had very bright silver, red, green, and yellow mauve lights that were spinning and flashing. The object suddenly vanished.

- 29 July 1997 at 13:15: In the town of Newton-le-Willows in Merseyside, a straight line was seen; it had no wings and was moving southwards.

- 31 July 1997 at 17:00: In the town of Keal Cotes in Lincolnshire, a shiny silver disc was seen. The object came out of a cornfield vertically and then disappeared.

- 31 July 1997 at 22:20: Town unknown in Bressay Island/Scotland, a round object was seen. The object had a flat bottom and was a very bright colour.

- 1 August 1997 at 23:45: In the town of Chesterfield in Derbyshire, three lights were seen. Two of the lights were dim and the third was bright. The two dim lights moved off, leaving the one bright light stationary and hovering.

- 1 August 1997 at 12:00: In the town of Erdington/Birmingham in the West Midlands, one object the size of a small car was seen. The object looked like an upside-down plate. The object was a very bright white colour and was stationary for a few minutes before disappearing.

- 1 August 1997 at 22:24: In the town of Worcester in Worcestershire, a UFO was seen that was described to look similar to a conventional aircraft travelling at high speeds.

- 1 August 1997 at 00:00: In the town of Daventry in Northamptonshire, a large light object with multiple lights on it was seen. The object was making an unusual sound as the witness was looking at it; something shot out of the object. The object hovered outside the witness's bedroom window.

- 2 August 1997 at 22:18: In the town of Twickenham in Middlesex, two UFOs were seen, both were white in colour and moving west, making erratic movements.

- 2 August 1997 at 08:47: In the town of Rochester, Kent, a massive UFO was seen. It was described that the object broke up into two parts that looked like fireballs.

- 2 August 1997 at 00:00: In the town of Balham in London, a very bright football-shaped object was seen to leave behind a trail in the sky. The object disappeared.

- 2 August 1997 at 23:20: In the town of Wootton Bassett in Wiltshire, one round-shaped object was seen. The object was a very bright white colour and was described to be as bright as the moon. The object had a halo around it.

- 2 August 1997 at 22:30: In the town of Bracknell in Berkshire two, saucer-shaped objects were seen. Both objects had a dome top, and both objects were described to be the width of a large dog. The objects were an illuminous green colour and were flying around, chasing each other.

- 2 August 1997 at 22:15: In the town of Hindhead in Surrey, four circular/elliptical-shaped objects were seen. The objects were smaller than a normal aeroplane and were a very bright white colour.

- 3 August 1997, time unknown: In the town of Swindon in Wiltshire, one cigar-shaped object was seen. The object was described to have a bobble centrally above and below it. The object glowed with a consistent very bright white light. The object moved very fast vertically into the clouds.

- 3 August 1997 at 20:50: In the town of Bexley, Kent, a huge UFO was seen. It came down to the woods.

- 4 August 1997 at 21:30: In the town of Lancaster in Lancashire, two independent bright white lights were seen. Both lights were moving fast and were heading north.

- 4 August 1997 at 22:30: In the town of Bampton in Oxfordshire, one rectangular-shaped object was seen. The object had three bright lights and a red light near its rear. The object lifted up straight into the sky.

- 5 August 1997 at 20:00: In the town of North Weald in Essex one diamond-shaped object was seen. The object was black in colour with green edges. The object was 700 ft high in the sky and moved at a very fast speed.

- 5 August 1997 at 21:23: In the town of Addlestone in Surrey, there was a burning light going across the sky; it was described to look like a fireball. The object vaporised after 10–15 seconds.

- 5 August 1997 at 22:50: In the town of Wisbech, Norfolk, a bright orange sphere-shaped object was seen. The object was a pale colour and was described as having half-moon-shaped wings. The object descended rapidly, moved across the horizon, and then suddenly disappeared.

- 5 August 1997 at 09:05: In the town of Deal in Kent, a circular-shaped ball of white light was seen. The object was described as having the same amount of brightness as a star. The object was silent. The object dropped down very fast and then blinked out.

- 6 August 1997 at 22:05: In the town of Bridgehall/Stockport in Cheshire, one large, very bright white light was seen then followed by a smaller white light. They were moving northeast.

- 6 August 1997 at 22:05: In the town of Rochdale in Cheshire, one large, bright light was seen which was then followed by a smaller light. It moved from the southwest to the east.

- 6 August 1997 at 22:10: In the town of Darnhill/Heywood in Lancashire, one large white light was seen followed by a smaller light. It came from a Westerly direction.

- 6 August 1997, at 21:50: In the town of Woking in Surrey, one object shaped like a horizontal cylinder was seen. The object was the size of an aircraft. The object was white in colour and very bright. It was hovering.

- 6 August 1997, at 03:00: In the town of Hale, Greater in Manchester, a very bright star was seen. The star came towards the witness, lit up the whole area, and then went back in the direction it had come from.

- 6 August 1997, time unknown: In the town of St Ives in Cornwall, a large, saucer-shaped object was seen. It was the size of a hot air balloon, with two pods on either side and a central bright light/fiery glow.

- 6 August 1997 at 22:40: In the town of Glasgow in Lanarkshire, a pair of stars appeared to be moving in an Easterly direction. They moved almost in a straight line.

- 7 August 1997 at 16:00: In the town of Whitby in North Yorkshire, a circular object that was spinning and glinting was seen. It was moving from East to West very fast.

- 7 August 1997 at 22:03: In the town of Northwich in Cheshire, one bright, white light in the sky was seen.

- 7 August 1997 at 22:40: In the town of West Ewell in Surrey, one object that was a greenish colour was seen. The object then turned red and was very bright. There was erratic movement. It moved very quickly backwards and forwards, creating a 'W' effect.

- 8 August 1997 at 23:30: In the town of Abergavenny in Monmouthshire, one object that was bigger than a car was seen. It was white and very bright. It came down the road.

- 8 August 1997 at 23:30: In the town of Kingstown in London, two objects were seen, both the size of a saloon car. Both were very bright. They were bouncing all over the sky.

- 8 August 1997 at 01:15: In the town of Durham in Durham, two lights in the sky were seen. They were yellow/orange in colour. They moved in various directions – straight lines, curved lines, and definite turns.

- 8 August 1997 at 21:30: In the town of Ripon in North Yorkshire, a bright circular light was seen. It was stationary for 40 minutes, and then it started to move slowly.

- 9 August 1997 at 14:00: In the town of Southsea/Portsmouth in Hampshire, twenty-five to thirty small metallic objects were seen. The objects were very high and moving very fast.

- 9 August 1997 at 21:50: In the town of Dorking in Surrey, one object was seen. The object was yellow and red in colour. It was stationary and then made erratic movements. It was going backwards, up and down, and kept changing speed.

- 9 August 1997 at 21:45: In the town of Leeds in West Yorkshire, three objects were seen. They looked around. They were white and all as bright as a star. The objects moved from East to West and back to East again.

- 9 August 1997 at 21:32: In the town of Staines in Middlesex. one star-like-shaped object was seen. It had a bright, white light. Brighter than any star. The object moved to the right and then upward.

- 9 August 1997 at 18:26: In the town of Solihull in the West Midlands, two objects, which were star-shaped, were seen. The objects were metal colour. They were drifting across the sky.

- 9 August 1997 at 21:25: In the town of Wilmslow in Cheshire, a bright light in the sky was seen. It disappeared quickly, leaving a glow behind.

- 9 August 1997 at 18:00: In the town of Molesey/Hampton in Surrey, one angular object was seen. It was moving eastward and was rising in the sky.

- 9 August 1997 at 23: In the town of Ashford in Middlesex, two fighter jet-sized objects were seen. The objects looked a bit like normal aircraft. They were pale and glowing pink. The objects were moving from West to East very fast.

- 10 August 1997 at 02:30: In the town of Taunton in Somerset, one bright yellow light was seen. It looked similar to a street lamp. It rose and kept rising until it disappeared into a black hole in the sky.

- 11 August 1997 at 20:15: In the town of Muswell Hill in London, there was a triangular-shaped object seen. It was a very bright white colour with red and green flashing lights. It was roughly stationary, with some horizontal movement.

- 11 August 1997 at 22:00: In the town of Pembury in Kent, a luminous, triangular-shaped object was seen hovering in the sky. There were four other luminous objects flying near it. The first object then disappeared.

- 11 August 1997 at 09:30: In the town of Culham/Abingdon in Oxfordshire, one object that was white and very bright was seen about 10 ft above the ground. It circled the witness twice and then disappeared.
- 11 August 1997, time unknown: In the town of Cardiff in Glamorgan, one star-shaped object was seen to zig-zag across the sky and then disappear.

- 12 August 1997, time unknown: in the town of Tunbridge Wells in Kent, an object much bigger than a star was seen. The object was described to look like a large apple. It exploded and sparkled like a firework and then fizzled out.

- 12 August 1997 at 21:20: Town unknown and county unknown, a white flash in the sky was seen, and this was repeated about every five minutes four times. It got brighter, and then the last time, it looked like a very bright ball in the sky.

- 12 August 1997 at 22:20: In the town of Bletchley/Milton Keynes in Buckinghamshire, an object the size of a golf ball was seen at 3–4000 ft in the sky. It was very bright and yellow in colour. It moved over the witness's house at high speed.

- 12 August 1997 at 00:45: In the town of Leicester in Leicestershire, one large, round object was seen. The object was white and very bright. It was moving from right to left and then back again, quickly. There was a low humming noise.

- 12 August 1997 at 01:00: In the town of Corsham in Wiltshire, a triangular-shaped object was seen. It had two red lights on the rear. On the front was a white light, but it didn't give off a beam of light. A second object joined it, and they moved off at a fast speed.

- 12 August 1997 at 21:00: In the town of Stourbridge in the West Midlands, one object was seen that looked triangular and moved in a manner similar to a 'jellyfish'. It was moving in an Easterly direction.

- 12 August 1997 at 17:30: In the town of Cumbran/Newport in Gwent, a small triangular-shaped object was seen. It had black wings and was sausage-shaped in the middle. It was moving very fast.

- 13 August 1997 at 19:45: In the town of Rutherglen/Glasgow in Lanarkshire, a black, disc-shaped object was seen. It was low in the sky and was pulsating. It was moving in a straight line and then climbed vertically.

- 13 August 1997 at 21:00: In the town of Oxford in Oxfordshire, one large, orange, saucer-shaped object was seen. It was very bright. The object was moving downwards in the sky.

- 13 August 1997 at 23:50: In the town of Marston/Oxford in Oxfordshire, one round-shaped object was seen. It had red and white bits on it that were glistening. The object was very bright. It moved in a straight line, then landed at the witness's feet.

- 13 August 1997 at 23:10: In the town of Feltham in Middlesex, a circular blue light contained within an object the size of a double-decker bus was seen. It moved slowly without making noise and then disappeared.

- 14 August 1997 at 22:00: In the town of Newington/Ramsgate in Kent, one object as large as a B747 was seen. It was triangular/V-shaped. The object was orange in colour. The object was brighter than aircraft navigation lights.

- 14 August 1997 at 21:00: In the town of Great Yarmouth in Norfolk, four spherical objects that were green on top and red and white at the bottom were seen. The objects were very bright. They made erratic movements, and it was like an aerial ballet in the sky.

- 14 August 1997 at 00:00: In the town of Northampton in Northamptonshire, three red, green, and white flashing lights were seen. They moved faster than a plane. They flew along, stopped, and then carried on.

- 14 August 1997 at 22:00: In the town of Ramsgate in Kent, a black, triangle-shaped object with three orange lights was seen. It was the size of a jumbo jet. The object moved as fast as a jet aircraft.

- 15 August 1997 at 12:00: In the town of Fraserburgh in Aberdeenshire, a singular, round, flat-bodied shiny object was seen. The object approached the witness's boat for a short period and then returned to its original position.

- 15 August 1997 at 15:45: In the town of Erdington/Birmingham in the West Midlands, one round-shaped object was seen. It was silvery white. It was going in a north-easterly direction.

- 15 August 1997 at 01:10: In the town of Birmingham in the West Midlands, one circular-shaped object was seen. It was blue in colour and quite bright. It was moving in an Easterly direction.

- 15 August 1997 at 22:00: In the town of Ashton/Mersey in Greater Manchester, one circular, red, blue, and white object was seen. It was brighter than a star. It moved in a triangular/diamond-shaped pattern.

- 15 August 1997 at 00:35: In the town of Edinburgh in Fife, a round, bright object was seen. It had flashing blue, red, and white lights. It was slow-moving.

- 16 August 1997 at 22:30: In the town of Aston Clinton in Buckinghamshire, one object about two inches square was seen. It was red and very bright. It went into the witness's house through the window and moved around the living room.

- 16 August 1997 at 21:40: In the town of Leeds in West Yorkshire, one round-shaped object was seen. It had a strobe light that was white with a red tint. The object was dimmer than a star. The object was very high up, and the strobe light was very fast.

- 16 August 1997 at 23:10: In the town of Knottingley in North Yorkshire, a sequence of red and blue lights in a spiral effect was seen.

- 16 August 1997 at 09:50: In the town of Bletchley/Milton Keynes in Buckinghamshire, a black triangle-shaped object was seen. The object was described to be smaller than an airliner but faster than a normal airliner. The object had a large wingspan with triangular indentations and a trailing wingspan.

- 17 August 1997 at 21:18: In the town of Grouville/Jersey in the Channel Islands, two white lights similar in brilliance were seen. The second light was half the size of the first light. They disappeared over the horizon.

- 17 August 1997 at 22:49: In the town of Staithes in Cleveland, two slow-moving lights were seen. The two lights kept together and descended slowly then rose at the same speed. This happened three times. The lights then just disappeared.

- 17 August 1997 at 02:30: In the town of Kelso in Roxburghshire, an oval object was seen. It had a green light in the centre and was glowing orange. There was a rushing wind sound. The object was going faster than a jet.

- 17 August 1997 at 00:25: In the town of Knottingley in North Yorkshire, four separate white lights, which then changed to red, were seen. The objects were very bright. They were moving northeast.

- 18 August 1997 at 01:16: In the town of Rawmarsh/Rotherham in South Yorkshire, a light aircraft that was silent was seen. It had a beam of light coming down from it. It circled the Rawmarsh area and then vanished.

- 18 August 1997 at 21:30: In the town of Raunds in Northamptonshire, one blue, disc-shaped object the size of an aircraft was seen. The object was about 45000 ft high in the sky.

- 21 August 1997 at 23:00: In the town of Cowlinge in Norfolk a circular object about 30–40 feet across was seen. The lights on the object were spaced approximately 1–2 ft apart. It moved up and away to the left before disappearing.

- 21 August 1997 time unknown: In the town of Blacon/Chester in Cheshire, there was one large circular object with two smaller ones beside it. The larger one kept moving from side to side.

- 21 August 1997 at 21:00: In the town of Edinburgh in Fife, one very large object was seen. The object was red, green, and yellow in colour. It was very bright. It moved very fast westward and then disappeared.

- 22 August 1997 at 21:20: In the town of Edinburgh in Fife, one large circle-shaped object in the sky was seen. It was eight times bigger than the triangular-shaped object that followed afterwards.

- 25 August 1997 at 22:30: In the town of Birchwood/Lincoln in Lincolnshire, a bright light glowed and then became smaller. It was high in the sky.

- 25 August 1997 at 22:00: In the town of Paignton in Devon, a star-shaped object was seen. It was very high. It moved in an 'inhuman way' on a curved path. Slowed down and then disappeared into outer space.

- 26 August 1997 at 02:00: In the town of Trowbridge in Wiltshire, one 20-inch circular object was seen. It had red and green lights and was very vivid. The object was moving westward.

- 29 August 1997 at 07:55: In the town of Stamford in Cambridgeshire, one balloon-like object was seen. It was crossing over the AI from West to East and was moving very fast.

- 30 August 1997 at 20:50: In the town of Ben Lomond in Stirlingshire, a comet with a fiery trail was seen. It was red at the end. The trail was quite short. It was seen westward going down.

- 30 August 1997 at 22:12: In the town of Arborfield/Reading in Berkshire, the witness saw a hovering red light with a strong white light coming from it.

- 30 August 1997 at 00:45: In the town of Aberdeen in Aberdeenshire, four roundish lights the size of a single bed were seen. White and fairly bright. The lights moved in a small circle at evenly spaced intervals. Then they rotated in a clockwise direction.

- 4 September 1997 at 20:00: In the town of Heighington/Lincoln in Lincolnshire, a five-pointed star about four times bigger than a star was seen. It was very bright and lit up the whole sky. It moved along the sky, appeared to get higher, and then picked up speed.

- 5 September 1997 at 02:15: In the town of Brighton in East Sussex, one triangular-shaped object was seen to be similar in size to an airliner 747. It was white, with red lights flashing on and off underneath. Was very bright. It was flying straight and level.

- 7 September 1997 at 20:50: In the town of Grassington in North Yorkshire, a bright object that was similar in size to a star was seen. It was a lot brighter, though. The object began to zig-zag erratically across the sky at high speed and then disappeared over the valley.

- 7 September 1997 at 03:11: In the town of Barking in Essex, one large object was seen. The object was similar in shape to an aeroplane. It had bright white lights along the bottom. A very loud aircraft noise. It was miles away but then shot over the town at a very high speed.

- 7 September 1997 at 21:47: In the town of Crawley in West Sussex, a cluster of lights was flashing green, red, and orange. They were ball-shaped. There was static in the air. They made erratic movements.

- 7 Sep 1997 at 22:20: In the town of Mynydd Caerau in Glamorgan, one round object with a white light was seen. It also had flashing/rotating blue and red lights. It moved up and down.

- 7 September 1997 at 20:30: In the town of Tamworth in the West Midlands, one small rocket-shaped object was seen. It was dark and dull. It was going fast and was moving straight up.

- 8 September 1997 at 23:00: In the town of Erdington/Birmingham in the West Midlands, five orbs and triangle-shaped objects were seen. One of them was white, and the rest were red. They were bright. They were moving southward.

- 8 September 1997 at 03:50: In the town of Brooksby Village in Leicestershire, one small oval-shaped object was seen. It was white with blue and red lights. The brightness was glaring. It hovered, then disappeared behind a church.

- 9 September 1997 at 06:40: In the town of Matlock in Derbyshire, two silver objects which formed the letter H were seen. They were bright. They were moving slowly in a straight line.

- 12 September 1997 at 03:30: In the town of Peterborough in Cambridgeshire, a white bumble bee-shaped object with lights all over was seen. It was 1000 ft high and was moving very fast.

- 14 September 1997 at 22:20: In the town of Colby Corner/Walsham in Norfolk, a single light to the naked eye was seen. When seen through binoculars, there was a group of coloured lights moving around. Lights were moving around each other.

- 14 September 1997 at 11:30: In the town of Chalfont St. Giles in Buckinghamshire, one ball-shaped object with indentations on the top was seen. The object was white and bright. It was higher than a normal aircraft. It was slow and steady and went upward.

- 14 September 1997 at 22:00: In the town of Dover in Kent, a bright silver object with red and green lights at the back was seen. It changed to an egg shape, went bright yellow, and then vanished. Moved quickly across the sky.

- 18 September 1997 at 07:37: In the town of Altrincham in Cheshire, a flashing/revolving light was seen. It was white. Was slowly moving above the horizon.

- 18 September 1997 at 18:20: In the town of Winchelsea Beach in East Sussex, a disc-shaped object with a 20ft wingspan was seen. The object was flying in controlled circular motions.

- 19 September 1997 at 21:00: In the town of Thame in Oxfordshire, two circular-shaped objects were seen. They were rotating in a cloud of smoke. They were very bright. The object was spinning and following the witnesses' car.

- 20 September 1997 at 23:05: In the town of Maidstone in Kent, one object 20 times the size of a jumbo jet was seen. It was bird-shaped and very bright orange in colour. It was moving in a straight line, banking from left to right.

- 21 September 1997 at 01:15: In the town of Werrington/Peterborough in Cambridgeshire, two revolving lights that were moving around each other were seen. They were flashing at different speeds. Were 200–500ft in the sky and moving from East to West.

- 21 September 1997 at 23:00: In the town of Chalfont St. Peter in Buckinghamshire one oval-shaped object eight times larger than a star was seen. It was white and yellow in colour and very bright. It was south-west in the sky.

- 21 September 1997 at 01:44: In the town of Cauldon Lowe in Staffordshire, a circular or oval-shaped object was seen. The object was mauve/silver in colour. The craft was illuminated in some way. It was travelling at a very high speed from left to right.

- 22 September 1997 at 21:56: In the town of Bodicote/Banbury in Oxfordshire, a flying saucer with red, green, and gold lights was seen. It had been hovering.

- 22 September 1997 at 02:30: In the town of Acton in West London, a Policeman saw a round object. The object was bigger than a star and bright white colour. It moved horizontally, from south to east at a very high speed. It was similar to a shooting star.

- 23 September 1997 at 08:57: In the town of Kilmarnock in Ayrshire, one meteorite-like object was seen. The object had a fiery tail and was quite big. It was moving in a straight line and heading West.

- 1 October 1997 at 11:50: In the town of Brize Norton in Oxfordshire, there were two objects glinting in the sun. One object was following the other.

- 1 October 1997 at 04:45: In the town of Brongest in Dyfed, three round, star-sized objects in a triangular formation were seen. They circled around each other and then went back to their original position. The objects were white in colour and very bright. They were moving South.

- 2 October 1997 at 02:30: In the town of Bretton/Peterborough in Cambridgeshire, one glowing light with a short trail was seen. The object was at a 45-degree angle and about 20000 ft in the sky.

- 2 October 1997 at 20:19: In the town of Townhill/Swansea in West Glamorgan, one round-shaped object was seen. The object was red, orange, and green in colour and very bright. The object was stationary.

- 2 October 1997 at 20:45: In the town of Leven in Fife, four red lights were seen. One was larger in size and was 3ft by 3ft. They moved very fast.

- 3 October 1997 at 20:55: In the town of Oswestry in Shropshire, one saucer-shaped object with a swirling spiral of white/grey luminous light was seen. The lights turned blue and then back to their original colour. It moved towards the witness's windscreen and then sped off at high speed.

- 4 October 1997 at 18:16: In the town of Chippenham in Wiltshire, one object larger than a person was seen. The object was flat, like a playing card, and had no depth. The object looked like it had two legs hanging from it. The object was dark in colour, but there was a glimmer at the rear. It disappeared due to the east.

- 5 October 1997 at 20:45: In the town of Salisbury, Wiltshire, one object was seen. The object was circular and then changed to a triangular shape. The object was white, red, and green in colour and bright. The object was about 35,000ft up in the sky.

- 5 October 1997 at 19:50: In the town of Coupar Angus/Blairgowrie in Perthshire, one ball of fire with a tail was seen. The object was orange-coloured. It was above the horizon, quite far away, but dropping down.

- 5 October 1997 at 20:47: In the town of Palmers Green North in London, two spherical pinky-red illuminated objects were seen. The objects were going from SW to NE. The objects were three thousand feet high in the sky and were travelling at a fast speed of approximately 1500–2000 mph.

- 6 October 1997 at 22:17: In the town of Stantonbury in Buckinghamshire, seven small round-shaped objects were seen in a line. They had red lights on them. They came from the West and then moved to the East slowly, then departed at speed.

- 7 October 1997 at 13:00: In the town of Lochans/ Stranraer in Dumfriesshire, one bright white star-shaped object was seen. The object was moving from east to west and very fast.

- 7 October 1997 at 19:55: In the town of Crowle in Lincolnshire, a semi-circle of six to seven red lights that were sixty to seventy yards apart was seen. They maintained a level height.

- 7 October 1997 at 19:55: In the town of Hull East in Yorkshire, a triangle formation of flashing red lights was seen. They were moving from West to East at a constant speed.

- 7 October 1997 at 19:00: At Sandtoft Airfield in Lincolnshire, a delta formation of thirteen flashing red lights was seen. They were moving slowly from southeast to northwest.

- 7 October 1997 at 19:03: In the town of Raynham in Norfolk, a very bright orange ball was seen. The object was silent with a dim, flashing white light. It moved very slowly and smoothly to the East.

- 7 October 1997 at 21:45: In the town of River Humber/Brough in East Yorkshire, two objects not seen together were seen. There was a bright light at random intervals. The light was bigger than the stars. The objects zig-zagged across the sky on a continual flight path.

- 10 October 1997 at 19:30: In the town of River Humber/Brough in East Yorkshire one diamond-shaped object with a bright light in the centre of the undercarriage was seen. The object travelled from West to East in a straight line.

- 10 October 1997 at 19:25: In the town of Newsham Park/Liverpool Mersexy in Merseyside, a bright white star was seen. It was 70,000ft high and was moving in a straight line. It was too fast to be an aircraft.

- 13 October 1997 at 21:20: In the town of Bury in Lancashire, a bright white light was seen. It eventually moved Southward, towards Saddleworth.

- 13 October 1997 at 8:50: In the town of Walton in Surrey, one star-shaped object was seen. The object was white in colour. It moved from the south west to north east.

- 14 Oct 1997 at 01:05: In the town of Scunthorpe in Lincolnshire, a fireball was seen. It was approximately 35 degrees from horizontal. It made a steady downward movement.

- 18 October 1997 at 22:30: In the town of Great Munden/Ware in Hertfordshire, a large, wide bell-shaped object was seen. It had white lights. Was approximately 15 ft off the ground and 25ft to 30ft long.

- 18 October 1997 at 19:20: In the town of Grimsby in North East Lincolnshire three triangular-shaped objects which were amber in colour were seen. They were travelling quite fast. They were overtaking each other. The objects moved westward until they disappeared.

- 21 October 1997 at 10:30: In the town of Batley in West Yorkshire, a silver dome in the sky above the clouds was seen. The sunlight was reflecting off it. It skimmed above the clouds.

- 21 October 1997 at 23:55: In the town of Leighton Village in Shropshire, one triangular-shaped object was seen. It was 40 ft in size. It had orange and green lights along the edges. It was not very bright but was pulsating. It was moving downward and made a humming noise.

- 21 October 1997 at 19:45: In the town of Morris Grange/Richmond in North Yorkshire, approximately 30 to 40 small white lights were seen. They were moving erratically.

- 22 October 1997 at 19:45: In the town of Hutton Magna/Richmond in North Yorkshire, six objects that looked like 'fancy rats' were seen. The objects were green and white in colour. They made circular patterns in the sky.

- 22 October 1997 at 02:49: In the town of Caernarfon in Caernarfonshire, one object that had four lights on it was seen. The lights were green, white, red, and blue. The object was spinning in the sky.

- 24 October 1997 at 15:00: In the town of Harrogate in North Yorkshire, two white objects were seen. They were motionless in the sky. They then started drifting slowly to the East.

- 25 October 1997 at 16:30: In the town of Camberwell in Surrey, an object was hovering in the sky. It then moved up and down and from side to side. It had bright lights.

- 28 October 1997 at 19:30: In the town of Stafford in Staffordshire, one very big and round-shaped object was seen. The object was green, red, and yellow in colour. It had lights that looked like a normal aircraft's lights. It moved North, hovered, and then slowly moved away.

- 28 October 1997 at 16:45: In the town of Kirby Wiske in North Yorkshire, one star-shaped object was seen. The object was orange and very bright. The object was moving south-west.

- 28 October 1997 at 20:10: In the town of Madley/Crewe in Cheshire, one triangular-shaped object was seen. The object was larger than a normal aircraft. It had three lights, and one of them was red. It was stationary at first but moved quickly away.

- 29 October 1997 at 21:00: In the town of Covenham Reservoir in Lincolnshire, two very large crafts were seen. The objects were yellow/golden in colour. There was a hovercraft-type noise. There were 30 lights per craft, and they were arranged in horizontal and vertical patterns. They stopped and then moved away quickly.

- 29 October 1997 at 21:00: In the town of Dawley/Telford in Shropshire, three objects in a triangular formation were seen. They were white, and one of them was bright. The lights were stationary and then split up and went in different directions.

71

- 29 October 1997 at 18:00: In the town of Newport in Shropshire, two objects were seen. Both objects looked like triangular shapes of lights. Both objects were a dull amber colour. They made fast and erratic movements and then disappeared.

- 30 October 1997 at 20:30: In the town of Dawley/Telford in Shropshire, there was an object that had a light at either end that was seen. There was a flashing white light that was very bright. It made constant turning movements and then erratic movements.

- 31 October 1997 at 19:05: In the town of Hanwell in Middlesex, one triangular-shaped object that was a similar size to an airliner was seen. It was black in colour. It was moving in a NorthWesterly direction.

- 31 October 1997 at 11:45: In the town of Marske in North Yorkshire, a cylindrical object with a dome on it was seen. The object was 2000ft high in the sky.

- 4 November 1997 at 18:00: In the town of Minehead in Somerset, a circle of light appeared on the witness's car bonnet. The electricity was lost for a short time.

- 5 November 1997 at 19:45: In the town of Blackpool, Lancashire, a big red ball floated slowly to the ground.

- 6 November 1997 at 18:35: In the town of Whitecrook/Glasgow in Lanarkshire, a grey saucer-shaped object was seen. It was spinning. It hovered and then shot straight up.

- 6 November 1997 at 19:45: In the town of Strathmartin in Angus, one black object which had blue lights on it was seen.

- 6 November 1997 at 21:20: In the town of Arncroach in Fife, one large circular white ball was seen. The object was very bright and was moving East and going very fast.

- 9 November 1997 at 21:50: In the town of Stretford in Greater Manchester, one white star-shaped object was seen. The object was very bright. It was moving East.

- 11 November 1997 at 21:45: In the town of Newark in Nottinghamshire, an 'A' frame-shaped object was seen. The object was moving northeast over Newark and was very high in the sky.

- 12 November 1997 at 04:13: In the town of Kirkham in Lancashire, two lights that were stationary were seen. Then there were a further three lights in a triangle formation, with a red strobe observed in the centre.

- 12 November 1997 at 23:55: In the town of Watchet in Somerset, at first it looked like a very bright spot of light, but after a while, it became a stack of four different coloured lights.

- 12 November 1997 at 20:00: In the town of Scotch Corner in County Durham, two large red triangles were seen. The objects were stationary.

- 13 November 1997 at 18:45: In the town of Stoke-on-Trent in Staffordshire, a Pilot saw one object that was large and that had an undiscernible shape. The object was white, like "white hot". It was descending.

- 13 November 1997 at 20:00: In the town of Bo'ness in Central, two bright lights were hovering. The object swooped down and then hovered just above ground level, and then rose up into the sky.

- 19 November 1997 at 17:25: In the town of Livingston in West Lothian, one glowing white and orange round object was seen. The object moved up, down, and around, then moved in a Westerly direction.

- 22 November 1997 at 18:20: In the town of Bideford in Devon, one ball-shaped object that was mainly yellow with a red side light was seen. The object was very bright. It had a tail. It moved upward, then started falling.

- 22 November 1997 at 17:00: In the town of Northampton in Northamptonshire, a round, spinning silver object was seen. It had white lights around it with red circular lights in between them. It moved slowly.

- 22 November 1997 at 05:00: In the town of Beckenham in Kent, one round-shaped object was seen. The object had red, green, and blue colours and was very bright. The object was moving East.

- 22 November 1997 at 00:04: In the town of Bredenbury in Herefordshire, one round-shaped object was seen. The object was green and dim. The object was moving West and then fell from the sky at a steady rate.

- 22 November 1997 at 18:32: In the town of Brixham in Devon, a shadow of a delta-winged aircraft moved across the stars. It had a steady pink light on the front and two at the back. It was silent.

- 24 November 1997 at 18:15: In the town of Preston in Lancashire, a green star-shaped object was seen.

- 25 November 1997 at 18:00: In Grove Park in London, a huge light in the sky with a smaller light above it was seen. The light went on and off three times, then disappeared.

- 30 November 1997 at 17:27: In the town of Bridgend in Glamorgan, one large circular object was seen. The object is white and very bright. The object was moving backward and forward.

- 30 November 1997 at 18:03: In the town of Ingleby in Derbyshire, one bright light was seen. The object was not high enough to be a star.

- 30 November 1997 at 22:30: In the town of Fauldhouse/Edinburgh in West Lothian, an orange, green, and yellow object was seen. The object was flying low and erratically.

- 30 November 1997 at 17:30: In the town of Stirling in Stirlingshire, eight bright orange objects like stars or pinpricks were seen. They split into four and then reformed. They were moving fast from left to right.

- 1 December 1997 at 20:34: In the town of Hull in Humberside, a streak of light was seen. It went in a straight direction and then faded out.

- 1 December 1997 at 20:35: In the town of Pocklington in East Yorkshire, there was a light with sparks coming from the rear. It was heading for the ground.

- 1 December 1997 at 20:56: In the town of Houghton in Norfolk, a bright circular light at approximately 1000 feet above the ground was seen. It had a short tail and was silent. It was travelling about 500mph.

- 1 December 1997, time unknown: In the town of Rosyth in Fife, a single object was seen. It changed colours from purple, red, yellow, and green. The object appeared stationary for long periods, then disappeared.

- 2 December 1997 at 02:27: In the town of Middleton in Staffordshire, twelve semi-circular-shaped craft flying in formation were seen. They were flying from North to South.

- 3 December 1997 at 05:30: In the town of Harrow in Middlesex, a white light was travelling at high speed in a South-Westerly direction. It circled the moon and then disappeared.

- 4 December 1997 at 20:22: Town unknown in Devon, two jet-sized objects were seen. They had two red lights and one white light. They were very bright. There was a rushing sound. Flying West and very slow.

- 4 December 1997 at 20:35: In the town of Whorlton in County Durham, a stationary white light was seen. It appeared to be rotating, with rays coming from it. It was moving East.

- 5 December 1997 at 02:09: 8 Miles west Isle of Anglesey, a Pilot saw a bright circular red light about 3mm in diameter relative to the cockpit windscreen. It was moving in a Westerly direction.

- 8 December 1997 at 23:37: In the town of Walthamstow in East London, a triangular-shaped object was seen. It was hovering in the sky.

- 11 December 1997 at 21:45: In the town of Elgin in Morayshire, a bright orange light was seen. The object was moving West. It was low on the horizon.

- 14 December 1997 at 17:20: In the town of South Raynham in Norfolk, a very bright white light was seen. The object changed shade and also looked like a gas cloud. The object was about 6–7,000ft high and was moving South-West.

- 18 December 1997 at 20:10: In the town of Newmilns in Ayrshire, a circle of red lights with a purple centre was seen. They were far away and then got closer.

- 19 December 1997 at 08:20: At Heathrow in Middlesex, a Pilot saw one object like a parachute or flying-wing shape. It was dark green.

- 25 December 1997 at 19:45: In the town of Froxfield in Wiltshire, one very large disc-shaped object was seen; it was red, white, and blue in colour. The object was bright but got duller as you got nearer.

- 27 December 1997 at 17:30: In the town of Craigshill/Livingston in West Lothian, a witness saw two huge explosions and moments later saw a very bright light. The explosions made no sound, though, and were miles high and directly above.

- 28 December 1997 at 19:48: In the town of Malby in Ireland, a Pilot and co-pilot saw one object that was very bright. The objects' colours were changing in sequence from white, yellow, and red. The UFO remained near the aircraft then disappeared.

- 29 December 1997 at 02:40: In the town of Bletchingley in Surrey, one object no bigger than a star was seen. The object was white and very bright, brighter than a star. The object was moving South-West.

- 29 December 1997 at 10:50: In the town of Nottingham in Nottinghamshire, a Pilot saw a single spherical object approx. 5–7 feet in diameter. It was Metallic and had a high-gloss finish, but with signs of grime on the underside. A machined appearance.

- 30 December 1997 at 13:09: In the town of Exeter, Devon, a red and yellow fiercely burning ball of fire with embers falling off of it was seen. It looked like the size of two dinner plates with tennis balls falling off it and burning out.

- 3 January 1998 at 22:05: In the town of Knutsford in Cheshire, one small kite-sized leaf-shaped object was seen. The object was bright red in colour and moved very fast.

- 4 January 1998 at 01:50: In the town of Raglan in Gwent, one circular-shaped object was seen. The object had a tail and was extremely bright. It moved incredibly fast in different directions across the sky.

- 5 January 1998 at 19:30: In the town of Calne in Wiltshire, one elongated object was seen that was described to be larger than a Hercules. The object was red/green in colour and had long lights with white lights at the back, in squares. The object was very bright.

- 5 January 1998 at 05:45: In the town of Rayleigh, Essex, three white lights were seen. One red light on top was rocking from side to side and then faded.

- 13 January 1998 at 18:49: In the town of Coulsdon in Surrey, a beam of light was shining upwards. Then a crescent-shaped object was seen. It moved slowly across the sky.

- 14 January 1998 time unknown: In the town of Calne in Wiltshire, a cigar-shaped object was seen. It was white with a green tinge and was seen for a few seconds before it accelerated extremely fast and then disappeared.

- 14 January 1998 at 07:40: In the town of Falkirk in Central, a large object was seen to be the same size as the moon. It went vertically straight through the cloud.

- 14 January 1998 at 21:56: In the town of Glasgow in Lanarkshire, a meteor-shaped object was seen that was a silent sphere of light. The object was moving in an arc going from southeast to northeast. It then disappeared.

- 14 January 1998 at 21:50: In the town of Kennoway in Fife, a light orange ball was seen that looked like a dull shooting star. It was silent and was heading northeast.

- 15 January 1998 at 22:30: In the town of Framlingham, Suffolk, a long, dark object in the sky was seen. The object had two bright lights at either end and several red ones in the middle. It moved vertically and then horizontally.

- 16 January 1998, 21:15: In the town of Stirling in Central, a low-flying white light with multi-coloured flashing lights on the underside was seen hovering.

- 16 January 1998 at 02:50: In the town of Gorton in Greater Manchester, lots of red lights were seen together and were flashing very fast in a cluster. They were very bright, and they appeared large.

- 20 January 1998 at 17:58: In the town of Airdrie in S'clyde, one object in the shape of a triangular defined by three flashing lights was seen. The light on the right was green, and the others white.

- 24 January 1998 at 15:00: In the town of Swansea in West Glamorgan, a black triangular-shaped object with two fins was seen.

- 25 January 1998 at 20:25: In the town of Newport in Gwent, one object in the shape of a star was seen with stud-like lights underneath in a circle. The object was travelling North in a straight line.

- 26 January 1998 at 05:45: In the town of Corby in Northamptonshire, three red lights in a triangular formation were seen. There was a silver star-shaped object below the lights.

- 26 January 1998 at 21:00: In the town of Ruislip in Middlesex, a spherical-shaped object was seen. The object was bright and pulsating. The object was larger than a light bulb and was 100 ft in diameter.

- 26 January 1998 at 22:02: In the town of New Cross in South London, one airline-sized cigar-shaped object with a bright red light was seen. The object was moving erratically.

- 1 February 1998 at 19:15: On the A272 near Winchester in Hampshire, one main object was seen to be a large red/orange luminous ball. There were two smaller objects that had totally different flight paths.

- 3 February 1998 at 07:30: In Birmingham, West Midlands, one object the size of a passenger plane was seen. The object was triangular in shape and silver. The object was very bright.

- 4 February 1998 at 22:55: In the town of Southend in London, one red and green object was. It was still and made noise.

- 5 February 1998 at 02:30: In the town of Sutton Coldfield in West Midlands, one oval-shaped object that was a bright green/blue colour was seen. The object was half as bright as the moon. It shot up vertically in the sky.

- 6 February 1998 at 07:15: On the A281 near Guildford in Surrey, three circular objects that were 20–30 feet high were seen. They were orange and very bright. They were stationary for a short time, then disappeared.

- 7 February 1998 at 06:40: In the town of Fleet in Hampshire, one triangular-shaped object like the end of a plane or concord was seen. The object gave off three brilliant white lights.

- 9 February 1998 at 15:40: In the town of Barry in South Glamorgan, a blast of orange light was seen. In the same direction, three golden balls appeared that were brighter, and then they disappeared.
- 13 February 1998 at 07:00: In Grove Park in London, a black ruler-shaped object was seen. It moved across the moon and then disappeared.

- 13 February 1998 at 21:30: On the A34 near Abingdon in Oxfordshire, one huge star-shaped object was seen descending down with the exhaust burning.

- 15 February 1998 at 03:10: In the town of Finchamstead in Berkshire, a twenty-eight-foot circular object with a dome on top which had a bright yellowish/whitish light was seen travelling very fast northeast.

- 16 February 1998 at 07:35: In the town of Methill in Fife, two circles of light that were very bright and very close together were seen. They moved at fast speeds vertically up into the sky.

- 17 February 1998 at 18:45: In the town of Lincoln in Lincolnshire, a single black triangle was seen.

- 19 February 1998 at 20:06: In the town of Heartburn/Stockton in Cleveland, a central disc with lights shooting off of it was seen hovering.

- 21 February 1998 at 02:20: In the town of Evesham in Worcestershire, one oval-shaped object which was extremely bright with a dark blodge was seen slowly moving across the sky.

- 22 February 1998 at 21:00: In the town of Ladysbridge in Aberdeenshire, one orange object with a very intense bright light was seen moving very slowly, and then it just disappeared.

- 24 February 1998 at 18:30: In the town of Hemel Hempstead in Hertfordshire, two large yellow lights surrounded by smaller blue/green, and yellow lights were seen. They made vertical and horizontal movements.

- 24 February 1998 at 17:00: In the town of Halifax in West Yorkshire, a purple diamond-shaped object was seen with a circle in the middle of it.
- 24 February 1998 at 22:30: In the town of Hull in East Yorkshire, a blue circular intermittent light was seen.

- 27 February 1998 at 20:45: In the North of M898/Glasgow in Lanarkshire, a bright light was seen falling to earth very fast.

- 4 March 1998 at 13:06: In the town of Gibraltar Point/Skegness in Lincolnshire, a large cylindrical solid object was seen. It was silver in colour and very bright. The object shot up in the air and disappeared.

- 4 March 1998 at 00:04: On the A12/Wyton in Cambridgeshire, lights were seen dancing in the sky. The lights went up and down in the sky and seemed to keep pace with the witness's car.

- 8 March 1998 at 20:06: In the town of Skirlaugh in East Yorkshire, one object was seen. It had a bright white light and an inner red light. It was moving up, down, backwards, and forwards.

- 9 March 1998 at 19:45: In the town of Maidstone in Kent, a round-shaped object with red and white flashing lights was seen. There were sometimes two and three of them moving around.

- 10 March 1998 at 20:55: In the town of Cheam in Surrey, a very bright pink light that shot off at high speed was seen.

- 11 March 1998 at 19:45: In the town of Bwlchgwyn in Clwyd, a large black oblong-shaped object that was 40ft long was seen. It was about 25ft off the ground.

- 14 March 1998 at 19:20: In the town of Newton Stewart in Wigtonshire, an object was seen. The object was like the sun setting; it had an orange glow, and three lights shot off from it.

- 16 March 1998 at 02:05: In the town of Leven in Fife, one object was seen. The object looked like a red dome. It had a white flashing light which was small and bright.

- 18 March 1998 at 17:40: In the town of Bolton in Greater Manchester, a round and very bright object was seen that was equivalent to a 5p coin in size at arm's length. the object was stationary and then disappeared.

- 19 March 1998 at 18:17: In the town of Hull in Humberside, one object was seen that looked like two lights. The width of the object was about 10 metres across, and it was hovering.

- 22 March 1998 at 21:20: In South Brent, Devon, an object in the shape of a T was seen. The object was bright, like a star. Then a bright orange light was seen high in the sky. The object was descending slowly.

- 23 March 1998 at 19:15: In the town of Histon/Cambridge in Cambridgeshire, five-round, smooth objects were seen. The objects had flashing red and blue lights going around in a circle and another light in the centre. The object was quite fast.

- 27 March 1998 at 00:30: In the town of Harrogate in North Yorkshire, a very large spherical object with multi-coloured lights was seen moving at high speed.

- 30 March 1998 at 22:25: In the town of Bury St Edmunds in Suffolk, twenty-five to thirty small disc-shaped objects that were illuminated were seen. They veered away.

- 30 March 1998 at 23:20: In the town of Wrexham in Clwyd, one large, square-ish very bright object was seen. The object was blue-ish with lights around it. There was a humming sound and a nasty smell.

- 30 March 1998 at 22:50: In the town of Malpas in Cheshire, one object was seen. The object was silent, was changing from pale blue to green, then yellow, and had one bright light. It moved erratically in the sky.

- 31 March 1998 at 04:20: In the town of Clywd Mountains/Clywd in Powys, an object was seen that had blue lights on the top and white lights on the bottom. The object was 40 ft in length and 600 ft high.

- 5 April 1998 at 01:30: In the town of Liverpool in Merseyside, one round grey object that was the size of a helicopter was seen revolving clockwise like a plate spinning. The witnesses could see windows and a glow coming through them.

- 10 April 1998 at 21:20: In the town of Kelty in Fife, one large star-shaped object was seen to have colours that were constantly changing.

- 12 April 1998 at 23:45: In the town of Much Marcle/Ledbury in Herefordshire, a UFO was seen hovering; it had numerous flashing lights of all different colours. The object hovered in the sky for 10 minutes.

- 15 April 1998 at 02:00: In the town of Musselburgh in Midlothian, two jellyfish-shaped objects were seen. The objects were very bright and were moving in a south-easterly direction.

- 16 April 1998 at 01:00: Town unknown Coutney unknown: one triangular-shaped object with flashing green and red lights was seen.

- 16 April 1998 at 21:00: In the town of Falkirk in Stirlingshire, one oval-shaped object displaying five bright searchlight-type lights was seen. The object was straight and level and moving slowly.

- 17 April 1998 at 23:00: In the town of Aviemore Village/Aviemore in Inverness-Shire, an object was seen to be moving in slow motion with twelve to fifteen lights around the perimeter. 50ft in size. The object descended behind trees.

- 21 April 1998 at 01:00: On the A19/Darlington in County Durham, numerous crescent-shaped very bright white lights were seen. There was one red light. They moved slowly at first and then picked up speed.

- 28 April 1998 at 23:40: In the town of Twickenham in Middlesex, a single white light was seen. It had a faint light behind it and was moving slowly.

- 9 May 1998 at 21:40: In the town of Crumlin in Gwent, a huge meccano/round-type looking structure/object was seen with pulsing red, green, and white lights. Very slow-moving.

- 10 May 1998 at 02:00: In the town of Nantwich in Cheshire, a very large object was seen.

- 13 May 1998, time unknown: In the town of Hawley in Hampshire, a black rectangular-shaped object with a small fuselage was seen moving very fast.

- 16 May 1998 at 22:00: In the town of Amersham in Buckinghamshire, an orange ball of light with a white ring around the outside of it was seen travelling along in a straight line.

- 16 May 1998 at 22:45: In the town of Wimbourne in Dorset, three flare-shaped objects were seen. They were yellow in colour and very bright. They were about 500ft up and moving in the same direction.

- 16 May 1998 at 01:30: In the town of Worthing in West Sussex, one oval/bell-shaped object was seen. The object was light in colour and very bright. It made a humming sound, which drew the witness's attention to it.

- 17 May 1998 at 17:00: In the town of Wigan in Greater Manchester, five white objects that were very high in the sky were seen moving very slowly.

- 17 May 1998 at 15:00: In Market Harborough, Leicestershire, one flattened rugby ball-shaped object with a long needle hanging from it was seen. It was white and silver in colour and was moving extremely fast.

- 17 May 1998 at 17:05: In the town of Hull in Humberside, seven lights were seen; six were together and one was in front. The lights merged and moved in formation. They were very high.

- 18 May 1998 at 03:15: In the town of Llanfair in Gwynedd, one long-shaped object with six flashing lights was seen. They were flashing from faded to very bright. They were moving from North to South.

- 18 May 1998 at 23:00: In the town of Erdington/Birmingham in the West Midlands, three red lights in a triangle shape 200ft up were seen. They were moving very slowly and changing patterns. There was a low-humming monotone sound.

- 28 May 1998 at 00:32: In the town of Bangor in Gwynedd, one light, golden in appearance and larger and brighter than a planet, was seen travelling from southwest to the east.

- 29 May 1998 at 02:15: In the town of Ogmore Vale/Bridgend in Mid Glamorgan, one object was seen that had no distinctive shape but was extremely bright red. The object had white and blue flashing lights. It was extremely noisy, then shot off at great speed.

- 31 May 1998 at 22:48: In the town of Sheffield in South Yorkshire, a strange group of lights was seen by various witnesses. The lights were moving in irregular patterns. They shot off at great speed.

- 2 June 1998 at 23:45: In the town of Melksham in Wiltshire, two star-sized lights about 15 feet apart were seen. There was also one red light. They had the intensity of the North Star.

- 6 June 1998 at 23:00: In the town of Sheffield in South Yorkshire, orange discs that were the size of tennis balls were seen. There were two seen side by side; the one on the right-hand side was catching up, and there was one behind.

- 11 June 1998 at 03:10: In the town of Birmingham in the West Midlands, one oval-shaped object the size of a small car was seen. The object was blue-ish green in colour and very bright. It was stationary for a while, and there was a burning coal smell.

- 12 June 1998 at 21:00: In the town of Benllech on the Isle of Anglesey, one white ball of light the size of a 5p piece at arm's length was seen. Plus, there were two smaller, faint objects in the trail too.

- 13 June 1998 at 22:00: In the town of Battersea in South London, one square-shaped object was seen. The object had blue, red, and white lights and was pretty bright. The object was stationary and then floated/glided along.

- 25 June 1998 at 03:30: In the town of Warminster/Westbury in Wiltshire, a flying saucer was seen.

- 26 June 1998 at 00:35: In the town of Hull in Humberside, a ball of white light was seen. It was travelling East before it disappeared. The ball of light changed colour to red.

- 28 June 1998 at 23:15: In the town of Uttoxeter in Devon, a saucer-shaped object that was revolving in the sky was seen. The object was greyish-white in colour and was hovering and rotating.

- 1 July 1998 at 00:05: In the town of Windsor in Berkshire, one oval-shaped object was seen. The object was orange in colour but was quite dim. It was travelling West and was very fast.

- 3 July 1998 at 07:15: In the town of Bradford-on-Avon in Wiltshire, one oval-shaped object that was charcoal grey in colour was seen.

- 8 July 1998 at 00:15: In the town of Eastbourne in East Sussex, one star-shaped object was seen. The object was white and blue in colour and very bright and was moving to the North from the south-west.

- 12 July 1998 at 23:09: In the town of Manchester in Greater Manchester, a round object was seen. The object was a bright white colour and was 400 ft up in the sky. The object stayed level as it moved across the sky.

- 13 July 1998 at 20:40: In the town of Barking in Essex, two diamond-shaped objects were seen. The objects were yellow in colour and very bright. The objects were zigzagging in the sky.

- 15 July 1998 at 00:40: In the town of Sudbury in Suffolk, an arrow-shaped object with a light at each corner plus one underneath was seen. The object went in a north, north-west direction.

- 15 July 1998 at 21:35: In the town of Abronhill in North Lanarkshire, a star-shaped object was seen. The object was very bright and was almost vertical and descending.

- 18 July 1998 at 23:26: In the town of Whitby in North Yorkshire, a witness saw lights in the sky.

- 18 July 1998 at 01:06: In the town of Lydney in Gloucestershire, a round-shaped object was seen. The object had a very intense white light and was moving slowly.

- 18 July 1998 at 22:11: In the town of Whitby in North Yorkshire, a bright, large, cone-shaped object was seen. The object was one and a half inches in size. There was static coming from it, and it was moving in a straight line downward.

- 19 July 1998 at 08:45: On the A3/Guildford in Surrey, one jelly bean-shaped object was seen. The object had a mirror finish and was reflecting the sun.

- 19 July 1998 at 00:15: In the town of Gulworth/Tavistock in Devon, three hundred foot sphere-shaped white objects were seen. They were moving from North to South in a straight line.

- 19 July 1998 at 02:20: In the town of Southall in Middlesex, one object larger than a star was seen. It was round, white, and brighter than Venus and had three tails.

- 19 July 1998 at 02:00: In the town of Southminster in Essex one very large flying saucer was seen. The object had thousands of lights on the underside, with one larger, centrally placed red light. It moved slowly away.

- 22 July 1998 at 23:44: In the town of Hythe Bay in Kent, a squashed, elongated disc with a yellow glow was seen to fade away and then brighten.

- 23 July 1998 at 00:15: In the town of Eastbourne in Sussex, a bright white was seen to change speed very fast and easily.

- 23 July 1998 at 22:40: In the town of Suffolk/Cambs County, unknown a witness saw dim lights in a circular shape spinning round.

- 26 July 1998 at 01:58: On the A386/Horrabridge in Devon, one very large disc-shaped object that was pale blue in colour was seen.

- 27 July 1998 at 23:20: In the town of Twickenham in Middlesex, one large circular object that had blue lights that were spinning was seen.

- 27 July 1998 at 23:10: Town unknown, county unknown, one dim object that had two white lights and two red lights was seen.

- 1 August 1998 at 23:41: In the town of Cleethorpes in Lincolnshire, lights were seen in the sky that looked suspicious.

- 2 August 1998 at 01:30: In Bury St Edmunds, Suffolk, 10 white lights were seen rotating around one similar light in the sky.

- 2 August 1998 at 00:30: In the town of Milton Keynes in Buckinghamshire, one circular object with square lights and windows from the outside going to the centre was large and seen to be revolving.

- 2 August 1998 at 01:40: In the town of Wrexham in Clwyd, one glowing outer ring surrounding an oval structure with pulsating lights was seen.

- 3 August 1998 at 22:08: In the town of Livingston in West Lothian, one bright light that was star-shaped which dimmed then brightened then dimmed again was seen.

- 4 August 1998 at 22:00: In the town of Eastbourne in Sussex, one small, bright, star-shaped object which was moving upward very slowly was seen.

- 5 August 1998 at 00:30: In the town of Brecon in Dyfed, a vortex with white, red, and green flashing lights was seen. The object rose straight up vertically from behind woods in the form of an arc. The object left a smokey trail.

- 6 August 1998 at 20:35: In the town of Dagenham in Essex, a witness saw a light travelling very fast in a south-westerly direction towards Barking.

- 7 August 1998 at 22:10: In the town of Shipley in West Yorkshire, one very bright object was seen.

- 7 August 1998 at 21:30: In the town of Aldershot in Hants, two spot-shaped star-coloured objects were spotted moving through the sky very fast.

- 7 August 1998 at 21:40: In the town of Hounslow in Middlesex, a shooting star-shaped object was seen making unsynchronised flashing lights in the sky.

- 8 August 1998 at 15:10: In the town of Ludgershall in Hants, one small spherical silver object that was very bright and the size of a football was seen.

- 8 August 1998 at 20:25: In the town of Laleham in Middlesex, a like jet fighter-shaped object, but very low and with no wings, was seen. It accelerated away.

- 9 August 1998 at 23:00: In the town of Horsham in West Sussex, one object with three flashing lights was seen.

- 9 August 1998 at 00:00: In the town of Keighley in West Yorkshire, one object that resembled a coloured star was seen. The object was red, orange, and green in colour. The object made erratic movements, then vanished.

- 10 August 1998 at 22:45: In the town of Hadley Wood in Hertfordshire There were three twinkling-like lights seen.

- 12 August 1998 at 03:45: In the town of Trotton in West Sussex, one spherical object that had various colours and was very bright was seen.

- 12 August 1998 at 22:00: In the town of Barry in South Glamorgan, four main lights formed a cross. There were bright green and orange lights in the centre of the object. The object was larger than a 747.

- 13 August 1998 at 04:45: In the town of Llanrhaeaedr in Clwyd, one huge silver star-shaped object was seen.

- 13 August 1998 at 12:15: In the town of Louth in Lincolnshire, a witness described seeing a yellow/white 'glow' with flashing lights that was moving very fast.

- 13 August 1998 at 22:45: In the town of Highcliffe in Dorset, one white circle travelling in a straight line was seen. There was then an extremely loud explosion over the sea.

- 15 August 1998 at 02:30: In the town of Conningsby in Lincolnshire, a bright green light that had three large green windows 8 ft apart and in an oval shape and was a quarter of a mile long.

- 16 August 1998 at 22:00: In the town of Frome in Somerset, one object looked like a yellow moon, the second one looked like a triangle with red flashing lights, and the other three looked like silver balls moving in a circle formation. The noise was a very loud noise, like the roar of many engines.

- 16 August 1998 at 22:30: In the town of Bristol, Somerset, many white small beams were seen flickering.

- 17 August 1998 at 10:00: In the town of Frome in Somerset, a witness saw many white small beams that were flickering.

- 17 August 1998 at 04:45: In the town of Slinford in West Sussex, two points of light that were too big to be stars were seen, as well as circles of yellow light. They were hovering and pulsating.

- 17 August 1998 at 23:26: In the town of Hensbridge in Somerset, one white star-shaped object was seen. The object was much brighter than a star.

- 19 August 1998 at 00:10: In the town of Elgin in Morayshire, a bright flickering light that changed colours from red, white, and green was seen.

- 19 August 1998 at 08:35: In the town of Shrewsbury in Shropshire, one circular gold-coloured object was seen.

- 21 August 1998 at 09:50: In the town of Porthcawl in Mid Glamorgan, a star size, bright object was seen. The object was blue/white in colour.

- 21 August 1998 at 23:45: In the town of Walthamstow in London, lights in the sky were seen moving. They stopped and then zoomed off.

- 22 August 1998 at 19:10: In the town of Bristol in Somerset, one object in the shape of an oval pebble that was white on top and black underneath was seen.

- 24 August 1998 at 00:30: In the town of Swansea in West Glamorgan, a very bright white light in the sky was seen moving very fast.

- 24 August 1998 at 00:00: In the town of Wakefield in West Yorkshire, one bright white light that was moving very slowly in an unusual way was seen.

- 25 August 1998 at 02:30: In the town of Hull in North Yorkshire, a hazy-shaped object was seen. It had three lights at the bottom, like traffic lights.

- 26 August 1998 at 22:45: In Wallingford, Oxfordshire, one white object with diffused light was seen.

- 29 August 1998 at 23:15: In the town of Cumnock in S'clyde, an object that looked similar to a division sign was seen with two stars on either side of the line.

- 30 August 1998 at 22:00: In the town of Yatton/Bristol in Somerset, one object that was bigger than a star and very bright but had no colours was seen.

- 30 August 1998 at 09:00: In the town of Kilmarnock in Ayrshire, a red and white flashing light that was moving extremely fast was seen.

- 30 August 1998 at 18:55: In the town of Eckington in South Yorkshire, two black spheres that were close to each other were seen. The objects had no lights at all, and they were moving fast.

- 31 August 1998, time unknown: In the town of Mottram in Cheshire, one to four bright triangular objects that then changed to a round shape were seen. They were all white and were there for one hour.

- 31 August 1998 at 16:00: In the town of Bewdley in Hereford and Worcester, one black teddy bear-shaped object was seen. The object was moving very fast through the sky.

- 1 September 1998 at 20:15: In the town of Callestick/Truro in Cornwall, one 8 ft long 3 ft wide oval, greyish-solid object that circled around the witness's house was seen.

- 1 September 1998 at 22:00: In the town of Mixenden in West Yorkshire, several round, elliptical, bright lights were shining upwards. The objects were moving backwards and forward.

- 5 September 1998 at 16:30: In the town of Esher in Surrey, several pairs of small elliptical silver objects descending from the sky were seen.

- 7 September 1998 at 20:25: In the town of Cumnock in S'clyde, an extremely bright flash of light was seen and was there for 2 seconds.

- 8 September 1998 at 20:35: In the town of Barnetby in North Lincolnshire, a large, round, circular object with orange lights on the outside which changed colour and green lights in the centre that changed colour was seen.

- 9 September 1998 at 01:00: In the town of Trowbridge in Wiltshire, bright lights were seen through the witness's bedroom curtains.

- 10 September 1998 at 00:30: In the town of Erith in Kent, two objects larger than planes were seen; both had round fronts going to points. The objects were red and had blue lights on the front of objects.

- 11 September 1998 at 20:15: In the town of Surbiton/Southampton in Hants, one object rushed over the witness house.

- 14 September 1998 at 03:00: In the town of Salisbury in Wiltshire, one car-sized cloud-shaped yellow luminous object was seen. The object had flashing lights and was 100 ft up.

- 16 September 1998 at 22:20: In the town of Norwich in Norfolk, one object was seen flashing a bright light.

- 16 September 1998 at 20:50: In the town of Blackridge in West Lothian, one sparkly light that was blue/white and very bright. The object was jumping back and forth but not moving any distance.

- 16 September 1998 at 20:35: In the town of Barking in Essex, four small white star-shaped objects were seen.

- 17 September 1998 at 05:22: In the town of New Milton in Hants, one object with a bright light and another object with it that had three bright lights was seen.

- 18 September 1998 at 21:00: In the town of Farm/Henfield in West Sussex, one large cylinder-shaped object 40m wide emitted misty white lights.

- 19 September 1998 at 22:45: In the town of Kidderminster in Worcestershire, one round white object that had the brightness of a star was seen making erratic movement when it moved.

- 19 September 1998 at 19:25: In the town of Redruth in Cornwall, two oval white objects were seen.

- 21 September 1998 at 21:30: In the town of Waunfawr in Gwynedd, spheres that changed colours on and off in sequences were seen.

- 25 September 1998 at 01:45: In the town of Blackstone in West Sussex, six circles and one object larger than a jumbo jet were seen rotating.

- 10 October 1998 at 23:25: In the town of Stanwell in Middlesex, two objects that were orange and had a dull glow were seen.

- 10 October 1998 at 18:30: In the town of Borough Bridge in North Yorkshire, one object that was a golf ball shape and had triangular lights on either side was seen.

- 10 October 1998 at 05:30: In the town of Horndean in Hants, one triangular-shaped object was seen rotating. The object had three to five lights underneath it that were also rotating.

- 11 October 1998 at 04:05: In the town of Edinburgh in West Lothian, a very large oval/round-shaped object was seen illuminating the sky.

- 12 October 1998 at 00:30: In the town of Gravesend in Kent, one global object that was pulsating and was very bright was seen.

- 13 October 1998 at 19:00: In the town of Staines in Surrey, one bright orange flashing light was seen. The object hovered for a while, then sped off faster than a conventional aircraft or helicopter.

- 19 October 1998 at 01:00: In the town of Basingstoke in Hampshire, lots of bright lights were seen.

- 19 October 1998 at 00:10: In the town of Waterlooville in Hampshire, a witness saw flashes of light every few minutes plus one long silver beam.

- 20 October 1998 at 00:45: Town unknown in Ayrshire, one single bright red light that was square and oblong shaped was seen. The object was emitting a humming noise.

- 23 October 1998 at 14:07: In the town of Aberdeen in Grampian, two objects that were spherical, shiny, and silver were seen. The objects looked approx. a quarter of an inch across.

- 25 October 1998 at 09:35: In the town of Boscombe in Dorset, one object that then split into two objects was seen. The object was the size of a minibus and was silvery white in colour.

- 26 October 1998 at 20:20: In the town of Whisby in Lincolnshire, one object the same size as a Harrier, but there was no noise. The object was brightish, with lights flashing underneath.

- 26 October 1998 at 19:10: In the town of Crewe in Cheshire, four triangular objects in formation were seen. They were yellow/white in colour and were moving across the sky.

- 27 October 1998 at 15:30: In the town of Kings Lynn in Norfolk, a small white cloud was seen that looked unnatural and had a reflection coming from it which appeared to revolve. It disappeared after 20 seconds.

- 28 October 1998 at 22:40: In the town of Thirsk in North Yorkshire, a very bright white light was seen.

- 29 October 1998 at 20:54: In the town of St. Andrews in Fife, a dull orange elliptical object was seen that arced across the sky 10 times.

- 30 October 1998 at 12:47: In the town of Harlow in Essex, a long cylindrical object with no defined edges was seen. The object was black and very dull. The object looked like it had three layers.

- 1 November 1998 at 20:30: In the town of Farnham in Hampshire, a very large cigar-shaped object with six sets of lights underneath was seen.

- 4 November 1998 at 18:00: In the town of Hull in Humberside, five star-shaped objects in a perfect line were seen. The object was at a very high altitude.

- 4 November 1998 at 04:00: In the town of Morden in Surrey, a ball of changing colour with lots of different coloured lights around it was seen. The object made helicopter sounds and stayed in place for about two hours.

- 4 November 1998 at 12:35: In the town of Bishops Waltham in Hampshire, one object that was round and white was seen. It had an orange underside.

- 6 November 1998 at 17:50: In the town of Hanham in Somerset, one object in the shape of an oval/eye with very bright white light was seen.

- 6 November 1998 at 04:30: In the town of Deal in Kent, two white fireballs in the sky were seen. The first fireball went in an arc. The second fireball went vertically.

- 9 November 1998 at 15:45: In the town of Bury in Greater Manchester, one object with flames, black smoke, and a defined mass was seen.

- 9 November 1998 at 19:40: In the town of Walsall in the West Midlands, one object bigger than a jumbo jet was seen. The object had two red lights, one white, and one blue. The object was very bright.

- 10 November 1998 at 19:45: In the town of Chichester in West Sussex, one object the size of a house with a pinnacle top with a dome was seen. The object was orange but dull in colour. The object moved very erratically and fast.

- 10 November 1998 at 21:15: In the town of Salisbury in Wiltshire, one star-shaped object was seen. The object was red and green, and the lights were flickering on the object.

- 11 November 1998 at 00:12: In the town of Reading in Berkshire, one object with tentacles was seen 300 ft in the air.

- 12 November 1998 at 06:35: On the A3 in East Hampshire, one quite large pear-shaped flat-fronted object was seen. The object was white with red sparkles and a blue tinge. The object had a very intense brightness.

- 15 November 1998 at 03:45: In the town of Cardiff in South Glamorgan, one huge 'aura' was seen tapered to one end, like a pen. The object was multi-coloured and shimmering.

- 15 November 1998 at 12:30: In the town of St Neots in Cambridgeshire, two shapes the size of a car that looked like they were burning were seen. They were spinning and silent.

- 16 November 1998 at 06:40: On the A12/Romford in Essex, one smallish blue-ish circle that was very bright was seen moving quickly from West to East.

- 16 November 1998 at 06:45: In the town of Llandrinio in Powys, one beam of blue light that was very bright was seen. The object then turned white and then disappeared, leaving a vapour trail.

- 16 November 1998 at 06:40: In the town of Stow Bardolph/Kings Lynn in Norfolk, an explosion was seen with a fast-disappearing tail.

- 16 November 1998 at 06:40: In the town of Marlborough in Wiltshire, a plume with a tail like a rocket that looked like a white flame with orange and pink edges was seen. The object was very bright and moved vertically up.

- 16 November 1998 at 05:50: In the town of Somersham/Huntingdon in Cambridgeshire, a white bright light was seen for 3 seconds.

- 16 November 1998 at 06:40: On the A17/Boston in Lincolnshire, a white ball with a long tail was seen.

- 16 November 1998 at 06:40: In the town of Cardiff in South Glamorgan, one bright white light in the shape of a circle with a vapour trail was seen.

- 16 November 1998 at 12:50: In the town of Brockley Green in Suffolk, a silver object with a short tethered tail was seen.

- 16 November 1998 at 04:15: In the town of Bow in East London, one round, dim orange object was seen moving from North to South.

- 16 November 1998 at 04:15: Town unknown in East London, a dim orange light in the sky was seen.

- 16 November 1998 at 22:20: In the town of Edinburgh in Lothian, one white, shining light was seen. The object made a whoosh sound.

- 16 November 1998 at 06:40: In the town of Tayport in Fife, an elongated pear-shaped turquoise in colour object was seen. The object was very low and large.

- 16 November 1998 at 05:15: In the town of Penrhyn Bay/Conwy in Gwynedd, there were several blue-ish white-ish lights seen.

- 17 November 1998 at 20:33: In the town of Sheffield in South Yorkshire, a red ball-type object like the sun going around in a circle behind the clouds was seen.

- 17 November 1998 at 00:01: In the town of Edmonton in North London, one object, two miles wide-ish and V-shaped, was seen. The object had 11 white and orange lights and was very bright.

- 17 November 1998 at 03:45: In the town of Chippenham in Wiltshire, lots of shooting star-shaped objects that were gold, green, and white in colour were seen. The objects were very bright.

- 18 November 1998 at 23:30: In the town of Minehead in Somerset, a large circular object was seen with silver, red, green, and blue lights.

- 18 November 1998 at 23:00: In the town of Newmarket in Suffolk, a large unidentified object like a reflection on a car windscreen was seen. The object was smokey and silvery in colour. The object rotated and moved parallel to the A14.

- 19 November 1998 at 19:10: In the town of Stirling in Central, one object was seen to have a very bright strobe light.

- 19 November 1998 at 22:50: In the town of Newmarket, Suffolk, one huge, dull, greenish object was seen. The object had a circular shape when it moved.

- 19 November 1998 at 23:10: On the A11/Newmarket in Suffolk, one huge circle with another circle in it and several smaller circles inside this circle were seen.

- 20 November 1998 at 12:03: On the A11 in Suffolk, two very large ring squares of dull blue-ish light that were spinning very fast and tilting were seen. The objects changed into a cigar shape.

- 21 November 1998 at 18:58: In the town of Hampton Poyle/Oxford in Oxfordshire, one large white oval object with 200 lights was seen. The object was still and then started spinning.

- 29 November 1998 at 17:45: In the town of Abergevenny in Gwent, one large dark hexagonal object with two white lights was seen. The object made a humming sound and then flew low over the witness's house.

- 29 November 1998 at 07:35: In the town of Hull in East Yorkshire, a round-shaped object with a pale yellow vapour trail was seen. The object was travelling in a vertical, downward direction.

- 30 November 1998 at 15:18: Town unknown, county unknown, a witness saw a UFO.

- 30 November 1998 at 22:10: In the town of Sutton Coldfield in the West Midlands, one very big, bright white triangular object with a light on each point was seen.

- 2 December 1998 at 00:10: In the town of Blairgowrie in Perthshire, an unusual light in the sky was seen. The object was not a star or a plane. The object did not move for the hour in which the witness watched it.

- 5 December 1998 at 05:10: In the town of Blaenau in Gwent, one very bright white light at a very high altitude was seen.

- 6 December 1998 at 04:10: In the town of Sutton Coldfield in the West Midlands, one enormous dark triangular object with three green/blue-ish lights was seen.

- 7 December 1998 at 23:00: In the town of Stanford Le Hope in Essex, several white lines and dots of medium size were seen flashing.

- 12 December 1998 at 21:30: In the town of Horsham in West Sussex, one very bright circular white light was seen moving from East to West.

- 12 December 1998 at 23:30: In the town of Walthamstow in East London, flashing lights were seen before they disappeared and then reappeared at midnight.

- 15 December 1998 at 07:50: In the town of Moseley in the West Midlands, a very bright star-shaped object was seen. The object moved very fast, too fast to be a plane.

- 17 December 1998 at 08:00: In the town of New Haven in East Sussex, a witness saw strange vapour trails plus unusual objects that came from the horizon that wiggled around a bit then went again. They came from across the English Channel.

- 18 December 1998 at 08:00: In the town of Bury St Edmunds in Suffolk, multiple objects were seen to be smaller than aircraft and moving around high in the sky.

- 18 December 1998 at 23:59: In the town of Burghead in the Highlands, a single object much larger than a star was seen. The object was in the shape of a spider's web and was very bright with glorious rainbow colours. The object was stationary.

- 19 December 1998 at 22:30: In the town of Leeds in West Yorkshire, one bright circular white, red, and green object was seen pulsating in the sky.

- 20 December 1998 at 18:00: In the town of Warrington in Cheshire, a large, bright triangle that was grey on the perimeter was seen. The object had three orange lights on each point and travelled across the sky, not particularly fast.

- 20 December 1998 at 23:15: In the town of Ventnor/Isle of Wight in Hampshire, one diamond-shaped object with red circles on it was seen.

- 20 December 1998 at 03:00: In the town of Edinburgh in Lothian, a line of four lights that were orange in colour were seen in the sky.

- 20 December 1998 at 03:00: In the town of Edinburgh in Lothian, a gold-coloured ball with a tail was very bright and was seen.

- 20 December 1998 at 16:30: In the town of Knutsford in Cheshire, an oval grey object was seen that was 6ft and was heading South.

- 21 December 1998 at 00:30: In the town of Tedburn St Mary in Devon, one disc-shaped object with a bright light was seen.

- 21 December 1998 at 00:45: In the town of Edinburgh in Lothian, an object that was changing colour was seen. The object had green lights/lasers on it and was stationary, hovered, and then moved.

- 22 December 1998 at 19:00: In the town of Bradford in West Yorkshire, four large objects (each one was three times larger than a Hercules) were seen.

- 22 December 1998 at 20:44: In the town of Whitwell/Isle of Wight in Hampshire, a boomerang-shaped object was seen. The object flew overhead very quickly and then disappeared.

- 22 December 1998 at 23:45: In the town of Newton Mearns/Glasgow in Lanarkshire, there were a series of lights that were moving very fast that were seen.

- No date, no time: In the town of Farnborough in Kent, objects that appeared from nowhere flew erratically and were pilotless, sometimes accompanied by a bright flash. The witness has seen these objects every day for the last three years.

- 4 January 1999 at 18:30: In the town of Folkestone in Kent, one oval-shaped object was seen. The object did not have the usual aircraft lights on it.

- 4 January 1999 at 06:45: In the town of Bournemouth in Dorset, one disc-shaped object was seen. The object had two bright blue flashing lights on it.

- 7 January 1999 at 18:30: In the town of Glanarfon in Wales, one flat triangular object shaped like a shield that was white in colour was seen. The object had coloured lights mainly around the edge of the craft and a spotlight beneath.

- 9 January 1999 at 22:00: In the town of Bolton in Lancashire, one main object that was blue, red, and white was seen.

- 9 January 1999 at 02:00: In The Rhondda in Mid Glamorgan, one large oval object with a sphere in the middle was seen. The object had bright blue, green, and white lights on top of the craft. There was a humming noise.

- 9 January 1999 at 01:20: In the town of Dukinfield in Cheshire, one or two round, star-sized objects were seen. They were multi-coloured.

- 9 January 1999 at 21:37: In the town of Dunbar in East Lothian, one light with red, green, and yellow alternating lights on it was seen.

- 9 January 1999 at 21:46: In the town of Kennoway in Fife, one sphere-shaped object that was alternating in the colours red, white, green, and blue was seen.

- 10 January 1999 at 01:30: In the town of Llanelli in Dyfed, one object was seen. It had a pinprick of light that was changing colour between red, green, and orange.

- 10 January 1999 at 10:07: In the town of Hednesford in Staffordshire, a bright star-shaped object with red, green, and blue lights flashing in it was seen hovering silently.

- 10 January 1999 at 21:54: In the town of West Kilbride in Ayrshire, a bright multi-coloured light was seen in the sky.

- 11 January 1999 at 01:30: In the town of Ballater in Aberdeenshire, two round ball-shaped objects that were four times larger than the largest star and that were shiny and glittery were seen. They had blue, red, and green lights on them.

- 11 January 1999 at 01:15: In the town of Holyhead in Merseyside, a bright light larger than a star was seen changing colours from white to orange, blue, and green and back again. It appeared to be moving slowly.

- 12 January 1999 at 09:15: In the town of Cambuslong in Lanarkshire, a bright light in the shape of a star was seen.

- 12 January 1999 at 05:55: In Shoreham-by-Sea, West Sussex, two oval-shaped objects that were bright white were seen. Then later, another two objects that looked the same appeared.

- 17 January 1999 at 06:20: In the town of Hanworth in Middlesex, flashes of light came through the witness's bedroom window, and a bright star-like object was then seen outside.

- 21 January 1999 at 20:45: In the town of Corwen in Denbighshire, a flying saucer-shaped object with three square windows was seen. The object got lighter, then dimmed and slightly tilted.

- 21 January 1999 at 21:00: In the town of Harleston in London, one large "L" shaped object was seen to be very bright.

- 22 January 1999 at 00:30: In the town of Shrewsbury in Shropshire, a white light with shimmering green and red lights was seen.

- 26 January 1999, time unknown: In the town of Henbury/Bristol in Somerset, a bright orange light was seen.

- 28 January 1999, time unknown: In the town of Shipston-on-Stour in Warwickshire, an object was seen to have wings but no propellers. It was silent, with red and blue lights on it, and was hovering above the treetops.

- 1 February 1999 at 15:10: In the town of Bramley in West Yorkshire, one object with grey/white tubular fins at both ends was seen.

- 2 February 1999 at 17:25: In the town of Swansea in West Glamorgan, a cross-shaped collection of five star-like objects that had gold-coloured lights were seen.

- 2 February 1999 at 18:00: In the town of North Finchley in London, two opaque spheres were seen. The two objects were chasing each other around.

- 2 February 1999 at 01:30: In the town of Hull in Humberside, a round-shaped object was seen. The object was coloured red, green, blue, white, and yellow.

- 4 February 1999 at 00:20: On the M56 towards Chester in Cheshire, one circular-shaped object that was very dark in colour with four permanent red lights and three to four pulsating lights on it was seen.

- 5 February 1999 at 01:30: In the town of Brighton in East Sussex, one round-shaped object with a very bright white light was seen hovering like a yo-yo in the sky.

- 5 February 1999, time unknown: In the town of Chiswick in London, seven unusual light objects were seen moving in all different directions.

- 6 February 1999 at 22:45: In the town of Hadleigh in Suffolk, a boomerang-shaped craft was seen. The object had a red flashing light on the front and a white consistent light on each side and was hovering.

- 7 February 1999 at 18:50: In the town of Brighton in East Sussex, one diamond-shaped object was seen. The object had white/blue colours on it. The object was very bright and was hovering and moved up and down too.

- 7 February 1999 at 18:20: In the town of Winchester in Hampshire, one indistinct-shaped object that was white and very bright was seen.

- 7 February 1999 at 22:45: In the town of West Hampstead in London, a silver ball of light was seen darting around and was very fast.

- 7 February 1999 at 22:25: On the M53/Hopsford in Warwickshire, a circular-shaped object the colour of a green traffic light was seen. It moved in a steady, straight line.

- 9 February 1999 at 20:06: In the town of Wandsworth in London, one object was seen hovering in the sky.

- 10 February 1999 at 02:45: In the town of Swansea in West Glamorgan, a retired Air Traffic Controller saw a single blue and red object. The object was very bright. It made an S pattern in the sky, and when finished, it moved northeast.

- 11 February 1999 at 18:45: In the town of Caernarvon in Gwynedd, a single object that had rotors was seen. It had blue, red, and white strobes.

- 11 February 1999 at 19:50: Near Ambury in Worcestershire, one oval spot light was seen.

- 12 February 1999 at 21:00: In the town of Wakefield in West Yorkshire, a single object in the shape of a rectangle was seen. The object had a fireball-like centre that was red and orange/yellow.

- 14 February 1999 at 05:30: In the town of Hastings in Sussex, a UFO was seen hovering and then shot off into the distance. It had red flashing lights!

- 14 February 1999 at 23:00: In the town of Brook in Surrey, four lights linked by a green lattice were seen.

- 15 February 1999 at 10:25: In the town of Prestwick in Ayrshire, a primary radar operator saw an object that was ten miles wide. The object was travelling very quickly.

- 15 February 1999 at 07:50: In the town of Didlington in Norfolk, a hub-cap-shaped object which was a very bright orange/yellow colour was seen.

- 17 February 1999 at 07:00: In the town of Canning in London, two large objects that changed from a water drop shape to a 'U' shape and then separated into squiggly lines were seen. The objects were a very bright orange/yellow colour.

- 20 February 1999 at 19:00: In East Horsley, Surrey, eight small circles forming one large circle, which was green in colour, were seen.

- 20 February 1999 at 07:20: In the town of Burt in Lancashire, one exceedingly bright white light approximately 10 metres in diameter was seen. The object was disc-shaped.

- 21 February 1999 at 18:45: In the town of Humber Bridge/Hull in East Yorkshire, one object was seen. The object looked like a dull orange ball, the size of a tennis ball. It made a jig movement.

- 22 February 1999, time unknown: In the town of Glasgow in Glasgow a silver ball was hovering for a few seconds and then shot off.

- 22 February 1999 at 20:20: In the town of Pickering in North Yorkshire, two objects diagonally above one another, initially blue in colour, were seen; they disappeared for a few minutes and then reappeared only to change to be orange in colour.

- 22 February 1999 at 23:45: In the town of Halifax in West Yorkshire, one big round-shaped object was seen. The object had bright lights, and there was a droning sound.

- 22 February 1999 at 18:00: In the town of Birkenhead in Merseyside, two lights in the sky, one bigger than the other, were seen.

- 22 February 1999 at 18:45: In the town of Ilkley in West Yorkshire, two very large, round, white objects were seen. The objects were very bright and were drifting across the sky in a Westerly direction.

- 22 February 1999 at 18:15: In the town of Great Missenden in Buckinghamshire, three very large round white objects were seen. The objects were extremely bright. The objects were stationary but then moved away very quickly.

- 22 February 1999 at 18:40: In the town of Skipton in North Yorkshire, two very large round white objects were seen. One object was larger than the other. The objects were very bright and just stayed stationary.

- 22 February 1999 at 19:13: In the town of Bradford in West Yorkshire, two very large round white objects were seen. The objects were very bright, were stationary, and then moved West.

- 22 February 1999 at 19:30: In the town of Leeds in West Yorkshire, two very large round white objects that were very bright were seen.

- 22 February 1999 at 20:20: In the town of Minard in North Argyll, some stationary lights were seen that then disappeared and then reappeared.

- 22 February 1999 at 19:40: Towards the West of Glasgow Airport in Strathclyde, two bright stationary lights, low on the horizon, were seen. The lower one was brighter. The objects were stationary in the sky for 30 minutes.

- 22 February 1999 at 18:30: In the town of Kings Langley in Hertfordshire, two static lights that were very bright and large were seen.

- 22 February 1999 at 18:50: In the town of Wraysbury in Middlesex, two very large, white objects that were very bright were seen. One object was larger than the other.

- 22 February 1999 at 19:45: In the town of Weston-super-Mare in Somerset, two large, round, white objects were seen. The objects were very bright. The objects remained stationary for about 15 minutes.

- 22 February 1999 at 19:30: In the town of Bristol in Somerset, two large, round, white objects were seen. The objects were very bright and were slowly moving West and lowering.

- 22 February 1999 at 18:50: In the town of St. Monans in Fife, a bright light that was pale blue and purple in the centre was seen.

- 22 February 1999 at 20:09: In the town of Derby in Derbyshire, a Police Officer saw two large round white/yellow lights.

- 22 February 1999 at 18:40: In the town of Glenrothes in Fife, two bright lights that were approximately one degree apart were seen.

- 22 February 1999 at 19:00: In the town of Bolton in Greater Manchester, two objects were seen. One object had a pale white light. The other object had a red/green light. They glided along the sky.

- 23 February 1999 at 19:00: In the town of Burnley in Lancashire, a disc-shaped object with lights was seen hovering.

- 24 February 1999 at 19:00: In the town of Chingford in Essex, an object that looked like Saturn and had a ring around it was seen. The object had lots of flashing lights.

- 25 February 1999 at 22:10: In Barnard Castle in County Durham, a bright yellow object was seen. The object was moving from South to North.

- 28 February 1999 at 22:00: On the A68/Corbridge in Northumberland, an object the size of ten football pitches, shaped like an arrowhead, was seen moving towards and upwards.

- 4 March 1999 at 21:15: In the town of Lichfield, Staffordshire, white lights were seen.

- 5 March 1999 at 21:00: On the M60/Manchester in Greater Manchester, a rectangle-shaped object that had a yellow light was seen.

- 5 March 1999 at 22:30: In the town of Falkirk in Stirlingshire, one dozen objects were seen. The objects were red, green, blue, and white in colour. The objects were stationary and revolving.

- 6 Mach 1999 at 01:15: In the town of Worthing in West Sussex, a black ball, metallic-shaped object was seen. The object changed the direction of travel from South to East quite fast.

- 7 March 1999, time unknown: In the town of Ballykinler in County Down, lights were seen at various times after dark. The lights were triangle and diamond-shaped. They were moving in different directions.

- 8 March 1999, time unknown: In the town of Seaforde Village in County Down, Lights in a circle shape were seen. They were spinning clockwise and oscillating.

- 9 March 1999 at 18:30: In the town of Ammanford in Dyfed, two dark grey translucent objects were seen. They were manoeuvring and then disappeared into the cloud.

- 9 March 1999 at 10:10: In the town of Newton Abbot in Devon, one large circle that constantly changed shape was seen. The object was yellow and very bright. The object was moving very slowly.

- 10 March 1999 at 20:30: In the town of Broughton/Scunthorpe in Lincolnshire, a bright star-shaped light about the size of a hot air balloon, was seen. The object was still, then dropped in height below the tree line.

- 10 March 1999 at 10:30: In the town of Bangor in Gwynedd flashing lights of various colours were seen. The object's shape is unknown.
- 10 March 1999 at 20:05: In the town of Chelsea, near the Football Club in London, a Police Officer saw four yellow lights. The objects changed from a square shape to a diamond shape.

- 11 March 1999 at 05:10: In the town of Newcastle Emlyn in Carmarthenshire, one large, round white light was seen. The object was very bright and was moving from West to East.

- 13 March 1999 at 21:25: In the town of Cardiff/Pontypridd in South Glamorgan, a set of red, blue, and yellow lights were seen in a straight line. The object was very bright and formed a triangle shape.

- 14 March 1999 at 23:25: In the town of Penheridge in Staffordshire, a low flying/hovering silent aircraft was seen.

- 17 March 1999 at 23:30: In the town of Shavington/Crewe in Cheshire, one star-sized object, brighter than a star, was seen. The object was stationary at first and then moved Westward.

- 18 March 1999 at 21:40: In the town of Bebbington in Merseyside, two round objects were seen. The objects had a faint red glow. One reversed on itself and then travelled North to join the other one.

- 20 March 1999 at 00:50: In the town of Frankwell/Shrewsbury in Shropshire, a triangle of lights that went across the witness with no sound were seen. They were travelling from North to South at a fast speed.

- 24 March 1999 at 21:25: In the town of Falkirk in Stirlingshire, a large, glowing object, brighter than a starry glow and bigger than a star, was seen. The object appeared to have a 'line' through it.

- 25 March 1999 at 21:30: In the town of Strathmiglo in Fife, one bright, white light was seen. The object was static to the South.

- 26 March 1999 at 20:45: In the town of Carshalton in Surrey, one large, round object was seen. The object was white and very bright and was travelling northwest.

- 26 March 1999 at 20:40: In the town of Alford in Hampshire, one large, round object was seen. The object was white and very bright and was travelling North West.

- 27 March 1999 at 21:00: In the town of Kilmarnock in Ayrshire, a bright light was seen.

- 29 March 1999 at 21:00: In the town of Tranent in East Lothian, a star-shaped object that was coloured red, green, and blue was seen.

- 29 March 1999 at 23:05: In the town of Newburgh in Fife, a triangular UFO weaving from side to side and changing colour over Newburgh for two hours was seen.

- 29 March 1999 at 21:30: In the town of Ardross in Ross-Shire, one object, four times larger than Venus, was seen. The object was halogen coloured and was brighter than Venus.

- 30 Mar 1999 at 21:35: In the town of Ardross in Ross-Shire, one object, four times larger than Venus, was seen. The object was halogen coloured and brighter than Venus. The object was stationary for quite a while.

- 1 April 1999 at 02:05: In the town of Llandovery in Dyfed, one capsule-shaped object was seen. The object was blue and silver.

- 6 April 1999 at 14:45: On the M2/Faversham in Kent, lots of swirly white lights that were 50 ft wide were seen. The objects were circular. transparent like jellyfish, and very bright. The object had lights that were coming and going on and off.

- 10 April 1999, time unknown: In the town of Wem, nr Shrewsbury, in Shropshire, a Pilot saw one large circular object with the bottom missing.

- 10 April 1999 at 10:30: In the town of Withernsea in Humberside, an irregular pattern of lights was seen. The lights were coloured white, blue, yellow, and red.

- 13 April 1999 at 21:15: In the town of East Belfast in Northern Ireland, a very bright, pointed light source was seen. The light was flashing white, with four quick flashes and then a gap. The object climbed rapidly in 30 seconds.

- 14 April 1999 at 11:18: In the town of Lewes in East Sussex, five circular objects were seen. The objects were green, red, and white in colour. The objects were extremely bright in colour and were moving North.

- 15 April 1999 at 02:19: In the town of Tooting in London, one circular bright white object was seen.

- 22 April 1999, time unknown: In the town of Dagenham in Essex, one large saucer-shaped object that looked like it was painted with a fine brush was seen. The object was flicking now and again.

- 29 April 1999 at 16:00: Town unknown in Mid-Glamorgan, a circular-shaped object was seen. The object was too high to be a bird and too low to be a plane. It was travelling from East to West.

- 29 April 1999 at 21:27: In the town of Brockley in London, a boomerang-shaped object that was silent was moving in a northeast direction.

- 1 May 1999 at 21:25: In the town of Greenock in Renfrewshire, five lights going into a centre and breaking away into a circle were seen circling in the sky.

- 4 May 1999 at 22:15: In the town of Modbury in Devon, one haze of light with two tyre-like spheres in the middle was seen. The object was white with a yellow haze and was very bright. It was stationary at first.

- 16 May 1999 at 00:15: In the town of Worcester in Worcestershire, one round-shaped object that was very bright was seen. The object was yellow with a red flash.

- 16 May 1999 at 21:20: In the town of Poole in Dorset, various rounded, orange/yellow objects were seen. The objects were very bright. There were fourteen at once, but they disappeared at high speed, only three stayed behind.

- 18 May 1999 at 12:45: In the town of Elgin/Moray in Morayshire, one balloon-shaped object was seen. The object had a bright white glow, moved slowly to the left, and then stayed stationary for a while.

- 19 May 1999 at 08:21: In the town of Bexhill in East Sussex, a bright light hanging in the sky was seen. The object had bits trailing off of it. It was stationary.

- 22 May 1999 at 22:00: In the town of Davyhulme in Greater Manchester, a round and dull orange object was seen. The object was swaying while moving upward and then changed direction as if guided.

- 23 May 1999 at 23:00: In the town of Oakham in Leicestershire, two large, yellow, bright lights were seen that were not moving.

- 24 May 1999 at 20:45: In the town of Craigie Village in Ayrshire, a star-shaped object with a tail above it was seen. The object was a yellow/white colour and very bright. The object was moving vertically.

- 26 May 1999 at 21:25: In the town of Liverpool in Merseyside, a very bright white light was seen approaching slowly from the south; it was stationary before heading east and then vanishing.

- 26 May 1999 at 21:35: In the town of Swansea in West Glamorgan, one object that was white and very bright was seen. The object was very high up and very fast.

- 29 May 1999 at 22:30: In the town of Bonny bridge in Stirlingshire, a very large, bright, star-shaped object was seen hovering low in the sky.

- 5 June 1999 at 22:58: In the town of Brighton in East Sussex, a very large circular set of lights that were circular in shape were seen. The

115

object split into two semicircular arcs, then joined up again. The object was white and very bright.

- 8 June 1999 at 00:00: In the town of Marlborough in Wiltshire, a Private Pilot saw one circular, red, yellow, blue and green object. It had a strong brightness and made sudden movements.

- 8 June 1999 at 22:35: In the town of Monmouth in Gwent, one object the size of a hot air balloon was seen. The object was bright, with a honeycomb of light. The object was stationary and then flew off.

- 8 June 1999 at 19:24: In the town of Rhymney Valley in Gwent, one metallic sphere, approximately five-six metres, was seen. It was flying erratically from South to North along the Rhymney Valley.

- 9 June 1999 at 23:15: In the town of Blithbury Reservoir in Admaston/Staffs, one round object was seen. The object was green, red, blue, and yellow in colour. It darted from left to right and towards the witness's vehicle.

- 11 June 1999 time unknown: In the town of Salisbury in Wiltshire, a very bright, highly reflective object was seen. The object was not like usual aircraft and did not have wings or a tail. The object was rotating horizontally.

- 12 June 1999 at 01:05: In the town of Flint in Clwyd, a disc/star shaped object with coloured lights, blue and green, spinning around it was seen. The object was like a sphere of light high in the atmosphere.

- 14 June 1999 at 16:15: In the town of Algate in London, one thirty-foot silver ball/sphere object was seen. The object was vertical at first and was still moving southward very gradually.

- 24 June 1999 at 22:19: In the town of Hove in East Sussex, one dome-shaped object was seen. The object had a bright white light and was flashing. The object was stationary for about 45 minutes.

- 25 June 1999 at 00:03: Town unknown in Derbyshire, a line of lights that were very intense were seen. They were steady and had red lights on top. They were moving away at an angle, moving to the right. They were horizontal.

- 26 June 1999 at 13:30: In the town of Blanefield in Ayrshire, a balloon-shaped object with bright yellow on top and a black, flat base was seen. The object was smooth, straight, and level.

- 30 June 1999 at 19:40: In the town of Kingsbury in London, one bullet-shaped object that had rounded at the sides was seen. It was jet black and very noticeable against the light evening sky. It was heading North.

- 30 June 1999, time unknown: In the town of Kingsbury in London, one large, black object glided across the sky. It was oscillating and climbing. It was moving North.

- 3 July 1999 at 22:10: In the town of Hemford in Shropshire, a single circular object the size of a golf/tennis ball was seen. The object was white and very bright. It was moving very slowly.

- 4 July 1999 at 20:00: In the town of Holland on Sea in Essex one oval transparent object was seen, which gave the whole appearance of a smoke ring. The object's outline was dark. The object changed shape when it moved.

- 5 July 1999 at 23:10: In the town of Scunthorpe in Lincolnshire, a bright, white light with a red tinge was seen. The object moved vertically, then started moving erratically.

- 6 July 1999 at 01:15: In the town of Eastbourne in East Sussex, one saucer-shaped object 80 ft in diameter was seen. The object was about 30ft off the ground. It made a rattling sound, and six beams, bright light came from the object.

- 10 July 1999 at 00:51: In the town of Rillington in North Yorkshire, a circular-shaped object was seen. It was surrounded by red and green lights, and there was a static sound.

- 10 July 1999 at 20:55: In the town of Porthcawl in Mid-Glamorgan, one cylindrical-shaped object was seen. The object was white and very bright. It was moving from left to right.

- 10 July 1999 at 19:00: In the town of Clayton in Greater Manchester, a 30ft, circular-shaped object was seen.

- 10 July 1999 at 02:45: In the town of Scunthorpe in Lincolnshire, a bright, white light with a red tinge was seen. The object was moving vertically and making erratic actions.
- 11 July 1999 at 00:00: In the town of Llangynog in Powys, a bright star-shaped object was seen. The object made an unusually gentle ark. Then some strange squiggles from left to right. The object was high up in the sky.

- 12 July 1999 at 11:45: In the town of Flint in Flintshire, one star-shaped object was seen. The object had coloured lights around it: green, blue, and red. It was spinning.

- 12 July 1999 at 13:45: In the town of Washingborough in Lincolnshire, one small kite-shaped object was seen. The object was bright white in colour. The object formed an arc shape and then moved away.

- 12 July 1999 at 23:10: In the town of Blandford St. Mary in Dorset, three star-shaped objects were seen. They were all white and very bright. They were faster than an aircraft.

- 12 July 1999 at 02:00: Town unknown in Wiltshire, a line of three orange lights was seen. Two of them were close together.

- 13 July 1999 at 02:15: In the town of Eyres Monsell in Leicestershire, two objects were seen: one was a triangle shape and the other a 'V' shape. Both had green and red lights. One was pulsating.

- 14 July 1999 at 21:45: In the town of Bushey in Hertfordshire, one object with four bright, white lights on it was seen. It moved in a straight line.

- 14 July 1999 at 15:00: In the town of Peterlee in Durham, a bright silver object that was stationary was seen.

- 15 July 1999 at 23:35: In the town of Halsted in Essex, blue lights darting around very quickly were seen.

- 15 July 1999 at 00:00: In the town of Eastbourne in East Sussex, numerous. Bright, flashing objects were seen moving very fast.

- 15 July 1999 at 01:10: In the town of Dwyfach in Gwynedd, a bright light was seen.

- 24 July 1999 at 23:30: In the town of Redcliff in Somerset, ten circular-shaped objects were seen. The object's brightness was less than that of a star. The objects were in line, doing zig-zags, and heading North.

- 25 July 1999 at 00:20: In the town of Coventry in the West Midlands, an illuminated disc-shaped object that was 4 inches in diameter was seen. The object was vertical and was moving fast in a straight line.

- 25 July 1999 at 23:05: In the town of Murthly in Tayside, one object the size of a football or melon was seen. The object was yellow/orange in colour. It went to a pinpoint and disappeared.

- 25 July 1999 at 22:25: In the town of Porthcawl in Mid Glamorgan, one disc-shaped object that was bluey-silver in colour was seen. The object moved in a straight line. It was definitely not a star or planet.

- 1 August 1999 at 10:30: In the town of Rochdale in Greater Manchester, a balloon-shaped object was seen. There were lights around the object. The object was hovering for some time.

- 2 August 1999 at 21:50: In the town of Boston in Lincolnshire, a very bright light that was orange in colour and much bigger than aircraft lights was seen.

- 3 August 1999 at 22:30: In the town of Slough in Berkshire, a single disc/star-sized object was seen. It was white in colour and bright like a star.

- 4 August 1999 at 23:30: In the town of Glenrothes in Fife, one small, very bright object with a tail was seen changing colours. It made slight movements from side to side.

- 6 August 1999 at 22:30: In the town of Loversall in South Yorkshire, two UFOs were seen, both UFOs were flashing different colours. They appeared to be hovering, but no shape could be seen.

- 8 August 1999 at 22:00: In the town of Ulverston in Cumbria, circular flashing lights were seen. They made extremely strange movements.

- 13 August 1999, time unknown: In the town of Tenterden in Kent, a large, brilliant light was stationary in the sky. It moved away fairly quickly and disappeared.

- 17 August 1999 at 20:50: Town unknown in Carlisle, two blue balls of light were seen dancing around in the sky.

- 21 August 1999 at 21:50: Town unknown in Middlesex, one very bright orange ball was seen. It made a humming sound and moved in a straight line.

- 21 August 1999 at 21:30: In the town of Kinloss in Morayshire, two very bright lights were seen in the sky.

- 22 August 1999 at 19:15: In the town of Thornton/Bradford in West Yorkshire, a black saucer/disc shape which was making no noise and had a bright silver light which appeared to rotate around the saucer was seen.

- 1 September 1999 at 18:30: In the town of Ealing in London, one object the size of an aircraft was seen. The object was long, thin, and black in colour.

- 10 September 1999 at 17:18: In the town of Oldham in Greater Manchester, one round ball-shaped object was seen. The object was bright white in colour and was horizontal.

- 11 September 1999 at 22:15: In the town of Livermead/Torquay in Devon, one large, cigar-shaped object was seen. The object was luminescent green and very bright. The object sort of glided along.

- 11 September 1999 at 19:45: In the town of Stowmarket in Suffolk, one yellow object was seen bouncing in the sky.

- 12 September 1999 at 19:42: In the town of Lower Stoneham in East Sussex, six groups of coloured lights were seen. The lights were white, green, and red in colour.

- 12 September 1999 at 21:20: In the town of Sellindge/Ashford in Kent, a bright light was seen heading South.

- 13 September 1999 at 16:30: Town unknown in Guernsey, one small circular-shaped object was seen. The object was white and extremely bright. The object appeared to be constructed of a lattice/trellis.

- 13 September 1999 at 01:40: In the town of Penarth/Cardiff in South Glamorgan, a large, bright object was seen.

- 13 September 1999 at 23:00: In the town of Newbiggin By-The-Sea in Northumbria, a large, bright light hovering near the coastline was seen.

The object looked like a large star with a smaller star on top. It had a red light coming from the middle.

- 18 September 1999 at 07:30: Town unknown in London, one small, round, white/silver object that was extremely bright was seen.

- 19 September 1999 at 20:20: In the town of Marlborough in Wiltshire, one car-sized object that was tubular-shaped was seen. It had three lights at the front, and they were very bright. It moved off at a high speed.

- 20 September 1999 at 23:30: In the town of Malton in North Yorkshire, one flat, rugby ball-shaped oval object was seen. It had two flashing red lights at the ends. It circled, then hovered, then headed off.

- 22 September 1999 at 21:25: In the town of Longden in Shropshire, one brilliant ball of light was seen. The object climbed very high and very fast in the sky and then disappeared.

- 23 September 1999 at 10:00: In the town of Leominster in Herefordshire, one large aircraft-size object was seen. The object had a bright light in front and had long wings. It had a jet that sounded very fast, and there was black smoke coming from the rear.

- 24 September 1999 at 22:10: In the town of Glengormley in Co. Antrim, one object with a red light flew level, then climbed vertically with a grey trail of smoke. It was very fast.

- 25 September 1999 at 01:30: In the town of Tinshill in West Yorkshire, one oblong, flexible object was seen. It was red in colour and was very bright, and then dimmed a little.

- 28 September 1999 at 04:55: In the town of Lochgreen in South Ayrshire, a very bright, intense light was seen. It flared up and moved from left to right very fast. It made sudden movements and quick direction changes.

- 29 September 1999, time unknown: In the town of Beddingham in East Sussex, one large, circular, flat, brown object was seen hovering.

- 2 October 1999, time unknown: In the town of Woolston/Warrington in Cheshire, a beam of light was seen over a school. A noise was then heard, but not that of a plane or helicopter.

- 3 October 1999 at 20:00: In the town of Dinnington in South Yorkshire, a light was seen in the sky, and then a square-shaped object appeared, with lights at each corner.

- 4 October 1999 at 21:09: In the town of Rosyth in Fife, one star-shaped object that was white was seen. It had a very bright light and moved fast in a straight line.

- 5 October 1999 at 21:55: In the town of Llanbedrog in Gwynedd, one tubular-shaped object that was larger than a normal aircraft was seen. It was bright green, tinged with blue. It moved downwards, leaving a trail behind.

- 9 October 1999 at 21:15: In the town of Calne in Wiltshire, two lights, one large and one small, were seen. They were white and very bright. They were moving from left to right and then to the left again.

- 10 October 1999 at 23:50: In the town of Foxham in Wiltshire, a single white light was seen being stationary for a while. Then fans of light began moving from left to right and back.

- 11 October 1999 at 11:20: In the town of Clitheroe in Lancashire one rounded saucer-shaped object that was smaller than a bi-plane was seen. It was dark on top and light underneath.

- 18 October 1999 at 06:25: In the town of Ilford in Essex, one cylindrical object that was the size of a fuselage or a small/medium aircraft was seen. It was bright white, moved rapidly upwards, and then disappeared.

- 18 October 1999 at 02:00: In the town of Bath in Somerset, one object, the size of a medium star shaped like a ball with three prongs on it, was seen. It was green, red, blue, and white in colour. It was very bright.

- 18 October 1999 at 19:21: In the town of Shotton in Flintshire, a UFO with a light was hovering. A second UFO appeared. It had a large, bright white light and also seemed to have a red and green fleck on it.

- 20 October 1999 at 02:45: In the town of Liverpool in Merseyside, one round, a football-sized object was seen. It was translucent green and extremely bright. It moved quite slowly in a straight line.

- 24 October 1999 at 21:00: In the town of Eppingham in Surrey, a long streak of light in the sky resembling six-eight windows was seen. It was moving from side to side very fast.

- 24 October 1999 at 19:40: In the town of Kingston Upon Thames in Surrey, a green light was seen projecting from the cloud, followed by a pulsed wave of green light. It was very bright. It was moving in a Southerly direction.

- 25 October 1999 at 23:59: In the town of Wetherby in West Yorkshire, a triangle formation of lights was seen. It suddenly gained speed and headed off north.

- 25 October 1999 at 05:45: In the town of Woolverstone in Suffolk, a very bright light, ten times the size of a star, was seen. It was very high in the sky and not moving or flashing. It was not an aircraft.

- 25 October 1999 at 08:00: In the town of Hipperholme/Halifax in West Yorkshire, a strange object was seen.

- 26 October 1999 at 18:40: In the town of Benllech in Anglesey, a white, onion-shaped object which was glowing white with sparks, was seen moving rapidly in a straight line.

- 27 October 1999 at 17:00: Town unknown, county unknown blue and green lights, with things falling out of the sky, were seen.

- 31 October 1999 at 21:00: In the town of Lisburn in County Antrim, one hexagon-shaped object the size of a bowling ball at arm's length was seen. It had red lines on it and was very bright. It moved fast, then vanished.

- 31 October 1999 at 16:15: In the town of Grantown-on-Spey in Morayshire, a large ball with two forks at the rear was seen. The ball and between the forks were lit. It was not as fast as a jet.

- 2 November 1999 at 19:43: In the town of Urmston in Greater Manchester, a star-shaped object, growing larger, then shrinking before disappearing. It was moving fast.

- 2 November 1999 at 06:20: In the town of Blurton/Stoke-on-Trent in Staffordshire, a small white light travelling in a straight line towards a second light, which appeared to be a star, was seen. The object fell, and the light dissipated.

- 6 November 1999 at 21:20: In the town of Heysham in Lancashire, four objects were sighted in the sky, moving at varying speeds. They moved erratically.

- 8 November 1999 at 18:00: In the town of Penicuik in Midlothian, one star-shaped object with blue and red flashing lights was seen keeping a constant position.

- 10 November 1999 at 20:25: In the town of Littlehampton in West Sussex, a witness described seeing a UFO 'unidentified foreign object'.

- 16 November 1999 at 04:00: In the town of Kirkham/Preston in Lancashire, a sphere of bright light the size of a tennis ball was seen falling from the sky towards the ground.

- 16 November 1999 at 18:00: In the town of Whitby in North Yorkshire, an RAF Pilot saw one bright red light flickering. There was static in the air. It was moving to the West.

- 17 November 1999 at 23:20: In the town of Maidenhead in Berkshire, a large circular light in the sky was seen. Then, after about eight minutes, it drifted off to the West.

- 18 November 1999 at 16:00: In the town of Crickhowell in Gwent, a vertical orange line near the horizon was seen moving to a horizontal position.

- 20 November 1999 at 08:12: In the town of Market Drayton in Shropshire, a craft with a bright, white light was seen. The craft was positioned once and then moved out of sight.

- 21 November 1999 at 22:25: In the town of Arbroath in Angus, a single, roundish, orange-glowing light was seen. It was moving horizontally across the sky and away in the distance.

- 22 November 1999 at 21:15: In the town of Skipton in North Yorkshire, two UFOs that were red in colour were seen, followed by two jets.

- 26 November 1999 at 17:30: In the town of Carcroft/Doncaster in South Yorkshire, a series of ten green lights in the sky were seen. They formed a formation, then broke formation and headed towards a large light.

- 28 November 1999 at 22:08: In the town of Pentraeth in Gwynedd, a giant dewdrop-shaped object was seen. It had a yellow centre and a green/blue haze around the outside. It was too big to be a shooting star.

- 29 November 1999 at 18:30: In the town of Durham in Tyne and Wear, two small, ball-shaped objects were seen. They were orange in colour. They were bright and then dim. They were moving upward.

- 29 November 1999 at 23:55: In the town of Tilbury in Essex, a Police Officer saw green, red, and white lights. The lights were brighter than on an aeroplane or a helicopter. They remained static in the sky.

- 29 November 1999, time unknown: In the town of Tilbury in Essex, a Police Officer saw one bright star-shaped object with a green hue surrounding it.

- 29 November 1999 at 23:55: In the town of Tilbury in Essex, a Police Officer saw a white, star-shaped object twinkling red and green. It did not move. It was brighter than the other stars.

- 29 November 1999 at 23:55: In the town of Chadwell St. Mary in Essex, a Police Officer saw one object flickering green and red.

- 29 November 1999 at 23:20: In the town of Dagenham in Essex, four lights of blue, yellow, red, and white in colour were seen.

- 29 November 1999 at 23:34: In the town of Dartford in Kent, a small light was glittering red, green, and white in the sky.

- 2 December 1999 at 02:05: In the town of Worthing in East Surrey, a UFO was seen.

- 2 December 1999 at 03:00: In the town of Thetford in Norfolk, one triangular-shaped object with two lights displayed in a similar manner to car headlights was seen. The object rotated about a vertical axis and descended.

- 3 December 1999 at 08:30: In the town of Deans/Livingston in West Lothian, the witness just said it was an object.

- 3 December 1999 at 13:50: In the town of Scunthorpe in Lincolnshire, a large cigar-shaped object was seen moving very fast.

- 4 December 1999 at 22:10: In the town of Newport in Gwent, a bright, Venus, pale orange object was seen. It was moving as a bird would, in and out of formation.

- 5 December 1999 at 21:55: In the town of St. Peter Port in Guernsey, eight orange blobs that resembled the flight of a bird were seen.

- 7 December 1999 at 17:45: In the town of Newport in Gwent, one star-shaped object was seen. It was white and very bright. It made very erratic movements.

- 9 December 1999 at 17:00: In the town of Melton/Woodbridge in Somerset, one very large object was seen. It had a tail. It was green in colour and glowing.

- 9 December 1999 at 16:55: In the town of Orsett in Essex, a large Crystal ball-shaped object was seen. It was the size of a light bulb. It was yellowy/white in colour and was travelling in a diagonal direction.

- 13 December 1999 at 06:00: In the town of Windlesham in Surrey, one star-shaped object was seen. It was white and very bright. It was very fast.

- 15 December 1999 at 08:00: In the town of Witham in Essex one large snowdrop-shaped object was seen. It was white and very bright and was moving South-East.

- 15 December 1999 at 03:30: In the town of Glasgow in Strathclyde, multiple bright lights were seen. They were red and green in colour. Some were moving and flashing. Separate streaks of light would come from them. They were erratic and would occasionally group in formation, then split up.

- 17 December 1999 at 18:45: In the town of Swindon in Wiltshire, two objects were seen. They had bright white lights. They were circling and spinning many times in the sky.

- 17 December 1999 at 10:00: In the town of Dundee in Angus, three extremely bright, piercing lights that then became four were seen.

- 18 December 1999 at 19:30: In the town of Forest Hill in London, a white glare was seen. Underneath it was another glare that was red and blue in colour.

- 19 December 1999 at 16:00: In the town of Whiteley in Hampshire, a large, bright object hovering in a southwest direction was seen. Then, a few seconds later, it vanished.

- 21 December 1999 at 08:45: In the town of Banchory in Aberdeenshire, one circular object was seen. It was white and very bright. The object was moving downward.

- 28 December 1999 at 06:10: In the town of Swindon in Wiltshire, one circular object, too big to be a star, was seen. It was mostly white, but it had coloured lights too. It moved from right to left at speed.

- 29 December 1999, time unknown: In the town of Dundee in Angus, one cylinder-shaped object that began to change shape into a V was seen. It had bright lights and was moving from East to West.

- 31 December 1999 at 18:45: In the town of Wigmore in Herefordshire, a large flashing light that looked like a white circle flashing in the sky was seen.

- No date, no time: In the town of Chobham in Surrey, a silver object darting back and forth was seen. It was moving fast and then disappeared quickly.

- No date, no time: In the town of Hanley in Staffordshire, two small dots that were cream-coloured were seen. The objects were moving as fast as a satellite or a shooting star.

- 1 January 2000 at 07:30: In the town of Tenbury Wells in Shropshire, a cigar-shaped object was seen. The object was grey in colour with two windows. There were bright lights shining from out the windows. The object was travelling from east to west.

- 3 January 2000 at 20:45: In the town of Evanton in Ross-Shire, a gold disc was seen. It flew through the clouds, reappeared, and then disappeared.

- 4 January 2000 at 00:30: In the town of Erdingham/Birmingham in the West Midlands, one large triangular-shaped object was seen. There were three red lights at each corner of the triangle. Also two-three white lights on the object.

- 5 January 2000 at 01:20: In the town of Wootton Bassett in Wiltshire, one single object was seen. It changed from white to green in colour with an orange tinge. It was brighter than any star and was flashing. It moved to the right.

- 9 January 2000 at 02:45: In the town of Runcorn in Cheshire, one round golf ball-shaped object was seen. It was orange and white in colour and very bright. It was moving East.

- 9 January 2000 at 21:36: In the town of Barnstable in Devon, one cylindrical-shaped object was seen. It was blue and green in colour. It was bright and pulsating. It was hovering and moving gradually from South to southeast.

- 9 January 2000 at 18:06: Town unknown in Cheshire, the object eclipsed the moon. The object was a ring shape.

- 13 January 2000 at 23:45: In the town of Motherwell in Lanarkshire, one pulsating orange ball was seen. The object was travelling from north to south.

- 14 January 2000, time unknown: Town unknown in London, a floating object sitting in front of a cloud formation was seen. It was flat and reflecting the sunlight.

- 17 January 2000 at 21:20: In the town of Leeds in West Yorkshire, a disc that was illuminated was seen. It was 200 ft up and 150 ft long.

- 17 January 2000 at 21:03: In the town of Newbridge in Dumfries and Galloway, two stationary oblong/cigar-shaped figures were seen. They were changing colour.

- 17 January 2000 at 21:40: In the town of Cottesmore in Leicestershire, several lights were seen falling to the ground, towards a brighter, larger light. The lights were white in colour.

- 19 January 2000 at 22:10: In the town of Birmingham in the West Midlands, a brilliant white light was travelling at extreme velocity.

- 20 January 2000 at 23:02: In the town of Coaltown/Balgonie in Fife, a ball-shaped object was seen. It was 40 feet in diameter. It was red, purple, green, and yellow in colour. A white light was pulsating from it. It was moving horizontally and vertically.

- 21 January 2000 at 00:40: In the town of Glen Rothes in Fife, a ball-shaped object was seen. It was 40 feet in diameter. It was bright orange and looked solid. It was stationary.

- 21 January 2000 at 20:30: In the town of Southampton, Hampshire, two objects the size of footballs were seen. They had tails that made them look like tadpoles. They were orange and very bright. They were moving rapidly.

- 22 January 2000 at 20:05: In the town of Fareham in Hampshire, an object the size of a 10-storey block of flats was seen. It had hundreds of white lights. It was moving very fast.

- 23 January 2000 at 02:30: In the town of Birmingham in the West Midlands, one single object the size of a mini car but round was seen. It was blue and very bright. The object was stationary and then shot upward.

- 23 January 2000 at 21:00: In the town of Whaplode in Lincolnshire, an object was flashing intermittently at regular intervals. It was hovering. It had an underside light, which remained static.

- 29 January 2000 at 16:15: In the town of Dibden/Southampton in Hampshire, three objects the size of airliners and many others that looked like large shadows were seen. They were all black and moved in a straight line.

- 1 February 2000, time unknown: In the town of Invergowrie in Angus, slow-moving lights were seen. They moved from the North to the South and then stopped.

- 1 February 2000 at 08:00: In the town of Colchester, Essex, a square-shaped object was seen. It was greyish in colour and was moving to the North.

- 2 February 2000 at 18:38: In the town of Hull in Humberside, four flashing lights were seen in the sky. They formed a square. They were moving north-northeast.

- 3 February 2000 at 19:10: In the town of Melksham in Wiltshire, four large round orange lights were seen. They were in symmetrical formation, and occasionally a light would black out and reappear.

- 6 February 2000 at 19:28: In the town of Bideford in North Devon, one triangular-shaped object was seen. It changed colour from red to green. The object swayed from side to side and then spun in the air.

- 10 February 2000 at 13:40: In the town of Shrewsbury in Shropshire, a saucer-shaped craft that was hovering and spinning was seen. It had protrusions on the outside and five dark circular areas in the middle.

- 11 February 2000 at 18:20: In the town of Banff in Banffshire, two star-shaped objects, with the larger emitting a light beam which was cone-shaped were seen. They were pinkish in colour.

- 11 February 2000 at 18:05: In the town of Banff in Banffshire, one object that was shrouded in a sort of mist was seen. It emitted a purple light for about five seconds. It was a very deep blue colour.

- 11 February 2000 at 18:00: In the town of Near Wick in Caithness, two white bright lights were seen. The lower of the two lights looked like a searchlight. They were very high.

- 11 February 2000 at 18:05: In the town of Bowness-on-Windermere in Cumbria, two lights that were bright and star-shaped were seen. They were white in colour. One was lighter than the other. They glowed from behind.

- 13 February 2000 at 18:30: In the town of Chapeltown/Leeds in West Yorkshire, two round objects that were bigger than the stars were seen. Both objects were red and white in colour and very bright. It was stationary.

- 14 February 2000 at 18:20: In the town of Coaltown/Balgonie in Fife, one mass of white light with a green and yellow outline was seen. It was flashing and was stationary in the sky.

- 19 February 2000 at 18:50: In the town of Little Town in West Yorkshire three large round-shaped objects were seen. They were dull in colour. They moved from North to South vertically up and then down.

- 23 February 2000 at 00:15: In the town of Colinton/Edinburgh in Midlothian, one very bright oval-shaped object was seen. It had a tail like a kite. It was moving very fast and travelling horizontally to the west when it dipped and then disappeared.

- 25 February 2000 at 19:30: In the town of Newport in Gwent, three objects/lights that were flickering on and off were seen. They moved West and then moved to the south.

- 26 February 2000 at 17:55: In the town of Finsbury Park in London, one odd-shaped object was seen. It was black in colour and was faster than a plane, and moved in a straight line.

- 1 March 2000 at 16:50: In the town of Westgate in Lancashire, one very bright cigar-shaped object was seen. It was very high up in the sky and was moving slowly.

- 1 March 2000 at 03:45: At Whitechapel Police Station in London, several Police Officers saw a small red light moving slowly to the South. It did a U-turn and moved off to the North at great speed. Then moved in tight circles.

- 7 March 2000 at 18:30: In the town of Wellingborough in Northants A UFO disc-shaped object was 33,000 feet up and was flying above a jumbo jet.

- 12 March 2000 at 20:00: In the town of Stamford Hill in London, one star-shaped object which was bright white was seen. It had steady movement and then did a 90-degree turn and headed North.

- 16 March 2000 at 21:37: In the town of Darlington in County Durham, a large number of lights flashing and moving around were seen. They were bright white in colour. They made a circular sweep.

- 17 March 2000 at 21:34: In the town of Blairgowrie in Perthshire, an object that made a similar trajectory to a satellite which brightened during the period of observation was seen. It moved in a Southerly direction.

- 18 March 2000 at 19:12: In the town of Falmouth in Cornwall, one object with a green bulbous front tapering off to a lighter green was seen. It had a huge yellow and red tail and was moving very fast horizontally.

- 18 March 2000 at 19:08: In the town of Pickering in North Yorkshire, a very bright, golden object was seen leaving a trail behind it.

- 20 March 2000 at 20:30: In the town of Wainford in Suffolk, five bright lights illuminated in the sky. They were constant, then disappeared.

- 20 March 2000 at 22:50: In the town of Saddleworth Moor in Greater Manchester, a cigar-shaped object descending at high speed was seen. The object was luminous green in colour. Then a second object appeared that was the same.

- 25 March 2000 at 21:40: In the town of Oxford in Oxfordshire, one oval-shaped object was seen. It had flashing red, green, and blue lights. It was brighter than a normal star, and it was still and then started to hover.

- 25 March 2000 at 21:20: In the town of Consett in County Durham, an object that looked like a cylinder was visible for several minutes.

- 29 March 2000 at 00:00: In the town of Welshpool in Powys, a round-shaped object with a one-foot-long flare was seen. It was six times bigger than a star and was moving from east to northeast.

- 4 April 2000 at 17:30: In the town of Bury in Greater Manchester, twelve small objects that were saucer-shaped were seen. They were silver and glinting in the sun and moved very erratically at high speed.

- 5 April 2000 at 22:30: In the town of Barnetby in Lincolnshire, a big chevron-shaped object was seen. It appeared solid, with many twinkling orange lights, and it was very fast and was silent.

- 7 April 2000 at 00:20: In the town of Leyburn in North Yorkshire, objects that were red changing to orange in colour were seen in the sky. They moved from the northeast to southwest and then disappeared.

- 13 April 2000 at 20:23: In the town of Crosskeys in Gwent, one star shaped object was seen moving West.

- 16 April 2000 at 20:00: In the town of Beeston in Cheshire, a very bright light in the sky was pulsing and changing shape. Then the object 'went out like a light and disappeared'.

- 17 April 2000, time unknown: In the town of Meppershall in Bedfordshire, bright lights heading through the sky were seen. They were moving towards the ground very fast.

- 26 April 2000 at 23:30: In the town of Whitby in North Yorkshire, one bright yellow and white object was seen. The object had variations in levels of brightness as it crossed the sky.

- 27 April 2000 at 21:00: On the A5104 in Flintshire, one large white ball-shaped object was seen. It hovered and then disappeared.

- 1 May 2000, time unknown: In the town of Marlow Bottom in Buckinghamshire, one object was seen. The object was moving like a satellite but more erratically, like a star moving towards other stars in the constellation.

- 8 May 2000 at 01:30: In the town of Glasgow in Strathclyde, one sun/circular-shaped object was seen. It was red in colour. It then changed shape from round, into elliptical.

- 21 May 2000 at 23:30: In the town of Havant in Hampshire, a bright flash in the sky was seen. It disappeared and reappeared every three seconds. It was followed by what looked like a satellite.

- 28 May 2000 at 01:30: In the town of Dartford in Kent, seven round but flat objects were seen. They were white, fairly bright, and also clearly visible. They made rapid and random movements.

- 28 May 2000 at 09:00: In the town of Sittingbourne in Kent, three lights were seen. They were moving West very fast and erratically.

- 29 May 2000 at 21:45: In the town of Gravesend in Kent Eight objects, approx. one metre in length, were seen. They were round/oval-shaped and light gold in colour. They were fast and smooth and made gliding movements.

- 5 June 2000 at 23:00: In the town of Brackley/Towcester in Northamptonshire, three that were rectangular, square, and hook in shape were seen. The objects were larger in size than a plane. They were all orange and brighter than Venus.

- 5 June 2000 at 14:15: On the M11 in Norfolk, a mysterious flying object was seen.

- 6 June 2000 at 15:00: In the town of Uley/Gloucester in Gloucestershire, an object appeared to follow an airliner. It was 1/8 of the size of the plane, with no vapour trail.

- 10 June 2000 at 23:05: In the town of Lowestoft in Suffolk, a bright light that was steady but decreasing in intensity was seen. The object then started to move northeast.

- 11 June 2000 at 21:10: In the town of Leeds in West Yorkshire, an object descended in an arc. It had three intense red lights, which seemed to make the whole thing glow red.

- 13 June 2000 at 17:00: In the town of Bolton in Lancashire, one round silver object was seen. It moved very rapidly in an Easterly direction.

- 17 June 2000 at 00:30: In the town of Burnley in Lancashire, one object that emitted a bright white light was seen. It was drifting slowly and making elaborate movements.

- 17 June 2000 at 01:00: In the town of Leven in Fife, three dull red domed-shaped objects were seen. They were described to be the size of a house. They were silent and moving together. They were low in the sky.

- 17 June 2000 at 21:00: In the town of Haversham in Buckinghamshire, one kite-shaped object was seen. It was very bright and was moving downward.

- 18 June 2000 at 19:20: In the town of Brighton in East Sussex, one large sphere-shaped object was seen. It looked like polished aluminium. It was very bright and was stationary at first, then moved off at high speed.

- 22 June 2000 at 02:03: In the town of Culross in Fife, one object that was cone-shaped was seen. It had four white lights at the top and two red lights at the base. It made a "hovering" sound.

- 23 June 2000 at 14:00: In the town of Felixstowe in Suffolk, a large object that looked like a dark silver rock was seen. It was definitely not an aircraft.

- 25 June 2000 at 17:30: In the town of Forest Hill in London, a round orange object which had orange fire coming off of it as it moved was seen. It was ten feet long and ten feet wide.

- 26 June 2000 at 00:30: In the town of Derby in Derbyshire, triangular lights with red centre lights were seen. They were going about 300mph on their course. They were heading north-north west.

- 1 July 2000 at 21:30: In the town of Putney in London, one circular-shaped object the size of a penny at arm's length was seen. It was a white/yellow colour and was very bright.

- 2 July 2000 at 01:45: In the town of Wirral in Cheshire, a large triangular-shaped object was seen, and on top of the triangle were two orange panels on each side. It had a dark blue top and was hovering.

- 3 July 2000 at 00:26: In the town of Consett in County Durham, a noise was heard that sounded like a popping explosion, and then a bright light in the sky was seen. The light was round and golden orange in colour.

- 8 July 2000 at 00:10: In the town of Harrogate in North Yorkshire, a small, bright light that was sphere-shaped was seen. Then another object appeared that was a seahorse shape that was blue, red, orange, and white in colour. Both objects disappeared.

- 8 July 2000 at 00:10: In the town of Harrogate in North Yorkshire, a small, bright light that was sphere-shaped was seen. It disappeared at a very high speed behind the clouds. Then a second object appeared in the shape of a seahorse.

- 9 July 2000 at 21:05: Town unknown in London, four helicopters were seen that looked like they could have been chasing an object.

- 9 July 2000, time unknown: In the town of Wilmslow in Cheshire, a UFO was seen.

- 11 July 2000 at 16:45: Town unknown in Fife, a silver ball hovering above a farmhouse was seen.

- 14 July 2000 at 19:58: Town unknown in West Yorkshire, one large circular, metallic, light bulb-shaped object was seen. It was silver in colour.

- 17 July 2000 at 01:25: In the town of Westlea in West Yorkshire, one spherical, white, and very bright object was seen.

- 17 July 2000 at 15:20: In the town of Stairhaven in Dumfries and Galloway, one beehive-shaped and cream-coloured object was seen hovering.

- 21 July 2000 at 00:00: In the town of Bideford in North Devon, a UFO/flying saucer and two lights were seen.

- 21 July 2000 at 00:10: In the town of Neath in West Glamorgan, one object the size of a Malteser when held at arm's length was seen. The object was spherical and very bright. It had orange, red, green, and white colours on it. It was pulsating.

- 22 July 2000 at 12:20: In the town of Crewe in Cheshire, something in the sky lighting up the witness's back garden was seen. The light went with it when the object moved.

- 22 July 2000 at 23:45: In the town of Birkenhead in Merseyside, two flare-sized objects were seen. They were extremely bright and falling from the sky.

- 27 July 2000 at 10:15: In Osterley Park/Hounslow in Middlesex, white, rounded, bright lights were seen.

- 27 July 2000 at 10:50: In the town of Salisbury in Wiltshire, a fairly large cluster of shapes was changing shape from triangular to crosses. They changed direction.

- 27 July 2000 at 21:30: In the town of Southall in Middlesex, one dome-shaped object was seen. It was the size of a jumbo jet. It was white in colour and very bright. It was moving slowly in a straight line.

- 31 July 2000 at 16:40: Town unknown in West London, one silver diamond/squid-shaped object was seen hissing.

- 1 August 2000 at 15:30: In the town of Cardiff in Glamorgan, one circular silvery-white disc was seen. It was right above the witness and then shot off.

- 5 August 2000 at 23:30: In the Ferrybridge area on the A1 in West Yorkshire, a bright white light moved across the sky before disappearing.

- 6 August 2000 at 09:15: In the town of Southsea in Hampshire, a black rectangle with a red glow was seen. It took a minute and a half to go across the sky.

- 6 August 2000 at 10:30: In the town of Dane End/Ware in Hertfordshire, a fireball in the sky with debris/lights behind it was seen.

- 6 August 2000 at 18:45: In the town of Rainham in Kent, two small flattened figures of eight objects with links of red were seen. They were dull in brightness. They were stationary and then moved slowly.

- 8 Aug 2000, time unknown: In the town of New Crosby/Carlisle in Cumbria, a disc shape with a hump on top was seen. It was definitely not an aeroplane. It was low down in the sky.

- 11 August 2000 at 19:00: In the town of Hastings in East Sussex, one spherical, dark grey object that was moving South was seen.

- 16 August 2000 at 21:50: In the town of Forest Hill in London, red and blue lights flashing consecutively on large spheres two feet wide and four feet tall were seen.

- 16 August 2000 at 23:50: In the town of Spey Bay in Morayshire, a Corporal in the RAF saw one sphere varying and constantly changing that was brighter than the other stars.

- 18 August 2000 at 09:50: In the town of Forest Hill in London, red and blue singular flashing lights were seen.

- 18 August 2000 at 21:45: In the town of Fishpond in Bristol, one helicopter-shaped object was seen. It had gold and red lighting on it and was very bright.

- 20 August 2000 at 15:15: In the town of High Wycombe in Buckinghamshire, one black dot was seen up in the sky. It was bright, considering the colour.

- 20 August 2000 at 02:00: In the town of Callington in Cornwall, a cluster of lights was seen in the sky. They were vivid green, white and red in colour and moved erratically and adjusted their positions.

- 21 August 2000 at 10:45: In the town of Burgess Hill in West Sussex, a large arrowhead-shaped object was seen. It had four/five lights at the extremities. It moved very fast from North to South in a straight line.

- 24 August 2000 at 10:55: In the town of Ravenstone in Northants, an object that was not a star or a small planet was seen. It was moving around far above normal airspace.

- 24 August 2000, time unknown: In the town of Cheltenham in Gloucestershire, a UFO was seen and filmed onto a VHS tape.

- 26 August 2000 at 20:30: In the Snowdonia Mountains in North Wales, a large fireball was spotted over the mountains. It seemed to be flaming rather than glowing.

- 27 August 2000 at 00:47: In the town of Runcorn in Cheshire, red and other coloured lights going on and off were seen. They were moving from North to South.

- 29 August 2000 at 04:18: In the town of Runcorn in Cheshire, a silver dot moving through the sky was seen.

- 29 August 2000 at 20:30: In the town of Glasgow in Strathclyde, a bright blob which turned into a streak before disappearing to return approximately ten minutes later was seen.

- 31 August 2000, time unknown: In the town of Wells in Norfolk, an object glowing with coloured lights around it was seen. It was flashing with red, blue, and green lights.

- 2 September 2000 at 02:30: In the town of Blackwood in Gwent, a diamond-shaped object, with three lights was seen. One light was red, and two of the lights were changing colour.

- 3 September 2000 at 12:20: On the M3 around Sudbury in Suffolk, one round-shaped object with a dark shadow on it was seen.

- 7 September 2000 at 05:50: In the town of Seddlecombe in East Sussex, six lights flying in the sky flying in some kind of formation moving North were seen. The witnesses heard some sort of noise.

- 9 September 2000 at 15:20: In the town of Hunsbury in Northamptonshire, one small elongated object that was brown and fairly bright was seen.

- 10 September 2000 at 11:05: In the town of Basildon, Essex, six objects were seen orbiting around one object. They were changing shape and were grey in colour.

- 10 September 2000 at 21:00: In the town of Eggham in Surrey, three lights bigger than stars were seen. They were white and fairly bright, but not blinding. They made erratic movements around each other.

- 12 September 2000 at 23:30: In the town of Ilford in Essex, nine oblong-shaped red lights, then two red lights, converged over the witnesses' house. They moved faster than any aircraft.

- 16 September 2000 at 21:00: In the town of Chesterfield in Derbyshire, an orange ball was seen.

- 16 September 2000 at 04:00: In the town of Shell Island in North Wales, a triangular object was seen described to look like a stack of plates with triangular-shaped windows with lights.

- 24 September 2000 at 20:13: In the town of Royston in Cambridgeshire, one big object was seen. It was multi-coloured, flickering, and getting brighter by the minute.

- 24 September 2000 at 00:02: In the town of Twickenham in Middlesex two golden lights were seen moving incredibly fast and then disappeared.

- 24 September 2000 at 02:43: In the town of Wembley in Middlesex, one large object the size of a helicopter with a cluster of lights was seen. It was white and very bright and was making bouncing movements.

- 25 September 2000 at 05:30: In the town of Highbridge in Somerset, lots of flashing lights, like aircraft lights were seen, but no aircraft was seen in the area.

- 27 September 2000 at 21:10: In the town of Ramsgate in Kent revolving lights on the right-hand side of the road and then on the left-hand side were seen. They looked like a tornado spinning.

- 28 September 2000 at 20:10: In the town of Rhuddlan/Rhyl in Clwyd, a Police Officer saw a big explosion with an intense white light.

- 29 September 2000 at 09:15: Town unknown, county unknown, five lights in the sky that were very bright were seen. The object had six lights that were changing.

- 30 September 2000 at 11:25: In the town of Birkenhead in Merseyside, a black triangular-shaped object was seen.

- 4 October 2000 at 05:45: In the town of Henley-on-Thames in Oxfordshire, one circular white and very bright object was seen.

- 4 October 2000 at 16:20: In the town of High Wycombe in Buckinghamshire, a chrome silver dome-shaped object that was 40 feet across with a few small windows was seen. It had no wings and was very reflective.

- 4 October 2000 at 20:45: In the town of Finchley, London, eight large round objects were seen. They were a normal colour and very visible.

- 4 October 2000 at 22:30: In the town of Collingdale in London, lights were seen in the sky. They were moving in a circular/dancing pattern.

- 4 October 2000 time unknown: In the town of Exeter in Devon a sphere-shaped object was seen in the sky.

- 5 October 2000, time unknown: A woman named Sharon Rowlands from Bonsall in Derbyshire claimed to have seen a large, luminous pink object hovering and rotating over a nearby field. She filmed the object on her camcorder.

- 13 October 2000 at 01:15: In the town of Huddersfield in West Yorkshire, three cone-shaped saucers that were bright red and one that had a red beam like a searchlight were seen.

- 16 October 2000 at 21:31: In the town of Northallerton in North Yorkshire, a triangular-shaped object was seen. It was black in colour and had green lights underneath.

- 16 October 2000 at 19:20: In the town of Ramsgate in Kent, two quite big objects were seen; one was triangular in shape and one was round. The triangle one had blue, red, and white colours on it. The circle one had white, red and orange.

- 17 October 2000 at 08:55: In the town of Keswick in Cumbria, a bright metal star with no jet stream was seen.

- 17 October 2000 at 20:15: In the town of Blackhill in County Durham, two flashing lights were seen; they were red and green and appeared to be joined. They merged into one large red light.

- 18 October 2000 at 17:50: In the town of Northolt in Middlesex, a luminous green stripe appeared.

- 18 October 2000 at 19:21: In the town of Ilford in Essex, very distant red, blue, and white flashing lights were seen. The object hovered and then shot off.

- 18 October 2000 at 21:00: At Heathrow at Stand B10 in London, six lights were seen. They were green and flashing. One end was brighter than the other, and it was stationary.

- 18 October 2000 at 21:30: In the town of Iverheath in Buckinghamshire, four objects were seen, one object was extremely large. They had green lights and were very bright.

- 18 October 2000 at 21:45: In the town of Southall in London, one large spacecraft followed an observer home and parked outside his house with a green light flashing.

- 19 October 2000 at 17:55: In the town of Upminster, Essex, one reddish/gold star that was very bright was seen. It zigzagged in a downward movement and was flashing.

- 20 October 2000 at 19:04: In the town of Burgess Hill in West Sussex, a big, blue, bright, round circle was seen moving horizontally.

- 20 October 2000 at 19:40: In the town of Partick in Glasgow, two star-shaped and star-sized objects were seen. One object was behind the other. The objects were white in colour and travelling very fast.

- 21 October 2000 at 18:45: In the town of St Athan in South Glamorgan, a red light was seen hovering.

- 21 October 2000 at 06:45: In the town of Knutsford in Cheshire, a triangular-shaped object was seen. There was aa light on each point of the triangle. There was a large fluorescent tube that ran the full length of the trailing edge.

- 23 October 2000 at 22:05: In the town of Ilford, Essex, two ball-shaped objects were seen. The objects moved over the witness's house.

- 23 October 2000 at 19:04: In the town of Crawley in Sussex, a UFO was seen.

- 23 October 2000 at 20:10: In the town of Perth in Perthshire, a circular-shaped object was seen with five flashing underneath. It also had some lights on the side.

- 26 October 2000 at 22:20: On the A14/Cambridge in Cambridgeshire, one huge triangular-shaped object with two bright rings and two circles of light was seen. It was moving across the sky very fast.

- 30 October 2000 at 19:15: In the town of Belfast in Northern Ireland, two egg-shaped objects with red, blue, and green-coloured lights were seen. It had a dome-shaped top and a flat bottom. It was a blinding white colour.

- 30 October 2000 at 09:00: In the town of Plumstead in London, a round-shaped object the size of a small pea at arm's length was seen. It was illuminated from within, and a glowing white light was coming from inside the object. It looked three-dimensionally solid.

- 1 November 2000 at 09:31: In the town of Dartford in Kent, one pinpoint of light that was quite bright was seen. It made erratic movements from side to side.

- 2 November 2000 at 10:05: In the town of Rowsley/Matlock in Derbyshire, three silver shapes were seen. They were spinning.

- 3 November 2000 at 17:30: In the town of Walton Grands/Banbury in Oxfordshire, white lights were seen in a circle as well as blue lights. The lights were hovering.

- 3 November 2000 at 19:21: In the town of Scunthorpe in Lincolnshire, strange lights were seen in the sky.

- 5 November 2000 at 23:34: In the town of Pen Machno in West Glamorgan, one large round fireball that was very bright was seen.

- 7 November 2000 at 14:05: In the town of Stouport-on-Severn in the West Midlands, a black triangle craft was seen.

- 10 November 2000 at 10:38: In the town of Shepperton in Surrey, ten oval-shaped objects that were 20ft across were seen. They were green and white. They were quite bright and rotating. The objects varied in speed.

- 11 November 2000 at 04:36: In the town of Rotherwick Village in Hampshire, two very bright orange lights that were close together were seen moving slightly to the right and left slowly.

- 14 November 2000 at 16:00: In the town of Berrynarbor in North Devon, one very bright oval-shaped object was seen moving from left to right slowly.

- 14 November 2000 at 19:22: On the M18 at Thorne Junction in South Yorkshire, one football-shaped and sized object was seen. It was a brilliant light with a short 'trail' of lesser light. It made erratic movements from right to left. Then climbed vertically.

- 15 November 2000 at 09:00: In Eltham Park in London, a UFO came close to the witness.

- 15 November 2000 at 15:40: In the town of Crowmand in Lincolnshire, unusual air activity was seen in the sky. The object moved ten times faster than conventional aircraft.

- 17 November 2000 at 18:00: In the town of Taff's Well in South Glamorgan, a bright light was seen in the sky.

- 22 November 2000 at 17:03: In the town of Fulham/Hammersmith in London, three large objects were seen; one looked like a tornado. They were green, red, and white in colour and quite bright. The lights were flashing very fast.

- 23 November 2000 at 18:30: In the town of Pontypridd in Mid Glamorgan, one large round light was seen. It was gold, then changed to red/amber in colour. It was changing from one side to the other.

- 23 November 2000 at 22:35: In the town of Huntsmead in Northants, a Police Officer saw one large circular pink object. There were also ten circular objects attached to it.

- 24 November 2000 at 16:40: In the town of Almondbank in Perthshire, a cigar-shaped object with a bright white light and a red pulsating light was seen. It had two other red lights below the white light.

- 27 November 2000 at 10:11: In the town of Rochester in Kent, a round object that lit up the surrounding area was seen.

- 28 November 2000 at 04:05: In the town of Shipston in Warwickshire, a stationary, intermittent flashing of yellow light was seen. Then, at one point, there were three objects fixed in one position.
- 29 November 2000 at 06:00: In the town of Dereham in Norfolk, a UFO was seen on one side; it had five lights that were very bright. It moved around and there were three white lights that were six feet apart.

- 2 December 2000 at 08:18: In the town of Harracott in Devon, one silver cigar-shaped object was seen moving faster than a nearby plane.

- 2 December 2000 at 18:50: In the town of Stonehenge/Salisbury in Wiltshire, one sphere-shaped object that was bigger than a shooting star was seen. It was green and blue and was flashing and was also very bright.

- 3 December 2000 at 20:00: In the town of Eastbourne in East Sussex, three red stars were moving very fast and randomly at first. They were suddenly zooming around and doing acrobatic things.

- 7 December 2000 at 18:00: In the town of St. Mawgan in Cornwall, one object that was quite large and very bright was seen. It was silent and had no identifying colour. It looked like an elongated arrowhead.

- 8 December 2000 at 18:00: In the town of Truro in Cornwall, very bright lights were seen. A sequence of four lights, three lit at any one time. They were orange and were slowly moving in a straight line.

- 10 December 2000 at 16:00: In the town of Thorpe Bay in Essex, a rubber shape with a V on its side was seen. On one side, it was orange, and it had yellow flames coming out of it. On the other side, it had a red flashing light.

- 13 December 2000 at 23:30: In the town of Bloxham in Oxfordshire, eight very bright objects were seen moving very fast.

- 15 December 2000 at 18:05: On the A460/Rugeley in Staffordshire, a single object that seemed to hover above a tree line of a wooded area was seen. It changed from white in colour to blue, then red, then white again.

- 22 December 2000 at 01:15: In the town of Dursley in Gloucestershire, in a lorry, the witness saw a blue/white flash from within the woods. The sky took on a red glow.

- 22 December 2000 at 18:30: In the town of Blackpool in Lancashire, a white very bright light like a star was seen.

- 29 December 2000 at 23:00: In the town of Pantymwyn in Flintshire, a roundish object that was silvery white was seen. It was quite low down and enormously bright.

- No date, no time: Town unknown in Hertfordshire, a black domed-shaped object was seen. It stayed for a few seconds before shooting off at extreme speed.

- No date, no time: In the town of Yeovil in Somerset, a large silver metal shining ball with a dark mist surrounding it and a blinding light surrounding the mist was seen.

- No date, no time: Town unknown in Carlisle, objects are seen every day in the sky. They hold people in their homes and are a nuisance.

21st Century

2001

- 4 January 2001 at 03:30: In the town of Teignmouth in Devon, bright flashing lights were seen moving south.

- 5 January 2001 at 17:15: In the town of Ogwen Valley in North West Wales, an object that looked like a shooting star but with a burning tail was seen. It was about the size of a military aircraft. It looked like it was heading towards the ground.

- 5 January 2001 at 17:30: In the town of Hunmanby in North Yorkshire, twelve objects with pulsating coloured lights were seen. The objects split and moved in different directions.

- 9 January 2001 at 14:45: In the town of Humberside in East Yorkshire, a silver cigar-shaped object was seen. It was moving near a military aircraft and was stationary at first.

- 10 January 2001 at 18:22: In the town of Norwich in Norfolk, one object that looked a bit like a star at first was seen. It then split into about half a dozen lights before clouds crossed over them.

- 10 January 2001 at 18:30: In the town of Dundee in Scotland, two objects were seen. The first was triangular in shape and had three orange lights. The second was a bright white light.

- 10 January 2001 at 22:30: In the town of Chelmsford, Essex, 700 objects appeared among the stars. They were white and very bright. They formed an arc from horizon to horizon, east to west.

- 11 January 2001 at 11:20: In the town of Swinton in Manchester, a round silver ball was seen. The object was moving horizontally.

- 11 January 2001 at 20:29: In the town of Blackpool in Lancashire, a white light was seen flashing. It had a round shape. It was stationary, moved west, and then disappeared.

- 12 January 2001 at 21:15: In the town of Tottingham in East Yorkshire, seven objects flying in arrow formation were seen. They were moving at high speed from South to North.

- 12 January 2001 at 23:20: In the town of Bootle in Merseyside, one aircraft-type-shaped object was seen. It was dark red in colour and quite dim. It made no sound. It was very high up and was moving in fast, small movements.

- 12 January 2001 at 21:00: 30 miles over Bath in Somerset, a RAF Pilot saw a triangular-shaped object that was mainly stationary.

- 13 January 2001 at 05:22: In the town of Farnborough in Hampshire, bright lights were seen in the sky. Then followed what looked like people climbing down webbing into the house.

- 13 January 2001 at 19:00: In the town of Liverpool in Merseyside, one square-shaped object was seen. It had an orange light in the middle. It was moving from the south to the north and then to the west.

- 14 January 2001 at 21:00: In the town of Tarleton in Lancashire, a flashing red and blue pulsing light was seen. Then the object glowed orange and started to move towards the ground.

- 15 January 2001 at 16:00: In the town of Reading in Berkshire, a bright light that was changing shape and moving fast was seen. It was white in colour and made erratic movements.

- 15 January 2001 at 07:30: In the town of Kirkcaldy in Scotland, a single object that was bright white appeared to be moving North. The object went very bright, like an explosion.

- 15 January 2001 at 18:00: In the town of Southfields in London, a very large white light which turned the sky blue was seen.

- 20 January 2001 at 08:20: In the town of Girvan in Ayrshire, a white flashing ball with orange trails was seen falling.

- 20 January 2001 at 01:15: In the town of Canvey Island in Essex, a seven-foot silver dome with a blue glow was seen. It was climbing vertically in the sky, in stages.

- 24 January 2001 at 17:00: In the town of Battle in East Sussex, one round, star-shaped object with one white flashing light was seen. It was very bright. It was stationary but quivering.

- 24 January 2001 at 19:05: In Bush Hill Park, Enfield, Middlesex, a very bright, silvery light that was a Delta shape was seen. It was stationary, then circling, then moving back and forth.

- 25 January 2001 at 16:40: In the town of St Andrews in Fife, a strobe effect of lighting was seen one above the other. The object moved very fast.

- 28 January 2001 at 20:20: In the town of Liverpool in Merseyside, an orange object was seen doing circuits around the Liverpool area. There were flames coming out of the front, with burning bits falling off of it.

- 28 January 2001 at 20:20: In the town of Childwall/Liverpool in Merseyside, an object was moving slowly from left to right. The object had an orange glow. It had lights on it.

- 28 January 2001 at 09:34: In the town of Folkestone in Kent, a silver spin top-shaped object the size of a football was seen bobbing at a height of 300 feet.

- 29 January 2001 at 12:25: In the town of Dundee in Scotland, one object the size of a pin dot was seen. It was bright and shiny.

- 31 January 2001 at 21:10: In the town of South Clifton in Nottinghamshire, one object the size of a helicopter was seen. It had red and white stripes/lights, with wings like a Phantom. It was stationary, then darted about the woods.

- 4 February 2001 at 04:00: Town unknown in South Wales, one triangular-shaped object like an inverted ice cream cone was seen. The object disappeared down a country lane.

- 6 February 2001 at 06:00: In the town of St Columb in North Cornwall, a big, bright light was seen in the sky. It was making circular movements, and then it hit the ground.

- 7 February 2001 at 19:00: In the town of Dumbarton in Scotland an elliptical object that was bright like a star was seen. There was movement within the object. It was moving slowly.

- 7 February 2001 at 10:00: In the town of Morecambe Bay in Lancashire, lights were seen in the sky. They were in the shape of three triangles.

- 7 February 2001 at 19:40: In the town of Caernarfon in North Wales It initially looked like a star. It looked like it was going to crash into the witness's house. It was a green colour with red on the side.

- 7 February 2001 at 19:45: In the town of Amlwch/Anglesey in North Wales, one object with a blue glow which then turned green was seen. It broke up and left smoke. It seemed very large.

- 8 February 2001 at 19:30: Town unknown in Staffordshire, an object was seen burning up in the sky and breaking into two-three pieces; it looked like a shooting star, but lower in the sky. It turned green.

- 8 February 2001 at 20:00: In the town of Preston in Lancashire, an orange ball in the sky looked to be on fire. It was coming from an Easterly direction.

- 8 February 2001 at 19:40: In the town of Lincoln in Lincolnshire, the object looked like a rocket. It had a white/orange glow.

- 8 February 2001 at 19:20: In the town of Duffield in Derbyshire, a large blue, fluorescent, cigar-shaped object was seen. The object hovered and then moved away quickly.

- 8 February 2001 at 19:42: In the town of Wrangle in Lincolnshire, a bright ball-shaped object was seen; it was about the size of a tennis ball which was lit up. Behind it was a long tail that tapered off, with a smaller ball at the end of the object.

- 8 February 2001 at 19:45: In the town of Scunthorpe in Lincolnshire, a white ball of light was seen. It was moving from West to East. It stopped and then went up into the sky vertically.

- 8 February 2001 at 19:40: In the town of Aldborough in East Yorkshire, one main object, which was very bright and white in colour, was seen being stationary.

- 8 February 2001 at 19:40: Town unknown in West Yorkshire, a huge fireball streaking across the skies of West Yorkshire was seen.

- 9 February 2001 at 20:23: In the town of Kiltarlity in Inverness-shire, one multi-coloured object was seen. It was round at the front and tapered towards the tail. It was moving from left to right.

- 9 February 2001 at 06:15: In the town of Slough in Middlesex, three elongated objects were seen. They all had a white light at each end. They hovered and then moved in formation to the North.

- 9 February 2001 at 20:35: In the town of Stevenage in Hertfordshire, one object shaped like a half circle was seen. There were three lights on it, changing from white to green to red. It made a whirring sound.

- 9 February 2001 at 07:30: In the town of South Kirkby in West Yorkshire, a large orange ball with a triangle-like structure inside it and two white lights at the edge was seen.

- 12 February 2001 at 19:30: In the town of Trehafod/Ponty Pridd in Mid-Glamorgan, one bright star-shaped object was seen. It rose fast in the sky and then disappeared.

- 12 February 2001 at 21:25: In the town of Colchester, Essex, one very bright spherical object that had a reddish hue was seen. It was visible the whole time. It zig-zagged across the sky very fast.

- 13 February 2001 at 02:30: In the town of Morton in Lincolnshire, a circle of flashing white lights that were shaped like a bracelet were seen. It moved over to the right, then left. The lights turned green and red.

- 13 February 2001 at 10:15: In the town of Saltash in Cornwall, one object was seen. It was white in colour and was stationary for about 10 minutes.

- 13 February 2001 at 18:45: In the town of Liverpool in Merseyside, four very bright round-shaped objects with orange lights were seen. They were moving from left to right.

- 13 February 2001 at 22:10: In the town of Baschurch in Shropshire, one object, the same size as a star was seen. It was multi-coloured and very bright. It was fluctuating/glowing. There was a black hole in the centre. It made rapid movements.

- 13 February 2001 at 21:00: In the town of New Milton in Hampshire a bright orange ball in the sky which 'hopped', before disappearing was seen.

- 14 February 2001 at 00:15: In the town of Salisbury in Wiltshire, a very bright triangular-shaped object was seen. It had flashing lights in red, purple, and green. It was moving in a Southerly direction.

- 14 February 2001 at 19:15: In the town of North Kelsey in Lincolnshire, an object that looked like a very bright star was seen. They were still and then moved from side to side.

- 14 February 2001 at 20:00: In the town of North Muirton/Perth in Scotland, two objects with white lights were seen. The second object seemed dimmer. It was moving at 90-degree angles. They moved at high speed.

- 16 February 2001 at 21:00: In Bishops Castle in Shropshire, one object with red, yellow, and green lighting on it was seen. It was flying towards Shrewsbury.

- 16 February 2001 at 18:20: In the town of Ruskington in Shropshire, two lights that were white and constant were seen heading East.

- 16 February 2001 at 18:30: In the town of Ryhall in Lincolnshire, two very bright, large objects were seen. They were moving from North to South.

- 16 February 2001 at 18:20: In the town of Scarborough in North Yorkshire, two very bright balls of light were seen. They were moving from the west to the east.

- 18 February 2001 at 20:10: In the town of Starvation Island in Norfolk, one main object that was very bright was seen. It was white in colour and was stationary.

- 19 February 2001 at 23:00: In the town of Staithes in North Yorkshire, one large green ball which was shining brightly was seen. It was moving straight downward and would have hit the sea 3–4 miles from the coast.

- 22 February 2001 at 23:00: In the town of Woodford Green in Essex, two small orange lights, far away in the distance, were seen. The lights joined and then looked bigger. They looked like two sparklers.

- 23 February 2001 at 18:30: In the town of Hampstead in London, one object that was white in colour and was slow-moving was seen.

- 24 February 2001 at 11:00: In the town of Truro in Cornwall, an explosion in the sky, but with no sound, was seen. It looked like a rocket. It was very large and had a blue and red light.

- 24 February 2001 at 16:45: In the town of Bracknell in Berkshire a white ball, followed by a USAF jet, was seen. It was moving at high speed in a straight line.

- 26 February 2001 at 23:00: Town unknown in Leicestershire A UFO was seen. It had bright red, blue, and orange flashing lights, it was in the shape of a triangle. It remained stationary for 15 minutes.

- 28 February 2001 at 12:00: In the town of Whitchurch in Shropshire a white, circular object with a ring around it was seen. The object moved ten miles in about 2 seconds, then left to right, and then moved East.

- 1 March 2001 at 19:00: In the town of Fleetwood in Lancashire, an unconventional silent craft, consisting of four red lights, flying low over the witness's house was seen.

- 1 March 2001 at 19:00: In the town of Morecambe Bay in Lancashire, unusual lights were seen over the bay.

- 1 March 2001 at 10:00: In the town of Holyhead in North Wales, an object was seen that looked like a bright star. It had a pulsating red and green light. It was stationary and then moved off.

- 1 March 2001 at 19:05: In the town of Fleetwood in Lancashire, five flying saucers that were orange in colour were seen. They moved from East to West and then moved quickly over the sea.

- 2 March 2001 time unknown: Town unknown in the East Midlands, a UFO was running parallel to the landing lanes of an East Midlands Jet.

- 8 March 2001 at 18:45: In the town of Fleetwood in Lancashire, two very bright lights, surrounded by smaller lights, were seen.

- 12 March 2001 at 22:00: In the town of Finchley in London, soft orange lights in a formation were seen. They were moving fast to the southeast.

- 12 March 2001 at 18:00: In the town of Carnforth in Lancashire three small lights above a large star-shaped object were seen. They were very bright and were stationary.

- 20 March 2001 at 01:00: In the town of Moseley in the West Midlands, a very bright light was seen. A couple of hours later, a dark object was seen with lights underneath.

- 21 March 2001, time unknown: Town unknown, county unknown, a big, bright sphere that looked like Saturn was seen.

- 21 March 2001 at 19:15: In the town of Annan in Scotland, red lights were seen. It hovered for a short time, then headed southeast at speed.

160

- 26 March 2001 at 22:45: In the town of Leith/Edinburgh in Scotland, two fuzzy white lights dancing around each other were seen. They were moving to the East.

- 29 March 2001 at 09:00: In the town of Chesham in Buckinghamshire, two UFOs with flashing red lights were seen. The objects seemed to interfere with the witness's radio and television while heading south west.

- 29 March 2001 at 15:03: In Gunnersbury Park in London, fifty-five suspicious circles were seen in the sky.

- 31 March 2001 at 18:15: In the town of Whaplode in Lincolnshire, an object was seen to be like a bag with two hanging straps and one loose hanging strap. It was black and changing shape. It was stationary.

- 3 April 2001 at 02:35: In the town of Chippenham in Wiltshire, a pair of bright red lights were moving from the southeast towards the northwest. Each light had a double flashing pulse.

- 3 April 2001 at 22:29: In the town of Aberdeen, Scotland, a star-shaped object was seen in the sky. It was changing colours from red, blue, and green.

- 4 April 2001 at 02:15: In the town of Renfrew in Scotland, an object was seen to be like a spotlight in the sky.

- 4 April 2001 at 21:14: In the town of Aberdeen in Scotland, a star-shaped object was twinkling, but when seen through binoculars, it had a red, orange, and blue light.

- 4 April 2001, time unknown: In the town of Ashford in Kent, three fob-shaped objects bobbed about in the sky.

- 13 April 2001 at 23:15: In the town of Doncaster in South Yorkshire, an object was seen high in the sky and was described as having headlights along the side of it.

- 13 April 2001, time unknown: In the town of Syderstone in Norfolk, one bright light was seen. It was low on the horizon. It was seen for about 20 minutes.

- 16 April 2001 at 01:30: In the town of Grimsby in Lincolnshire, a ball-shaped object was seen. It gave off a glow, like a hot coal ember orange/red. It dropped through the air and then shot up and disappeared.

- 17 April 2001 at 22:00: In the town of Montrose in Scotland, big fans of light, which made a circle in the sky, were seen. There were flashes in the centre of it. It was stationary.

- 19 April 2001 at 19:35: Town unknown in the Isle of Man, three very large objects were seen. They were travelling in formation. The distinct formation separated, and they headed off southeast.

- 6 May 2001 at 19:50: In the town of Oxford in Oxfordshire, one object was white and bright. It had a halo above it. It was heading northwest.

- 7 May 2001 at 20:30: In the town of Dersingham in Norfolk, a large orange, tadpole-shaped object with a long tail was seen. It was followed shortly afterwards by two more similar objects.

- 12 May 2001 at 22:10: In the town of Bristol Channel in Somerset, two satellite-shaped objects that were a very bright white colour were seen.

- 14 May 2001 at 06:50: In the town of Rhonda Valley in Wales, one tennis ball-sized object was seen. It was round at the front and had a triangular back. It was rainbow-coloured and very bright.

- 20 May 2001 at 01:15: Town unknown in Humberside, small blobs of rings with a larger ring around them were seen. They were white and very bright. They were stationary.

- 24 May 2001 at 22:25: In the town of Forest Hill in London, an alien craft was near to the witness's house. It was disc-shaped with a beam of light coming from it. The electrical equipment was disturbed.

- 31 May 2001 at 01:35: In the town of Grimsby in Lincolnshire, a bright light travelling across the sky was seen. It was very high and going faster than a jet.

- 31 May 2001 at 03:00: In the town of Worcester in Worcestershire, one shooting star that was very bright was seen. The movements were slow and then very fast.

- 1 June 2001 at 10:30: In the town of Glasgow in Scotland, a black cylinder-shaped object was seen. It was moving West and making sharp movements.

- 3 June 2001 at 02:14: In the town of Hitchin in Hertfordshire, a witness saw an object. It was emitting a bright mauve light.

- 4 June 2001 at 14:00: In the town of Moota/Cockermouth in Cumbria, a large triangular craft hovered over a field. It was very colourful, with white and red lights.

- 8 June 2001 at 00:05: In the town of Keighley in West Yorkshire, three lights that are triangle-shaped were seen. There was a static red light. They moved slowly in a straight line.

- 10 June 2001 at 11:05: In the town of Kennoway in Scotland, a small to medium-sized object that was pebble-shaped was seen. It was black. It was travelling from the south to the north.

- 10 June 2001 at 18:00: In the town of Fenwick in Newcastle-upon-Tyne, a white spherical object was seen. The object was seen for about one minute.

- 10 June 2001 at 01:56: In the town of Arbroath in Scotland, one triangular-shaped, pulsing white light was seen. It was about twice the size of a star. The object was stationary.

- 16 June 2001 at 11:30: In the town of Diss in Norfolk, a hovering, orange light that was low in the sky was seen. It turned white.

- 17 June 2001 at 22:10: In the town of Weston-super-Mare in Somerset, a round, red, glowing ball which changed colour as it slowed down was seen. A second object then appeared.

- 19 June 2001 at 18:00: In the town of Golders Green in London, eighty jellyfish-shaped objects that were white were seen. There was also one single, pulsating red light amongst them.

- 25 June 2001 at 21:00: In the town of Llanelli in Wales, one large, disc-shaped object was seen. It was black in colour. It then changed to an oval shape. The object was moving fast to the West.

- 28 June 2001 at 23:59: In the town of Eynsham in Oxfordshire, one object, four times the size of a star, was seen. It was round in shape. It had a bright light that was yellow/white. It moved North.

- 29 June 2001, time unknown: In the town of Sutton Coldfield in the West Midlands, a UFO was floating high up in the sky over Sutton Park.

- 2 July 2001 at 19:30: In the town of Hampstead Gardens in London, one dome-shaped object was seen. It was very dark. It was directly above and moving slowly.

- 4 July 2001 at 07:00: Town unknown in Kent, one object was seen. It had a bright light, too. It was moving from West to East.

- 8 July 2001 at 22:15: In the town of Cricklewood in London, the object was like a star but was moving.

- 14 July 2001 at 09:08: In the town of Holmpton in Yorkshire, one circle-shaped object was seen. It was beige in colour. It was flying from north to southwest.

- 15 July 2001 at 16:55: In the town of Hellingly in East Sussex, a Pilot saw one large object, the size of an eagle. It looked like three circles joined together. It was dark brown and black. It was moving quite fast.

- 16 July 2001 at 10:55: In the town of Burton Joyce in Nottinghamshire, one round-shaped object was seen. It was silver and reflected the sun. It was high up and bobbed about.

- 18 July 2001 at 21:15: In the town of Milford Haven in South West Wales, eight star-sized objects with lights that were red, white, blue, and yellow were seen. Six were followed by two.

- 18 July 2001, time unknown: In the town of Exmouth in Devon, the object was cream-coloured. It was travelling at an altitude of about 8,000 feet.

- 18 July 2001 at 23:55: In the town of Barrhead/Glasgow in Scotland, one spherical-shaped object was seen. It was orange and yellow. It was stationary for a short amount of time.

- 21 July 2001 at 21:25: In the town of Countesthorpe in Leicestershire, a UFO was seen flying northeast.

- 21 July 2001 at 22:31: In the town of Letchworth in Hertfordshire, a sequence of bright lights was seen. They were moving from right to left, then back in a random fashion.

- 21 July 2001 at 20:50: In the town of Milton Keynes in Buckinghamshire, a kite-shaped object was seen. It was black in colour. It was heading West and often changed its speed.

- 23 July 2001 at 18:15: In the town of Harrow in London, one small, balloon-shaped object was seen. It was brown in colour. It was moving up and down and sideways.

- 23 July 2001 at 11:00: In the town of Perton in South Staffordshire, a dark, possibly circular object that looked like a rocket at first glance was seen. Part of the object was metallic and glistened.

- 25 July 2001 at 14:10: In the town of Folkstone in Kent, one circular-shaped object with flashing bright lights was seen. It was at a high altitude.

- 27 July 2001 at 19:00: In the town of Liverpool in Merseyside, one dome/bell-shaped object was seen. It had two red lights on either side, and other colours were seen on and off. It was stationary.

- 30 July 2001 at 23:10: In the town of Nottingham in Nottinghamshire, one circular object that was orangey/red in colour was seen. It was very bright. It was moving in a regular figure-of-eight pattern.

- 30 July 2001 at 23:30: In the town of Bath in Somerset, one oval-shaped object was seen. It had rotating lights. It was moving to the West.

- 1 August 2001 at 08:20: In the town of Ilkley in West Yorkshire, one silver, fountain pen-shaped object was seen; it was described as an aircraft without wings.

- 4 August 2001 at 00:40: In the town of Port Talbot in Wales, two large, shining golf ball-like objects were seen. They were moving in and out of the clouds.

- 4 August 2001 at 00:40: In the town of Rickmansworth in Hertfordshire, one large, circular object and a number of small fragments, the size of 10p pieces, were seen. They were white and had a glow of red and blue. They were very bright.

- 4 August 2001 at 01:40: In the town of Bushey in Hertfordshire, a strange formation of lights flying overhead was seen.

- 4 August 2001 at 02:30: In the town of Glasgow in Scotland, a big, bright, white light was seen. Then a smaller white light was moving towards and away from the bigger white light.

- 5 August 2001 at 23:40: In the town of Chipping Norton in Oxfordshire, several objects were seen. They were different colours: purple, green, and white. They were very bright. They were moving very fast to the South.

- 5 August 2001 at 02:00: In the town of Barnstable in Devon, two 18-inch across, round-shaped, spinning objects were seen. They were white and very bright.

- 6 August 2001 at 16:30: In the town of Ashton-Under-Lyne in Greater Manchester, the witness saw something that they could not identify, but it was not a plane.

- 6 August 2001 at 03:08: In the town of Berwick in Northumbria, two stationary cone-shaped objects were seen. One below the other. They were extremely bright.

- 11 August 2001 at 00:30: In the town of Tipton in the West Midlands, a bright round light that moved in steps was seen. It reduced in size, and then, when smaller, shot off to the left and disappeared.

- 14 August 2001 at 11:05: In the town of Buxton in Derbyshire, one circular ring-shaped object with a horizontal tail hanging below it with a black ball at the bottom was seen.

- 16 August 2001 at 21:30: In the town of Newport in Gwent, one large, round-shaped object was seen. It was white and very bright. It moved fast upward in the sky.

- 17 August 2001 at 21:45: In the town of Abbotskerswell in Devon, the object looked like a circle within a circle.

- 18 August 2001 at 02:10: In the town of Paisley in Scotland, a red flash fell from the sky. It was falling to the ground in a wide spiral.

- 19 August 2001 at 22:45: In the town of Shoeburyness in Essex, one large, square/grid-shaped object was seen. It was grey and orange and very bright. It was static and then moved North.

- 20 August 2001 at 10:00: Town unknown, county unknown, one 15 inches across, circular-shaped object was seen. It was a metallic grey colour. The witness got up close and touched it.

- 21 August 2001 at 01:20: In the town of Berwick in Northumbria, four cone-shaped objects which were brightly lit were seen. They were in a line, moving northeast.

- 22 August 2001 at 22:56: In the town of Newport Pagnell in Buckinghamshire, between two to three stars, there was something which exploded into a large mass.

- 27 August 2001 at 21:00: In the town of Nantwich in Cheshire, nine smokeless flares were seen. Two were falling in parallel.

- 27 August 2001 at 19:35: In the town of Poynton in Cheshire, a circular object with a depression in the middle was seen. It was a grey/metallic colour. It was very bright. It was emitting smoke.

- 28 August 2001 at 02:00: In the town of Cherry Valley/Belfast in Northern Ireland, one large, white, circular light, moving at high speed with no sound, at about 500 feet, was seen.

- 1 September 2001 at 16:30: In the town of Wallington in Surrey, one object that looked a bit like an inverted U was seen moving due West.

- 2 September 2001 at 01:00: In the town of Royston in Hertfordshire, one rectangular/triangle-shaped object was seen. It had a white light that was pulsating. It was of average brightness and was moving northeast.

- 3 September 2001 at 12:00: In the town of Gosport in Hampshire, a twinkling object in the air, in close proximity to a plane, was seen.

- 7 September 2001 at 19:45: In the town of Broadstairs in Kent, a red ball of fire was seen. It was low on the horizon and was moving to the East.

- 9 September 2001 at 23:45: In the town of Probus in Cornwall, a half-mile-long object that was very bright was seen. It was slow and moving in anticlockwise circles.

- 9 September 2001 at 04:35: In the town of Sheffield in South Yorkshire, the object was very large and about the size of a helicopter, which made no sound. It was seen by the witness on two consecutive nights.

- 10 September 2001 at 23:20: In the town of Sheffield in South Yorkshire, the object was very large and about the size of a helicopter, which made no sound. It was seen by the witness on two consecutive nights.

- 11 September 2001 at 00:10: In the town of Hailsham in East Sussex, a very large, round object, followed by another object which was green and conical in shape were seen. Both objects were travelling fast.

- 15 September 2001 at 05:00: In the town of Swindon in Wiltshire, one white and very bright object was seen. It was moving vertically, then remained stationary, with occasional bursts of light. It was seen for over an hour.

- 16 September 2001 at 04:45: In the town of Market Drayton in Shropshire, one mushroom/lampshade-shaped object, about six-eight feet was seen. It was white with a very bright base and was moving very fast.

- 17 September 2001 at 06:00: In the town of Aslockton in Nottinghamshire, there was a light through the witness's window, which seemed to be quite a distance away and moving slowly.

- 21 September 2001 at 04:00: In the town of Ashford in Kent, the ship/craft moved towards Ashford and then hovered over Ashford for some time. The craft was solid.

- 21 September 2001 at 05:30: In the town of Ashford Kent, One triangular-shaped object. The size of a 747, maybe bigger. It moved N-easterly, then became stationary.

- 3 October 2001 at 20:40: In the town of Plymouth in Devon, exactly fifty objects that looked like points of light were seen. They were very bright. They were in line formation and moving from East to West.

- 7 October 2001 at 03:16: In the town of Woodbridge in Cambridgeshire, a spaceship was seen that had lights on the top and bottom of it.

- 11 October 2001 at 15:20: Town unknown, county unknown, the witness was visited by an alien that mentioned that the planets are in danger from different things going on in our solar system.

- 21 October 2001 at 18:15: In the town of Torbay in Devon, the object was larger than Venus but smaller than the moon. It was very white. It was wiggling from side to side.

- 23 October 2001 at 23:40: In the town of Dorking in Surrey, a silent craft shone a light on the witness. There was a low humming noise.

- 27 October 2001 at 20:30: In the town of Great Yarmouth in Norfolk, a bright white light with an orange light at the rear was seen.

- 31 October 2001 at 04:00: In the town of Wisbech in Cambridgeshire, a well-defined blue object, which was fat at both ends but slim in the middle, was seen.

- 1 November 2001 at 18:45: In the town of Wirral, county unknown, a vast number of lights flashing in the sky were seen. The lights then became still.

- 5 November 2001 at 18:30: In the town of South Croydon, Surrey, four objects that were smaller than a large aircraft were seen. They were triangular in shape and very bright colour.

- 5 November 2001 at 00:30: In the town of Hamilton in Lanarkshire, a Police Officer saw the object; it looked like half of a saucer; it had red and green lights, but mostly white. It also appeared to have rings around it.

- 9 November 2001 at 18:00: In the town of Welshpool in Powys, one triangular-shaped object with lights was seen.

- 11 November 2001 at 08:40: Flying over Seaford in Sussex, the Captain of the aircraft saw one red object sighted by the Captain in flight.

- 15 November 2001 at 05:59: In the town of Armthorpe in South Yorkshire a Police Officer saw a tennis ball-sized and shaped object with an orange centre and a black inner line around the circle. It had two bright green flare trails at its rear.

- 19 November 2001 at 17:10: Town unknown, county unknown, a small star-shaped object was seen.

- 25 November 2001 at 06:20: In the town of Inverness in the High Lands, one large torpedo-shaped object with red and white lights was seen. There were bright lights at the front, and also amber flashing lights.

- 25 November 2001 at 06:30: In the town of Nairnside in the High Lands, one roundish-shaped object that was glowing white and red was seen.

- 26 November 2001 at 11:20: On Briton Ferry in West Glamorgan, one long silver cylinder-shaped object was seen. It was very big and very high.

- 30 November 2001 at 15:40: In the town of Glasgow in S' clyde, strange lights in the sky were moving very erratically, making quick dart-like movements, then they stopped before moving off again.

- 2 December 2001 at 18:15: In the town of Torquay in Devon, one object the size of a small room was seen. It was spinning on its own axis.

- 9 December 2001 at 17:00: In the town of Leven in Fife, an assortment of flashing lights was seen.

- 10 December 2001 at 23:00: In the town of Blairgowrie in Perthshire a triangular-shaped object that was multi-coloured and had lights on the sides and points of the shape was seen.

- 10 December 2001 at 18:15: In the town of Torfaen in Gwent, three lights that looked like an elongated triangle were seen. The lights were very bright.

- 18 December 2001, time unknown: In the town of Stockport in Greater Manchester, two grey plumes of smoke in the sky over Stockport Railway Station were seen. A grey triangle was then witnessed.

- 18 December 2001 at 20:00: In the town of Stockport in Greater Manchester, a red light moving fast high up in the sky was seen. It slowed down, got fast again, and then wobbled from side to side.

- 18 December 2001 at 20:50: In the town of Crawley in Sussex, an object was seen. The object looked like a rounded triangle, longer at one point, with a giant light in the centre.

- 25 December 2001 time unknown: Town unknown, county unknown, an unusual aerial phenomenon was witnessed.

- 30 December 2001 at 02:30: In the town of Baltonsborough in Somerset, two round, thirty-foot objects were seen. Each had one white light on the left and one red light on the right. There was a low rumbling sound.

- 31 December 2001 at 09:00: In the town of Leeds in West Yorkshire, an object in the shape of a teardrop was seen. It was bright orange in colour and appeared to have lightning coming from its sides.

- 31 December 2001, time unknown: In the town of Tipton in the West Midlands, a bright light that was covered in black spots was seen.

- 31 December 2001 at 20:30: In the town of Bingham in Notts, one opal-shaped object with lights that were orange, red, blue, and white was seen. It was very bright.

- 31 December 2001, time unknown: In the town of Enniskillen in Northern Ireland, an object was seen travelling from East to West.

- 31 December 2001 at 21:00: In the town of Malvern in Worcestershire, one star-shaped object was seen. It had triangular red lights. There were also yellow and blue rays. It was hovering. It pulsated and then vanished.

- 31 December 2001, time unknown: In the town of Castle Donington in Leicestershire, a bright, green light was moving at a very high speed. The object appeared to land near Kegworth, over the M1.

- 31 December 2001 at 18:45: In the town of Crewe/Leighton in Cheshire, a silver ball that was really bright was seen. It was lower than an aircraft and moving in a straight line.

2002

- 1 January 2002 at 22:30: In the town of St. Andrews in Fife, a glowing white light was seen flashing in the sky.

- 9 January 2002 at 23:30: In the town of Swansea in West Glamorgan, a green, circular object that was hovering in its position was seen.

- 15 January 2002 at 18:00: In the town of Preston, county unknown, white and red flashing lights were seen that looked like they were zig-zagging, and then they came to a stop. They hovered, then moved away.

- 19 January 2002 at 02:00: In the town of Urmston in Greater Manchester, a spherically shaped object that was white and very bright was seen. The object moved at speed in a straight line, then disappeared.

- 24 January 2002 at 16:12: In the town of Cromer, county unknown, nine lights that looked like they were close and then they separated were seen. They were not too bright. They looked like large fireworks.

- 27 January 2002 at 19:25: In the town of Leeds in West Yorkshire, four small, bright, white lights that looked like headlamps were seen.

- 28 January 2002 at 03:00: In the town of Telford in Shropshire, three triangle-shaped objects were seen. They looked like the Mitsubishi car sign. The middle triangle was brighter than the other two.

- 6 February 2002 at 19:05: In the town of Narborough in Leicestershire, one globe with an attachment that was white and very bright was seen.

- 13 February 2002 at 22:19: In the town of Enfield in Middlesex, twenty silver balls with an orange tinge were seen flying West of Enfield Wash.

- 14 February 2002 at 21:11: In the town of Rock in Shropshire, white lights were seen.

- 14 February 2002 at 11:05: In the town of Corby in Northamptonshire, a silver object was seen that appeared to be flying quite low. It was followed by two aeroplanes with streams of light behind them.

- 15 February 2002 at 15:56: In the town of Richmond, county unknown, a very odd flashing light on a moving object spinning above London in the Westminster area was seen.

- 16 February 2002 at 22:50: In the town of Walton-on-Thames in Surrey, one oval disc was seen with green and red flashing lights.

- 22 February 2002 at 22:30: In the town of Leven in Fife, one ball-shaped object which flashed and became very bright was seen.

- 23 February 2002 at 21:40: In the town of Cirencester in Gloucestershire, one quite bright, semi-circular object was seen moving across the sky in a straight line.

- 24 February 2002 at 19:00: In the town of Newport in Gwent, one large and three smaller triangular objects were seen with bright red and blue flashing lights.

- 27 February 2002, time unknown: In the town of Harrow in Middlesex, the witness just said it was a UFO.

- 28 February 2002 at 22:50: In the town of St. Austell in Cornwall, there was a flying triangle and 100ft from the base of the triangle to the apex, there were red lights on the right and blue lights on the left.

- 1 March 2002 at 20:00: In the town of Lancaster in Lancashire, six round shimmery spheres were seen racing across the night sky.

- 2 March 2002 at 20:40: In the town of Weston-super-Mare in Somerset large, numerous lights were seen that were white and very bright. They were wheel-shaped.

- 5 March 2002 at 21:50: In the town of Ripley in Derbyshire, a large triangle-shaped object with a large white light on the front of each 'tip' and a white light in the centre with a group of four static red lights was seen.

- 7 March 2002 at 19:45: In the town of Hornchurch in Essex, two semi-circular, elliptical shapes dully illuminated in yellow and white were seen. There was a faint murmur.

- 13 March 2002 at 20:05: In the town of Shotts in Strathclyde, a saucer-shaped object with a white tail was seen. It was the brightest thing the witness had ever seen.

- 14 March 2002 at 00:30: In the town of Leicester, Leicestershire, the object appeared larger than a star and was circular. It then turned and looked diamond-shaped. It had a blue light at the top.

- 25 March 2002 at 18:50: In the town of Newport-on-Tay in Fife, one bright orange/red cigar-shaped object that was seen over the sea.

- 31 March 2002 at 02:15: In the town of Scunthorpe in Humberside, two lights were circling around each other. They were yellow, red, green, and blue in colour.

- Date unknown April 2002, time unknown: In the town of Wisborough Green in Wiltshire, one cylindrical, upright object that was grey and had light grey stripes was seen.

- 7 April 2002 at 21:30: In the town of Walton-on-Thames in Surrey one round object with red and green flashing lights was seen bobbing from side to side.

- 7 April 2002 at 01:50: In the town of Scawby in Humberside, the witness saw a blue light, then yellow shooting stars, followed by a loud bang.

- 8 April 2002 at 22:00: In the town of Walton-on-Thames in Surrey, one small disc-shaped object with red and green flashing lights was seen.

- 8 April 2002 at 08:35: In the town of Port Talbot in West Glamorgan, one large, round, very bright green object going very fast to the East was seen.

- 15 April 2002 at 03:30: In the town of Nottingham in Nottinghamshire, three silver triangular objects in a triangle formation were seen. They were closely followed by a Police helicopter.

- 15 April 2002 at 21:50: In the town of Worcester in Worcestershire, one big, round, bright star-shaped object that was coloured yellow and red was seen moving upwards.

- 13 May 2002 at 22:00: In the town of Addlestone in Surrey, one very big circular object, that was white and very bright was seen.

- 15 May 2002 at 02:15: In the town of Uckfield in East Sussex, one object with red and green flashing lights was seen.

- 27 May 2002 at 12:45: In the town of St John's Wood in London, an object was seen floating up and down and the sun was shining off of it. Also, there were two black dots moving quickly.

- 30 May 2002 at 01:50: In the town of Dumfries, county unknown, one object that was white and very bright was seen. It was moving vertically, very fast.

- 31 May 2002 at 03:40: In the town of Stamford in Lincolnshire, one object with two white lights on the front was seen. It had a flashing blue light on one side and a purple one on the other.

- 31 May 2002 at 18:30: In the town of Woking in Surrey, a sausage-shaped object, that was twenty times larger than a normal aircraft was seen. It had different colours.

- 31 May 2002 at 23:00: In the town of Harlow in Essex, two very large disc-type aircraft that were white and had a dull glow were seen.

- 3 June 2002 at 23:40: In the town of Keighley in West Yorkshire, one large object that had a bright white light was seen. It was moving from West to East.

- 4 June 2002 at 03:20: In the town of Llansamlet in West Glamorgan, six objects were seen omitting a bright, white light. They travelled at a slow, steady speed.

- 10 June 2002 at 01:30: In the town of Carron in Morayshire, one flashing object that had blue, green, yellow, and red lighting was seen.

- 22 June 2002 at 01:00: In the town of Greenford in Middlesex, an oval-shaped object was seen. It was light and almost white in colour. It looked like it was rolling through the sky. It was rotating.

- 14 July 2002 at 18:15: County unknown in London, one pinpoint object was seen that was very bright and was metallic that was reflecting the sunlight. It left a vapour trail behind.

- 28 July 2002 at 20:55: In the town of Salisbury in Wiltshire, a witness saw a bright red light. It vanished after five minutes.

- 3 August 2002, time unknown: Town unknown, county unknown; the witness said it looked like there were Harriers following moving lights, over the village after dusk.

- 10 August 2002 at 23:00: Town unknown county unknown lights were seen circling and then reversing direction every few minutes.

- 12 August 2002 at 22:00: In the town of Hull in East Yorkshire, one purple and white pulsating jellyfish-like object with smaller light circles surrounding it was seen. A smaller, hazy object was attached.

- 13 August 2002 at 00:50: In the town of Ruislip Manor in Middlesex, three balls of light stuck together were seen. They were red, blue, yellow, and white. They were very still and very bright.

- 15 August 2002 at 21:55: In the town of Milton Keynes in Buckinghamshire, a glowing orange boomerang-shaped object was seen moving very fast.

- 16 August 2002 at 20:12: In the town of Brighton in East Sussex, a big flying object that looked like a glider but, when viewed on the camcorder, looked like a big horse tumbling around was seen.

- 17 August 2002 at 21:45: In the town, of Hull in East Yorkshire, a series of neon lights in two lines were seen. The objects were boomerang-shaped, in a V formation.

- 20 August 2002 at 11:00: Town unknown, county unknown, a green light was seen coming down from the sky. The witness had never seen anything like it before.

- 21 August 2002 at 11:00: In the town of Fortrose in Highlands, a small torpedo-shaped object with a white or silver triangular reflector to one side was seen.

- 22 August 2002 at 22:25: In the town of Heathfield in East Sussex, aerial lights were seen in the sky.

- 22 August 2002 at 21:30: In the town of Shropham, Norfolk, aerial lights were seen in the sky.

- 22 August 2002 at 22:25: In the town of Heathfield in East Sussex, anomalous aerial lights were seen.

- 22 August 2002 at 21:30: In the town of Shropham, Norfolk, anomalous aerial lights were seen.

- 26 August 2002 at 00:00: In the town of Dundee in Tayside, strange red and white lights were seen through curtains. Then there was a solid red beam outside the window for about five to ten seconds.

- 29 August 2002 at 00:30: In the town of Leicester, in Leicestershire, a star-shaped object was seen. It had four lights on each side, like a black shadow.

- 1 September 2002 at 17:00: In the town of Leicester in Leicestershire, one object that was golf ball size was seen. Then another three golf ball-sized objects were seen moving in an L formation.

- 5 September 2002, time unknown: In the town of Wisborough Green in West Sussex, interesting lights on an equilateral triangle were seen.

- 10 September 2002 at 23:23: In the town of Hamilton in Strathclyde, there were three objects, each of which had two bright orange lights, in a triangular formation. They seemed to swap places with each other.

- 10 September 2002 at 19:45: In the town of Tibbermore in Tayside, one small, bright, oval-shaped object was seen. The object seemed to elongate as it got closer.

- 11 September 2002 at 10:40: In the town of Kirkcaldy in Fife, there were three hanging silver rods. They were drifting slowly, then became bright silver, and then faded away.

- 18 September 2002 at 19:20: In the town of Halstead in Essex, a display of three lights in a sort of star shape were seen. The lights were in formation and circling.

- 19 September 2002 at 21:20: Town unknown, county unknown, a circle of twenty lights were seen outside the witnesses house for about twenty minutes.

- 19 September 2002 at 22:21: In the town of Bradford in West Yorkshire, two circles, one inside the other, were seen. They were 50/50 feet in diameter. The brightness varied as they passed through the clouds.

- 23 September 2002 at 17:40: In the town of Huddersfield in West Yorkshire, one silver cigar-shaped object that split into six small silver balls was seen. They were travelling erratically, but remained as a group.

- 23 September 2002 at 01:00: In the town of St John's Wood in London, a triangle-shaped object with red flashing/alternating lights that went around the inside edges of the object was seen.

- 30 September 2002 at 22:00: In the town of Exeter, Devon, an object was seen that had two neon blue lights at the rear.

- 30 September 2002 at 23:30: In the town of Cannock in Staffordshire, an object was seen that was described to be three times bigger than the size of a jumbo jet, like "a gigantic flying piece of street".

- 3 October 2002 at 20:20: In the town of Exeter, Devon, one ball of red glowing light was seen.

- 4 Octber 2002 at 21:30: In the town of Everett, USA, five objects were circling above the head of the witness at about fifty ft. The witness heard a low-pitched noise. There was a blue and white type nucleus centre.

- 4 October 2002 at 20:30: In the town of Southend in Essex, one white, very small object was seen very high up in the sky.

- 17 October 2002 at 02:54: In the town of Hull in East Yorkshire Two Police Officers saw a star-shaped that was blue, green, red, and white in colour. The object moved fast.

- 23 October 2002 at 07:04: In the town of Woodbridge in Suffolk, a large silver triangle which then changed shape was seen. It was clouded in a pink and green haze.

- 25 October 2002 at 01:30: In the town of Liverpool in Merseyside, an object that looked like an upturned saucer with a dome on top was seen. It had amber lights, and the dome had a light on top. It was hovering.

- Date unknown November 2002 at 14:30: In the town of Walcott in Lincolnshire, a dark, black, torpedo-shaped object was seen. It left a white plume of smoke.

- 2 November 2002 at 23:00: In the town of Gors-goch in Dyfed, a round yellowish light followed by a green light was seen going up into the sky vertically.

- 2 November 2002 at 22:58: In the town of Llanerchymedd in Gwynedd, one light, the size of a football, was seen moving slowly at 2–3000ft.

- 7 November 2002 at 06:30: In the town of Wolverhampton in the West Midlands, two sets of lights with an aircraft in the middle of them were seen.

- 9 November 2002 at 22:00: In the town of Lechlade in Gloucestershire, a series of lights moving in an arc were seen. They were pink and spaced out.

- 11 November 2002 at 23:00: In the town of Nottingham in Nottinghamshire, eight objects joined into a circle, then separated. They moved independently, then joined together again in a circle.

- 14 November 2002 at 22:12: In the town of Saddleworth Moor in Greater Manchester, a small football-sized white light with a blue tail was seen.

- 15 November 2002 at 12:15: In the town of Eyam in Derbyshire, a large flying object was seen. The witness had never seen anything like it before. It had no lights whatsoever.

- 15 November 2002 at 21:30: In the town of Liverpool in Merseyside, a series of ten lights all tracing a pattern in the sky were seen.

- 24 November 2002 at 20:00: In the town of Bohuntine in the Highlands, a round orange-shaped object with pale green lights shining out in all directions was seen.

- 28 November 2002 at 14:26: On the Cardiff Docks in South Glamorgan, two sightings over Cardiff Docks happened. The objects were of different colours and were moving up and down.

- 9 December 2002 at 17:30: In the town of Bishop's Stortford in Hertfordshire, a small round, dull light was seen.

- 10 December 2002 at 18:27: In the town of Stoke-on-Trent in Staffordshire, the witness saw an orange disc shape.

- 16 December 2002 at 02:35: On the M62/near Rothwell in West Yorkshire, a number of objects that were quite large, long, thin, and shaped like cuttlefish were seen. They joined to become a rectangular, vertical light, skimming along.

- 18 December 2002 at 16:40: In the town of Coningsby, county unknown, a bright oval-shaped cluster of lights that grew brighter than the moon was seen.

- 19 December 2002 at 06:30: In the town of Chaldon in Surrey, a very bright object with an orange/yellow triangle behind it was seen.

- 19 December 2002 at 06:30: In the town of Notting Hill in London, a very large object was seen falling. Flames were coming out of the back.

- 19 December 2002 at 06:30: In the town of Brighton in East Sussex, a large cylindrical object with white flowing light from the front and flames coming from the rear was seen. It made some noise but was not loud.

- 19 December 2002 at 06:30: In the town of Newton Abbott in Devon, a strange object/light was seen; it made no sound.

- 24 December 2002 at 10:39: In the town of Aylesbury in Buckinghamshire, an orange object with a lighter-coloured trail about ten times the length of the head was seen.

- 28 December 2002 at 20:10: On the A31/Hogsback in Surrey, four pairs of lights were seen.

- 29 December 2002 at 00:00: 7 miles past Lancaster in Lancashire On that M6, a bright green light about the size of a traffic light arched over, came down to the ground, and broke up.

- Date unknown, time unknown: In the town of Solihull in the West Midlands, a witness saw two bright lights.

- Date unknown, time unknown: In the town of Welwyn Garden City in Hertfordshire, one disc-shaped object that was tangerine-coloured was seen. It zig-zagged for a while and then departed after fifteen seconds.

- Date unknown time unknown: In a Television Studio, a black tube appeared in the studio, two doors opened and then closed. It rose to the ceiling and then disappeared. It moved around.,

2003

- 4 January 2003 at 21:15: In the town of St Clares/Carmarthen in Dyfed, a white object with vivid flashing green, blue, and red lights was seen.

- 4 January 2003 at 19:20: At Benbecula Airport, a senior air traffic control officer saw one object with a very bright light, like an aircraft's landing light, with a smaller, dimmer light on top of the bright light.

- 6 January 2003 at 15:00: In the town of Huddersfield in West Yorkshire, three silver or white balls were seen in the sky, joined by another two. They were quite large and were travelling in a line.

- 7 January 2003 at 21:26: In the town of Blackpool in Lancashire, one bright white object, hovering at first, then moving quickly, was seen.

- 8 January 2003 at 22:00: In the town of Coaltown Balgonie in Fife, an object that was changing shape was seen. It had strong blue, green, and red lights pulsating lights. It was jumbo Jet-sized.

- 10 January 2003 at 03:00: In the town of Brighton, county unknown, a witness saw what looked like a satellite re-entering, moving across the sky, then it shot off like a shooting star.

- 10 January 2003, time unknown: In the town of Stirling in Scotland, two aircraft-type objects flying next to each other were seen. They both had vapour trails.

- 10 January 2003 at 01:00: In the town of East Dulwich in London, lights that were formed in a worm shape, wriggling around in the sky, were seen.

- 11 January 2003 at 23:45: In the town of Bridgnorth in Salop, an oblong in shape object that had with three vertical flashing lights, red, yellow, and green, all flashing at the same time, was seen.

- 13 January 2003 at 07:40: In the town of Dunkeld in Tayside, a distant object moving from side to side was seen. It had a bright light, brighter than any star. It went dim from time to time.

- 15 January 2003 at 22:10: In the town of Cowbridge in South Glamorgan, a large round disc, slightly smaller than the moon, was seen. It was creamy white, then changed to green.

- 19 January 2003 at 18:03: In the town of Stonehaven in Grampian, three bright lights forming a triangle were seen hovering, not moving.

- 25 January 2003 at 19:08: In the town of Chester in Cheshire, twelve bright lights moving from side to side in the sky were seen.

- 29 January 2003 at 18:15: In the town of Wolverhampton in the West Midlands, a Sergeant in the RAF saw two triangular-shaped objects flying in perfect synchronisation. They made a low humming noise; they were not like a normal commercial airliner.

- 3 February 2003, time unknown: In the town of Leyland in Lancashire, a bright light lit up the curtains and, for a split second, appeared to be heading for the window. Followed by a loud bang.

- 16 February 2003 at 17:20: In the town of Birmingham in the West Midlands, one object was seen. It was static.

- 19 February 2003 at 18:30: In the town of Huntingdon in Cambridgeshire, one object was seen; it looked like a shooting star falling to the ground.

- 21 February 2003 at 10:30: In the town of Penryn in Cornwall, a circular bright light that had three arms was seen, and in the middle of it was a red light.

- 25 February 2003 at 23:00: In the town of Southfields in London, an object that was not a plane, not on a flight path, and not a star was seen.

- 1 March 2003, time unknown: In the town of Northampton in Northamptonshire, two large white objects were seen close together; they looked like jets or refuelling planes. They were going at jet speed.

- 2 March 2003 at 15:54: In the town of Pontypridd in Mid-Glamorgan, a strange object, silver and shaped like a dart, was seen.

- 11 March 2003 at 21:50: In the town of Wellingborough in Northamptonshire an object was seen high up in the sky.

- 30 March 2003 at 20:00: In the town of Aldershot in Hampshire, a very large delta-shaped formation of steady red lights was seen they made no noise.

- 30 March 2003, time unknown: In the town of Glastonbury, Somerset, lights were seen in the sky.

- 31 March 2003 at 09:20: Town unknown in London, two silver objects that were stationary in the sky were seen. One seemed to be closer than the other.

- 5 April 2003 at 03:58: Town unknown, county unknown, a massive object about the size of two football pitches and triangular-shaped was seen. It took off very fast.

- 7 April 2003 at 02:30: In the town of Falmouth in Cornwall, one craft with three yellow lights on the port side and three red lights on the starboard side was seen. The shape was between circular and triangular, or Delta wing size.

- 11 April 2003 at 22:21: At Stansted Airport in Essex, the Captain and First Officer of an aircraft saw a ball of fire. It was very bright with no colour.

- 23 April 2003 at 18:15: At Heathrow Airport in London, a ball of light, with no colour, passed under an aircraft from front to back. It was very fast.

- 24 April 2003, time unknown: In the town of Shepherds Bush in London, crafts coming down from behind the clouds were seen.

- 5 May 2003 at 18:30: Town unknown, county unknown witness saw a black triangle flying quite fast and silently through the sky in a single direction.

- 13 May 2003 at 17:45: In the town of Belfast in Northern Ireland, two objects that looked like stars were seen.

- 25 May 2003 at 23:00: In the town of Sandyford in Lanarkshire, an object was seen. The object was high and bright and had no anti-collision lights.

- 25 May 2003 at 23:05: In the town of Kilmacolm in Strathclyde, a large, bright light was seen.

- 25 May 2003 at 23:20: In the town of St. Leonards in East Kilbride, a huge white ball that was glowing that looked like a flying jellyfish was seen.

- 28 May 2003 at 07:50: In the town of Great Yarmouth in Norfolk, an object was seen. The object was saucer-shaped.

- 30 May 2003 at 23:25: In the town of Kingston-upon-Hull in Humberside, a bright light was seen in the sky.

- 31 May 2003 at 21:00: In the town of Gateshead in Tyne and Wear, a black orb with five or six tassels underneath it was seen.

- 8 June 2003 at 17:00: In the town of Wellingborough in Northamptonshire, a white cylindrical object moving very fast up into the sky was seen.

- 9 June 2003 at 06:40: In the town of Isleworth in London, a silver object as bright as a star changed from a cylinder to a crescent moon shape with red and silver stripes.

- 14 June 2003 at 21:35: In the town of Llandrindod Wells in Powys, very big red light balls were hovering. One red light hung smaller and then dropped out.

- 14 June 2003 at 15:39: In the town of Walthamstow in London, a cylinder-shaped object with a radius around it of what looked like faint stars was seen. It was metal, as the light was shining off of it.

- 14 June 2003 at 06:00: In the town of Girton in Cambridgeshire, a small circular object was seen. It was blue and white and translucent.

- 20 June 2003 at 08:35: In the town of Dunstable in Bedfordshire, a string of two sets of two lights was seen.

- 21 June 2003 at 16:43: In the town of Richmond in London, a doughnut-shaped object was spotted moving from left to right and side to side. One side was shiny and reflective, and the other was black.

- 21 June 2003 at 12:32: In the town of Wimbledon in London, the witness said something was seen for three seconds.

- 26 June 2003 at 16:28: In the town of Melksham in Wiltshire, an object was seen. The object was a silvery white colour and non-reflective in the sunshine.

- 28 June 2003 at 23:22: In the town of Glastonbury, Somerset, orange lights moving as a group in a circular motion were seen. They moved slowly along.

- 8 July 2003 at 20:00: In the town of Hereford in Herefordshire, an MOD (Ministry of Defence) Police Officer saw a stationary triangular object. The object remained stationary for about 30 minutes at quite a height.

- 12 July 2003 at 22:05: In the town of Rhonda in Mid-Glamorgan, two round objects with legs which were black and spinning were seen.

- 13 July 2003, time unknown: In the town of Wellingborough in Northamptonshire, a witness saw a ball of light in the sky.

- 13 July 2003 at 20:30: In the town of Winterley in Cheshire, there appeared a star-like object.

- 14 July 2003 at 21:30: Town unknown in Northamptonshire, a witness saw the biggest white light that the witness had ever seen before. It shot off across the sky and then disappeared.

- 15 July 2003 at 03:25: In the town of Bermondsey in London, the witness saw an object, which the witness assumed to be a shooting star at first. It left no trail behind.

- 15 July 2003 at 21:40: In the town of Galston on Sea in Norfolk, a disc-like object moving in the sky slowly, poised once, and headed in a northeast direction was seen.

- 15 July 2003 at 00:30: In the town of Malvern in Worcestershire, one light was seen. It made erratic movements and was stationary.

- 20 July 2003 at 23:05: In the town of Bridlington in East Yorkshire, a bright white star-like light was seen. It moved from side to side, up and down, and in circles.

- 22 July 2003, time unknown: In the town of Bridlington in East Yorkshire, a silver or white object was seen. It moved at an unbelievable speed.

- 27 July 2003 at 18:00: In the town of Gravesend in Kent, a silver ball was seen up in the sky for about an hour. It disappeared and then returned again about an hour later.

- 4 August 2003 at 21:00: In the town of Wellingborough in Northamptonshire, a brilliant orange ball of light was seen 2000ft up in the sky.

- 8 August 2003 at 22:35: In the town of West Kilbride in Ayrshire a star-shaped object was seen. The witness watched for a few minutes, then it dropped from the sky like a bomb.

- 10 August 2003 at 23:15: In the town of West Kilbride in Ayrshire, a witness could see a few round spheres.

- 13 August 2003 at 22:55: In the town of Maesteg in Mid-Glamorgan, a roundish, football-shaped object was seen. It had flashing lights that were multi-coloured. The lights were on top, then moved around the object.

- 14 August 2003 at 18:00: In the town of Southfleet in Kent, an unusual object with flashing lights but not like an aircraft more like reflections from the sun, was seen. It left no trail.

- 14 August 2003 at 23:57: In the town of Worcester, county unknown, a very bright white light bigger than a star was seen but it began to quickly diminish in size until it completely disappeared.

- 14 August 2003 at 23:09: In the town of Newport in Gwent, an orange circular object was seen. It stayed stationary.

- 16 August 2003 at 21:00: In the town of Amesbury in Wiltshire, a flying saucer-shaped object was seen.

- 17 August 2003 at 23:45: In the town of Bonny bridge in Central, a witness just said a sighting had occurred.

- 19 August 2003 at 23:30: In the town of St Seithins in Perthshire, an object with two white lights and one red and one orange in the middle that were both flashing was seen.

- 21 August 2003 at 14:00: In the town of Lincoln, Lincolnshire, an object was seen. The object was cigar-shaped, grey in colour with domed ends, was silent and very slow.

- 27 August 2003 at 23:00: In the town of Worcester in Worcestershire, a helium-type balloon that was the size of a moon, with flashing blue and red lights, moving north along the line of the A38 over the area south of Worcester was seen.

- 3 September 2003 at 21:35: In the town of Wellingborough in Northamptonshire, an orange ball was seen 2000ft up in the sky.

- 4 September 2003 at 23:40: In the town of Todmorden in West Yorkshire, there were six lights that split, at one point becoming eight lights that were orange and red in colour.

- 13 September 2003 at 21:40: In the town of Heckmondwike in West Yorkshire, a Senior Curator at the Royal Armouries Museum saw two circular objects, about half the apparent size of the moon, that were a very dull yellow.

- 13 September 2003 at 22:40: In the town of Manchester in Greater Manchester, a round was seen which had white lights.

- 13 September 2003 at 20:15: In the town of Great Yarmouth in Norfolk, an object was seen that was as bright as Mars. It gave off a white light. It was a dim brightness. It moved in a southeast direction.

- 17 September 2003 at 20:45: In the town of Northampton in Northants, two small, star-sized objects that were a much darker orange or rust colour were seen, followed by another two doing manoeuvres.

- 17 September 2003 at 21:00: In the town of Northolt in London, one white extremely bright, brilliant object was seen, flickering yellow and red. It was moving from side to side.

- 18 September 2003 at 03:00: In the town of Wimbledon in London, a triangular-shaped object that was copper-coloured was seen. It hovered over the house for about a minute, then disappeared.

- 19 September 2003 at 22:30: In the town of Ashby De La Launde in Digby, Lincolnshire, an object was seen spinning whilst stationary above a house.

- 22 September 2003, time unknown: In the town of Hove in East Sussex, a red, unidentified flying object, definitely not an aeroplane, was seen.

- 24 September 2003 at 19:25: In the town of Barry in South Glamorgan, a witness saw an unusual object falling from a cloud, like it was burning, and it was very fast. It was viewed for five minutes.

- 24 September 2003 at 20:45: In the town of Northampton in Northamptonshire, a witness saw two pairs of objects that were not recognisable as aircraft and were purple in colour.

- 14 October 2003 at 06:56: In the town of Whitney in Oxfordshire, a very large object, was seen that had lights that were flashing on it.

- 26 October 2003 at 21:06: In the town of North Wirral in Merseyside, there were two objects travelling side by side overhead and were a dull red colour.

- 5 November 2003 at 16:30: Southbound on the A11, the Assistant Secretary in the RAF Dependants Fund saw two bright lights in the sky.

- 17 November 2003 at 02:25: In the town of Bromley in Kent, Police Officers and a Police helicopter crew saw that there were 20–30 red flashing lights in the sky accompanied by a whirring noise.

- 25 November 2003 at 14:25: In the town of Wem in Shropshire, a strange bright orange/red light was seen in the sky.

- 1 December 2003, time unknown: In the town of Woodbridge in Suffolk, an object that looked like an unusual aircraft but with strange lights was seen.

- 2 December 2003 at 01:20: In the town of Aylesbury in Buckinghamshire, nothing was seen, but a loud noise was heard, like a balloon letting out air.

- 2 December 2003 at 01:30: In the town of Thame in Oxfordshire, an Editor of a newspaper heard a loud noise like a hot air balloon, but nothing was seen.

- 17 December 2003 at 19:15: In the town of Wokingham in Berkshire, an object was seen. The object was black/dark with lights along the side and a weird strobe light. It was 60 ft across and very high in the sky.

- 29 December 2003 at 01:50: In Barnton Park in Edinburgh, a steady, bright light in the sky resembling the front of a helicopter was seen.

- Date unknown, time unknown: In the town of Ashburton in Devon, two strange lights were seen in the sky.

- Date unknown, time unknown: In the town of Wellingborough in Northamptonshire, a very bright white light with about five other lights around it that were moving was seen. They looked like a barrage balloon from World War 2.

- Date unknown, time unknown: In the town of Wigan, Lancashire, 17 spaceships were seen. They were V-shaped, oblong, with wings, and were different colours. The witness could see green aliens with cream-coloured bellies.

2004

- 2 January 2004 at 04:30: In the town of Ayr in Strathclyde, a square red object, pinkish at the front, was seen.

- 9 January 2004 at 14:00: In Market Harborough, Leicestershire, one large black triangular aircraft with three bright lights in a triangle formation was seen. There was a rumbling sound.

- 9 January 2004 at 22:30: In the town of Thaxted in Essex, a strange light that was watched for one and a half hours was seen.

- 12 January 2004 at 16:30: In the town of Huddersfield in West Yorkshire, a round object with white lights all around it was seen.

- 27 January 2004 at 21:00: In the town of Peterborough in Cambridgeshire, four dull red lights above the house, travelling fast and low, were seen.

- 27 January 2004 at 23:08: In the town of Retford in Nottinghamshire, one object was seen over Retford Town Hall.

- 28 January 2004 at 18:30: In the town of Peterborough in Cambridgeshire, flashing green lights were seen 1000–5000ft up in the sky.

- 28 January 2004 at 18:15: In the town of Billingsley in Shropshirel, Lights in the night sky were seen flying in formation.

- 4 February 2004 at 06:15: In the town of Grosmont in North Yorkshire, an object appeared to be a soundless pair of lights, one yellow, the other white. No discernible shape.

- 8 February 2004 at 21:45: In the town of Ely in Cambridgeshire, four lights, one brighter than the others, sometimes fading, were seen.

- 11 February 2004 at 21:05: In the town of Holbeach in Lincolnshire, two objects described as a fast pair of speeding lights that were very fast and very bright were seen.

- 18 February 2004 at 16:02: In the town of Rhyl in Clwyd, a large black object over was seen over Rhyl.

- 1 March 2004 at 20:00: In the town of Lowestoft in Suffolk, a yellow light in a circular formation was seen. The flash shot across the sky and the lights went out.

- 17 March 2004 at 20:20: In the town of Edinburgh in Lothian, a fast-moving bright light was seen.

- 25 March 2004 at 22:10: In the town of Leighton Buzzard in Bedfordshire, a large ball of light was seen. It looked like a rocket. It made no sound generally, but at times, a slight whirring sound.

- 27 March 2004 at 17:30: Town unknown in Sri Lanka, a witness saw an object. The object looked like a ring doughnut, was orange, and had other rings of colour surrounding it too.

- 2 April 2004 at 12:30: In the town of West Kilbride in Ayrshire, one sphere-shaped object was seen.

- 9 April 2004 at 17:57: In the town of Greater Chesterford in Essex, a 60ft long symmetrical object was seen.

- 9 April 2004 at 19:30: In the town of Dimchurch in Kent, the witness just said it was an object. That it was flying over very fast and then disappeared.

- 11 April 2004 at 20:43: In the town of Seaforth in Merseyside, the witness saw a UFO with a cluster of four bright lights in a ring shape on it. Three beams of white light shone upward and then disappeared.

- 14 April 2004 at 10:30: In the town of Wellingborough in Northamptonshire, z round object was flying overhead at a very fast speed.

- 14 April 2004 at 20:27: In the town of Honley in West Yorkshire, an object was seen that looked like a Jellyfish flying in the sky. It might have had two bright lights on the side of the object.

- 15 April 2004 at 22:20: In the town of West Kilbride in Ayrshire, a very bright, yellow, sphere-shaped object was seen.

- 16 April 2004 at 22:40: In the town of West Kilbride in Ayrshire, a yellow-shaped sphere was seen.

- 16 April 2004 at 22:55: In the town of West Kilbride in Ayrshire a yellow-shaped sphere was seen.

- 19 April 2004 at 22:10: In the town of Filey in North Yorkshire, two objects travelling together were seen. They climbed at an incredible speed and headed south down the coast.

- 22 April 2004 at 16:30: In the town of Goole in East Yorkshire, an object was seen. The object looked like a boomerang and was stationary over a power station. An aircraft was circling the object.

- 22 April 2004, time unknown: In the town of Queensbury in West Yorkshire, the witness just said an object was seen.

- 25 April 2004 at 08:50: In the town of Primrose Hill in London, an object was seen. The object was rectangular in shape with white light.

- 29 April 2004 at 22:30: In the town of Derby in Derbyshire, four bright lights plus the outer circle of the round object had eight lights going round in a clockwise direction.

- 5 May 2004 at 23:10: In the town of Kings Lynn in Norfolk, a bright, pulsing-spider-looking object was seen.

- 10 May 2004 at 22:45: In the town of Storth in Cumbria, an object was seen. The object looked like a bright star and was moving around like a kite.

- 10 May 2004 at 22:47: In the town of West Kilbride in Ayrshire, two yellow spheres going at a tremendous speed were seen.

- 14 May 2004 at 03:10: In the town of Leeds in West Yorkshire, a very bright light was seen, as well as strobe lights near the bright light.

- 15 May 2004, time unknown: In the town of West Kilbride in Ayrshire, two sphere-shaped objects were seen.

- 17 May 2004 time unknown: In the town of West Kilbride in Ayrshire, one sphere-shaped object was seen.

- 19 May 2004 at 23:20: In the town of West Kilbride in Ayrshire, a large, bright, sphere-shaped object was seen.

- 20 May 2004 at 09:43: Town unknown in Surrey, the witness had seen the object so clearly that grooves and windows could be seen, and there was no room for humans to fit within it.

- 20 May 2004 at 11:15: In the town of Nelson in Lancashire, an object was seen. The object was white in colour and 'chewy mint' shaped.

- 20 May 2004 at 13:30: In the town of Skipton in North Yorkshire, an object was seen. The object looked like a light/transparent ring.

- 22 May 2004 at 23:50: Town unknown, county unknown, two objects were seen; they were both orange colour and were disc-shaped. They looked like aircraft without wings and were very silent.

- 25 May 2004 at 17:00: In the town of Paignton in Devon, a long single, black cylinder-type object 200 ft long was seen.

- 25 May 2004, time unknown: In the town of West Kilbride in Ayrshire one sphere-shaped object was seen.

- 26 May 2004 time unknown: A 60-metre-long cigar-shaped object was seen over Torquay.

- 30 May 2004 at 12:15: In the town of West Kilbride in Ayrshire, five bright spheres flying beside each other were seen.

- 1 June 2004 at 00:00: In the town of Hamilton in Lanarkshire, an object was seen. The object was a bright light, and it was flashing and making engine noises.

- 2 June 2004 at 00:35: In the town of Hamilton in Lanarkshire, one object with a bright, white flashing light was seen, and it was making engine noises.

- 2 June 2004 at 01:00: In the town of Hayes in Middlesex, objects that looked like comets at first were seen. They were quite bright and got lighter as they grew bigger.

- 4 June 2004 at 21:07: In the town of Coventry in the West Midlands, an object was seen. The object was black and silver, and of cylindrical shape, and was flying below cloud level.

- 5 June 2004, time unknown: In the town of Wellingborough in Northamptonshire, a black 'UFO' was seen flying over a Methodist Church.

- 14 June 2004 at 09:30: In the town of Rushden in Northamptonshire, a 'UFO' was seen following an airliner.

- 14 June 2004 at 23:15: In the town of Bridgend county, an unknown object 70 ft long with brilliant bright lights was seen. The object changed shape just before the sight was lost.

- 21 June 2004 at 17:55: In the town of Oldham in Greater Manchester, one long, black, cigar-shaped object was seen.

- 13 July 2004 at 01:00: In the town of Winchmore Hill in London, an object was seen. The object was extremely large and completely circular, and the lights on it were pulsating different colours.

- 14 July 2004 at 23:10: In the town of Corby in Northamptonshire, a bright yellow light at a low level appeared from nowhere for about ten seconds.

- 19 July 2004 at 22:20: In the town of Wellford in Berkshire, the Press and the Newspaper were called about reports of a ball of flames with a solid underneath; the flames went out, came on again, and then plummeted to earth.

- 28 July 2004, time unknown: In the town of Lynton/Exmoor in Devon, an object was seen. The object looked like a big, white triangle on the horizon.

- 31 July 2004 at 22:45: In the town of Shepton Mallet in Somerset, three very strange, bright orange objects, which were quite large and going in an upward direction, were seen.

- 7 August 2004 at 04:30: In the town of Chingford in London, a strange-looking object, bigger than an aircraft, was seen. It had mesh around it and red, blue, green, and yellow lights around the outside.

- 7 August 2004, time unknown: In the town of Greenside in Newcastle, it was reported that a witness saw aliens above the house.

- 16 August 2004 at 23:35: In the town of West Kilbride in Ayrshire, five spheres were spotted flying together.

- 29 August 2004 at 03:05: In the town of Loughton in Essex, an object was seen. The object was white, hazy, and round, and there was no noise.

- 1 September 2004 at 15:55: In the town of Glossop in Derbyshire, a silver disc-shaped object was seen.

- 2 September 2004 at 23:50: In the town of Deal in Kent, an object was seen. The object was very bright and was of large proportions. It was large in velocity.

- 4 September 2004 at 14:30: In the town of White Hill in East Hampshire, an object was seen. The object was a black cylinder with a rectangular shape and was the size of a house. One minute, the colour was black and then changed to a silver colour.

- 5 September 2004 at 10:24: In the town of Birmingham in the West Midlands, an object was seen. The object was 2–3 mm wide with a domed top and bottom. It was metallic in appearance.

- 5 September 2004 at 15:20: In the town of Barry in South Glamorgan, an object was seen. The object was a bright light at first and then looked like a box kite. There was no sound, wings or fuselage.

- 7 September 2004 at 11:30: In the town of Holywell in Flintshire, two silvery objects were seen pulling apart and moving together, and they left vapour trails as they were moving.

- 8 September 2004 at 20:15: In the town of Cardiff in South Glamorgan, a large flash of light which turned into a grey object descending over Cardiff Bay with trailing smoke behind it was seen.

- 9 September 2004 at 23:20: In the town of Dumfries in Dumfries and Galloway, a witness spotted strange lights over the town.

- 16 September 2004 at 03:50: In the town of Iwerne Minster in Dorset, an object was seen. The object looked like a great bright light and was really intense, like a big ball of fire, rapidly moving towards the ground.

- 20 September 2004 at 22:00: In the town of Lutterworth in Leicestershire, flashing lights were seen.

- 24 September 2004 at 06:30: In the town of Devizes in Wiltshire, an object that looked like a big ball of fire coming down from the sky with a tail and sparks coming off of the end of it was seen.

- 24 September 2004 at 06:30: In the town of Newport in Dyfed/South Wales, one object that looked like a disc with a tail and was shiny was seen.

- 24 September 2004, time unknown: In the town of Swindon in Wiltshire, a witness saw a big orange disc going from East to West. The witness said the object was totally silent and moving quite slowly.

- 30 September 2004 at 21:10: In the town of Porchester, Hampshire, the witness just mentioned a sighting.

- 10 October 2004 at 10:15: In the town of Strath Bongo/Glasgow in Strathclyde, an object was seen. The object looked like a wide test tube shape that moved from the southeast.

- 10 October 2004 at 22:15: In the town of Colchester in Essex, a bright orange/red-coloured object was seen rapidly and randomly changing direction, from East to West.

- 11 October 2004 at 02:35: In the town of Preston in Lancashire, an object was seen. The object was a round sphere like the moo, it had green, and red flashing lights, and was very noisy.

- 12 October 2004 at 20:07: In the town of Dumfries in Dumfries and Galloway, strange lights over the town were seen.

- 18 October 2004, time unknown: In the town of Wimbledon in London, a few objects were seen.

- 6 November 2004 at 21:25: In the town of Driffield in East Yorkshire, an object was seen. The object had three to four different coloured lights.

- 9 November 2004, time unknown: In the town of Warmington in Northants, an object was seen. The object was very bright, like the sun, and it looked like the size of a space hopper. It had flames coming off of it.

- 11 November 2004 at 14:15: In the town of Ilford in Essex, an object was seen. The object was the size of a round beach ball and black. It looked disc-shaped when it became stationary in the sky. It had no wings.

- 19 November 2004 at 08:02: In the town of Douglas in the Isle of Man, an object was seen. The object was a silver disc, with solar panels.

- 26 November 2004 at 21:00: In the town of West Kilbride in Ayrshire, a witness saw 25 yellow spheres flying in groups of five. They were flying North over West Kilbride.

- 29 November 2004 at 17:15: In the town of Wellingborough in Northants, a group of lights were seen, and then a buzzing noise was heard.

- 10 December 2004 at 17:25: In the town of Broxburn/Edinburgh in Lothian, a ball of fire with a tail five to seven times the diameter of the ball was seen. It was bright orange with a weaker orange tail.

- 15 December 2004 at 08:30: In the town of Lisburn/Belfast in County Antrim, three bright lights were seen moving in the sky.

- 27 December 2004 at 17:15: In the town of Wellingborough in Northants, a 'UFO' was seen, and then it changed into a bright light.

- Date unknown, time unknown: In the town of Leicester in Leicestershire, four discs that looked oval-shaped when the discs moved to the side were seen. They moved in a triangular formation across the sky.

- Date unknown, time unknown: In the town of Letchworth in Bedfordshire, two objects flying around the sky for about two hours were seen, and they were going quite slowly.

2005

- 14 January 2005 at 00:24 In the town of Leeds in West Yorkshire, two round, orange, bright lights were seen.

- 10 January 2005, time unknown: In the town of Scarborough in North Yorkshire, an object was seen. The object was like a big silver ball/light that was seen in the sky, and it then moved off at speed to the northeast. It was seen at night time.

- 14 January 2005, time unknown: In the town of St. Clements in Cornwall, a bright light was seen heading towards the earth through the clouds.

- 15 January 2005 at 23:15: In the town of Stoke-on-Trent in Staffordshire The witness just said that it was a flying saucer.

- 19 January 2005 at 18:45: Town unknown in Shropshire, lights were seen in the sky.

- 19 January 2005 at 18:50: Town unknown in Shropshire, a beam of light was seen.

- 19 January 2005 at 18:35: Town unknown in Shropshire, a beam of light was seen.

- 24 January 2005 at 23:10: In the town of Portadown in Northern Ireland, there were eighteen lights moving across the sky.

- 31 January 2005 at 05:00: In the town of Port Talbot in West Glamorgan, an object was seen. It looked like an orange ball of light, like a big star in the sky, and it had spiderish legs.

- 31 January 2005 at 16:30: In the town of Scarborough in North Yorkshire, a light bulb-shaped object was seen in the sky.

- 1 February 2005 at 10:30: In the town of Stirling, county unknown, a black saucer was seen hovering in the sky.

- 2 February 2005 at 17:50: In the town of Wellingborough in Northamptonshire, a witness saw a V-shaped object which had bright lights, and sounded like bees.

- 4 February 2005 at 20:00: In the town of Bridlington, North Bay, in East Yorkshire, a group of lights in the sky were moving erratically to the West. They just seemed to fade away.

- 8 February 2005 at 22:55: In the town of Orpington in London, a massive light was seen. The object was shaped like an iron. It didn't move at all.

- 11 February 2005, time unknown: In the town of Huntingdon in Cambridgeshire, the witness just said that it was a 'UFO'.

- 14 February 2005 at 19:05: In the town of Selby in North Yorkshire, a crescent-shaped object was noticed.

- 14 February 2005 at 20:55: In the town of Selby in North Yorkshire, there was a crescent-shaped object in the sky.

- 15 February 2005 at 01:00: In the town of Greenock in Strathclyde, a large yellow conical shape was seen.

- 15 February 2005 at 05:15: In the town of Scarborough in North Yorkshire, two large, orange balls were seen in the sky.

- 15 February 2005 at 01:00: In the town of Selby in North Yorkshire, a white light was moving slowly in the direction of Hull like it was floating, but it stopped after a couple of minutes.

- 19 February 2005 at 19:45: In the town of Llangollen in Clwyd, a number of orange lights were seen in the sky.

- 20 February 2005, time unknown: In the town of Leicester in Leicestershire, an object was seen in the sky, but then the witness said it could have been a meteorite.

- 20 February 2005 at 10:00: In the town of Walthamstow in London, a light in the sky was seen.

- 20 February 2005 at 09:50: In the town of Cardiff in South Glamorgan, a bright blue object broke into about 3/4 segments and then disappeared.

- 20 February 2005 at 09:45: In the town of Minehead in Somerset, a 'swishing' sound, like a firework, was heard, and there was a bright green light travelling from East to West. It had a white trail.

- 20 February 2005, time unknown: In the town of Yeovil in Somerset, a bright blue flash was seen in the sky.

- 20 February 2005, time unknown: In the town of Sherborne, Dorset, a flash of green/blue colour was seen going across the sky. It looked like it was disintegrating. It looked like it had a tail.

- 20 February 2005 at 09:45: In the town of Barrington in Somerset, a witness saw an amazing blue light travelling very fast across the sky. It left a trail.

- 20 February 2005, time unknown: In the town of Kenton, Mandeville, county unknown, a blue flash of light was seen going across the sky.

- 20 February 2005, time unknown: Town unknown in Somerset, a blue flash was seen in the sky.

- 20 February 2005, time unknown: Town unknown in Dorset, a flash of blue light was seen.

- 20 February 2005, time unknown: In the town of East Coker/Yeovil in Somerset, a witness saw a flying object.

- 20 February 2005, time unknown: In the town of Yeldersley in Derbyshire, an object was seen. The object was missile-shaped. It was turquoise in colour, metallic, looked reflective, and was the length of an estate car.

- 21 February 2005, time unknown: In the town of Chivnal in Shropshire, a silver object/ball with a tail on it was seen. It was going very fast.

- 21 February 2005 at 10:00: In the town of Teddington in Middlesex, something was seen in the sky.

- 21 February 2005 at 09:56: In the town of Winkleigh in Devon, an object was seen in the sky.

- 27 February 2005, time unknown: In the town of Wokingham in Berkshire, a zoom of light which streaked across the sky from left to right, changed into a silver ball, then a flying saucer shape, before disappearing.

- 13 March 2005 at 23:00: In the town of Filey in North Yorkshire, a witness saw lights that seemed to be dancing in the sky.

- 14 March 2005 at 05:29: In the town of Immingham/Grimsby in Humberside, a witness saw one strange light that stayed there for about an hour. It dimmed, then got brighter again.

- 20 March 2005 at 19:35: Town unknown in North Wales; the witness just said they saw a UFO.

- 24 March 2005 at 21:30: Town unknown, county unknown, an object was seen. The object was star-shaped, had all the colours of the rainbow, and was dancing around.

- 31 March 2005 at 21:15: In the town of Woking in Surrey, a bright star that moved to the side was seen. It had bright lights.

- 4 April 2005, time unknown: In the town of Crosby, county unknown, the witness just said that there was something in the sky that could not be identified.

- 6 April 2005 at 23:00: In the town of West Kilbride in Ayrshire, the witness saw one yellow sphere that was very bright and fast. Moving from west to northeast.

- 7 April 2005 at 23:15: In the town of West Kilbride in Ayrshire, the witness saw three spheres within five minutes, moving from west to northeast.

- 11 April 2005 at 00:45: In the town of Shrewsbury in Shropshire, a triangular-shaped, huge craft with red lights on the stern was seen. It hovered over the southern suburbs of Shrewsbury.

- 18 April 2005 at 00:30: In the town of Matlock in Derbyshire, the witness said that there was a descending white light. Then rotating beams of light going upward from the ground.

- 18 April 2005 at 17:00: On the A64 a silver ball that was stationary and then disappeared into a cloud was seen.

- 21 April 2005 at 06:31: Town unknown in Norfolk, three objects were seen hovering in the sky.

- 22 April 2005, time unknown: In the town of Wellingborough in Northamptonshire, a UFO/bright light was seen at a high altitude.

- 29 April 2005, time unknown: Town unknown in Pembrokeshire, a witness saw a thing in the sky, like a white square box, travelling towards Newport.

- 2 May 2005 at 23:45: In the town of Flamborough Head in East Yorkshire, several lights were seen on the horizon moving from side to side and up and down. They were there for about 15 minutes and then stopped.

- 14 May 2005 at 21:43: Town unknown in South-East London, a black cigar-shaped object that looked like a disc side was seen. It accelerated to a great speed that would outstrip a fighter jet.

- 27 May 2005 at 15:15: Town unknown in Kent, there was a small white object that was moving parallel with an airliner.

- 4 June 2005 at 00:30: In the town of St Neots in Cambridgeshire, an object was seen. The object looked like a dim red light. It was zig-zagging across the sky in an easterly direction. It was faster than a plane.

- 7 June 2005 at 23:30: In the town of Filey in North Yorkshire, a flying triangle was seen.

- 8 June 2005 at 16:45: In the town of St Neots in Cambridgeshire, an object was seen that looked like a rod. Through binoculars, it appeared to shine silver but was grey to the naked eye. It was moving around.

- 18 June 2005 at 22:00: On the M62, two silver balls were seen, one after the other, travelling West.

- 23 June 2005 at 15:15: In the town of Stapleford in Nottinghamshire, two extremely bright, round lights were seen. They had an object to the left of them which was lozenge-shaped. It had the speed of an arrow.

- June 2005, time unknown: Three white objects were seen flying above the east of Glasgow on a cloudy sky around 00:00, and a man from Baillieston was reported to have heard spaceman-esque voices through his electronic equipment around the time of the sighting. Russian Antonov An-30s were proposed as explanations. A similar sighting was seen in Lockeridge, Wiltshire, in broad daylight; a man reported seeing three "white metallic craft" while cycling on the evening of June 21.

- 4 July 2005 at 21:00: In the town of Middlesbrough in Cleveland, an object was seen. The object was triangular, and the point was sort of rounded. It was silent and had no lights. It moved slowly in an Easterly direction.

- 4 July 2005 at 22:00: In the town of Scarborough in North Yorkshire, a UFO was seen.

- 11 July 2005 at 23:30: In the town of Nailsworth in Gloucestershire, the witness said that there were strange lights in the sky at a very high altitude.

- 2 August 2005 at 22:15: Town unknown, county unknown, there were two objects above the house, and they circled above it about five times.

- 3 August 2005 at 00:00: In the town of Peacehaven in East Sussex there were seven red and white flashing lights. They were moving in an erratic type of way.

- 6 August 2005 at 22:00: In the town of Rotherham in South Yorkshire, a thin band of cloud with beams of light coming down was seen. Lights moved from side to side like searchlights.

- 6 August 2005 at 22:15: Town unknown in Cumbria, a witness saw about forty orange and red lights in the sky.

- 7 August 2005 at 21:30: In the town of Kirby in Merseyside, a Sergeant in the Merseyside Police saw four very bright, oblong-shaped objects.

- 9 August 2005 at 23:00: In the town of Milton Keynes in Bucks a witness was travelling on the motorway and noticed objects/red balls in the sky. They were travelling North West.

- 10 August 2005, at 18:30: In the town of Walthamstow in London, an object was seen. The object was the size of a jumbo jet and was silver.

- 11 August 2005 at 02:00: In the town of Hurst in Berkshire, the witness didn't see the object but said that it sounded like a 1930s airship. There was a low humming noise over the house.

- 13 August 2005 at 17:11: 10 miles West of Gatwick in Sussex, a Pilot for Air France saw a cylinder-shaped object that was one–two metres in length. It was a yellow colour.

- 21 August 2005 at 11:50: In the town of Ripon in North Yorkshire, a round/football-shaped object that was shiny and metallic was seen.

- 23 August 2005, time unknown: Town unknown in the north of Derbyshire, there were eight to ten circular things/objects that looked quite low in the sky. They were uniform in shape, small, and opaque.

- 2 September 2005 at 21:30: In the town of Rhossili Bay in South Wales, a bright object was travelling at high speed, horizontally, from west to east. The object was matte white and looked like marble.

- 3 September 2005 at 17:45: In the town of Little Waltham in Essex, the witness saw a cylindrical-shaped object that changed from silver to black as it was moving across the sky. It was about 100 ft wide.

- 4 September 2005 at 22:00: In the town of Louth in Lincolnshire, two orange orbs were seen outside moving very slowly at first, then very fast, towards the North Sea.

- 4 September 2005 at 02:35: In the town of Wolsingham in Northumbria, four Police Officers saw a three-dimensional diamond-shaped object. It was the size of a large helicopter. It had green lights on either side.

- 5 September 2005 at 21:00: In the town of Hornchurch in Essex, a 'UFO' was seen.

- 9 September 2005 at 05:45: In the town of Little Hampton in West Sussex, there was one light in the sky that burst into four separate ones before disappearing.

- 10 September 2005 at 22:00: In the town of Loughton in Essex, three glowing lights were seen. They were a bright orange colour.

- 10 September 2005 at 22:00: In the town of Loughton in Essex three golden orbs were seen hovering in the sky for an hour, moving in a triangle formation.

- 10 September 2005 at 22:00: In the town of Loughton in Essex, the witness said that there were three very suspicious-looking lights up in the sky. They were orange and very bright.

- 10 September 2005 at 21:00: In the town of Loughton in Essex, three objects were seen in the sky. The objects appeared to be orange in colour.

- 10 September 2005 at 20:58: In the town of Loughton in Essex, three balls of fire were seen in the sky. They keep circling and then lining up.

- 14 September 2005 at 21:15: In the town of Lochgelly in Fife, bright, white lights that were moving in semi-circles were seen.

- 14 September 2005 at 21:45: In the town of Glenrothes in Fife, bright, white lights in circles were seen.

- 14 September 2005 at 23:15: In the town of Crieff in Perthshire, clear white lights, like a torch, but no beam, were seen.

- 14 September 2005 at 20:50: In the town of Letham in Fife, white circles were seen all over the sky.

- 14 September 2005 at 20:55: In the town of Blairgowrie in Perthshire, three white circles going clockwise and then anti-clockwise were seen.

- 14 September 2005 at 21:23: In the town of Kinross in Perthshire, two–three bright green and luminous lights circling were seen.

- 17 September 2005 at 15:58: Town unknown, county unknown, a Pilot saw one object that was dark brown in colour, was of military shape, and was fast moving.

- 20 September 2005 at 20:39: In the town of Romford, Essex, four orange lights were seen above the witness's house.

- 10 October 2005 time unknown: Town unknown, county unknown, the witness just said they had a sighting in the evening.

- 12 October 2005 at 17:40: In the town of Truro in Cornwall, a bright light was seen coming from the northwest heading southeast.

- 14 October 2005, time unknown: In the town of Keswick, A UFO was seen.

- 16 October 2005 at 22:40: In the town of Cayton Bay in North Yorkshire, an object was seen. The object was like a fireball in the sky. It was moving to the North.

- 16 October 2005 at 22:45: In the town of Muston in North Yorkshire, a ball-shaped object that was orange in colour with a tail was seen.

- 16 October 2005 at 23:45: In the town of Redcar in Cleveland, balls of lights and a streak were seen.

- 16 October 2005 at 23:40: In the town of Macclesfield in Cheshire, an object like a disc was in the sky heading West.

- 16 October 2005 at 19:30: In the town of Whitby in North Yorkshire, there was a silver object with a tail seen travelling North.

- 16 October 2005 at 21:00: In the town of Hull in North Yorkshire, five or six pulsing lights were seen in the sky that were moving to the South.

- 16 October 2005 at 20:00: In the town of Mablethorpe in Lincolnshire, a witness saw a silver light and then a flash.

- 18 October 2005 at 22:00: In the town of York in North Yorkshire, a witness saw an object like a big star moving northwest.

- 18 October 2005 at 22:00: In the town of Withernsea in East Yorkshire, exploding lights were seen in the sky.

- 18 October 2005 at 19:00: In the town of Filey in North Yorkshire, red and silver lights were seen in the sky.

- 18 October 2005 at 19:00: In the town of Selby in North Yorkshire, a witness saw lights that looked like Christmas tree decorations moving in the sky.

- 19 October 2005 at 20:50: In the town of Seamer in North Yorkshire, a globe-shaped object fell out of the sky. It was like a round, white light. It fell in the direction of Staxton.

- 20 October 2005 at 20:17: In the town of Chigwell in Essex, seven or eight orange glows above cloud cover with planes below were seen.

- 21 October 2005 at 21:15: In the town of Hunmanby in North Yorkshire, an object was seen in the sky that looked like a white ball of light.

- 23 October 2005, time unknown: In the town of Stapleford Abbots in Essex, a sighting in the evening was reported.

- 26 October 2005 at 19:15: In Malton, on the A64 in North Yorkshire, three red lights were seen in a triangle formation.

- 26 October 2005 at 23:58: Town unknown in Wales, an object was seen. The object looked like a red ball and was the size of a sixpence. It exploded, and the whole sky lit up.

- 27 October 2005 at 18:45: In the town of Scarborough in North Yorkshire, orange balls were seen on the way to Pickering.

- 29 October 2005 at 18:00: On the A171, a witness was travelling to Whitby on the A171 and saw an object that looked like an orange ball.

- 1 November 2005 at 19:00: In the town of RAF Coningsby/Lincoln in Lincolnshire, five large, star-sized objects that were orange. Were seen for four to five minutes.

- 5 November 2005 at 23:00: In the town of Cheltenham, Gloucestershire, three objects were seen in the sky. They all seemed to rotate.

- 8 November 2005 at 00:00: In the town of Cheltenham in Gloucestershire, two objects were seen.

- 9 November 2005 at 20:30: In the town of Sleights in North Yorkshire, a diamond-shaped craft/object was seen. The object had an unusually powerful, white/yellow, rotating beacon/searchlight at its rear.

- 14 November 2005 at 23:45: In the town of Selby in North Yorkshire, a flying triangle was seen in the sky.

- 19 November 2005, time unknown: In the town of Boston in Lincolnshire, lights were seen in the sky, moving in a straight line and were evenly spaced. The lights were glowing amber-like street lights.

- 22 November 2005, time unknown: In the town of Sheerness in Kent, a 'V' shape of dim lights, that went into a straight line and then back into a V again were seen.

- 22 November 2005 time unknown: In the town of Gillingham in Kent five lights in the sky that looked very strange were seen. The lights were flashing.

- 13 December 2005 at 19:45: In the town of Eastleigh in Hants, a trail of light was seen. It was almost luminous green in colour and looked like a rocket. It was high in the sky and was travelling at an amazing speed.

- 14 December 2005 at 07:15: Town unknown, county unknown, the witness saw an object and said that the object looked like a shooting star. It was very bright and had a trail behind it.

- 15 December 2005 at 21:15: In the town of Dunfermline in Fife, an object was seen that looked like a black triangle.

- 16 December 2005 at 14:10: In the town of Peebles in Borders, an object was seen. The object was small and silver in colour. It was flying twice the speed of a military aircraft in a very straight line.

- 18 December 2005 at 07:45: In the town of Leigh-on-Sea in Essex, a photograph of a dot in the sky was taken, and when magnified, looked like some strange craft.

- 24 December 2005 at 21:20: In the town of Whitstable in Kent, three bright, orange lights were seen in the sky, and then a fourth orange light appeared and followed the other three.

- 27 December 2005, time unknown: In the town of Rendlesham Forest in Suffolk, a plume of light was seen that was a yellowish/orange colour. It vanished after a few seconds.

- No date, no time: In the town of Chatteris in Cambridgeshire, the witness just said that it was a sighting.

- No date, no time: In the town of Whitstable in Kent, strange lights were seen in the sky.

- No date, no time: In the town of Port Talbot in West Glamorgan, the witness said it looked like a parachute flare.

- No date, no time: In the town of Swansea in West Glamorgan, a Coastguard said it looked like a parachute flare.

- No date, no time: In the town of Brighton, county unknown, the witness just said that it was a sighting.

- No date, no time: In the town of Briton Ferry in West Glamorgan the witness just said something was seen in the sky.

- No date, no time: In the town of Slough in Berkshire, the witness said it was like a big shooting star, amazing, but then said it was going too fast to be one.

- No date, no time: In the town of Shepton Mallet in Somerset, the witness just said that the object looked like a star but moved very slowly sideways.

- No date, no time: In the town of Basildon in Essex, the witness said that there was a spacecraft with aliens (the greys) sitting on top of it, above the bungalow.

- No date, no time: In the town of Kendal in Cumbria, witnesses think they saw a UFO.

- No date, no time: In the town of Brixton Hill in London, a witness thinks it was a UFO.

- No date at 09:34: In the town of Chevithorne in Devon, an object was seen. The object looked like a telegraph pole.

- No date, no time: In the town of Cardiff in South Wales, a UFO was seen.

- No date, no time: In the town of Pontyclun in South Wales, a UFO was seen.

- No date, no time: Town unknown, county unknown, two UFOs were spotted, and they were clearly not aeroplanes.

- No date, no time: In the town of Lichfield, Staffordshire, an object was seen. The object was circular and was a dull orange colour/light. It was the size of a medium aircraft.

- No date, no time: In the town of Ipswich in Suffolk, the witness just said that it was a 'UFO'.

- No date, no time: Town unknown in Somerset. The witness said that there was a bubble-like thing in the sky. It flashed across the sky.

- No date, no time: In the town of Croesyceiliog in Gwent, the witness saw five to six white lights flying very fast overhead. They looked a bit like bright stars.

- No date, no time: In the town of Bagshot in Surrey, the witness just said that it was a sighting.

- No date, no time: Town unknown, county unknown, a big, long-shaped object was seen. It looked like a long shaft.

- No date, no time: Town unknown, county unknown, the witness just said he/she had a UFO sighting.

- No date at 22:00: On the A5 in North Wales, a witness saw bright lights dancing in the sky on the way to Llandudno.

- No date at 23:10: In the town of Monmouth in Gwent, a flying saucer was seen while looking out of the witness's bedroom window.

- No date, no time: In the town of Waterlooville in Hampshire, twelve objects were seen in the sky in a sort of formation – three in a line, two in a line. Some flying above others.

- No date, no time: In the town of Harrington in East Lothian, the witness just said that it was a UFO.

- No date, no time: In the town of Louth in Lincolnshire, an object was seen. The object had red, blue, and white lights and was flickering; it was there for over half an hour.

- No date, no time: In the town of Ely in Cambs, the witness just said a sighting had happened.

- No date, no time: In the town of High Wycombe in Buckinghamshire, an object was seen.

2006

- 24 January 2006 at 16:20: Town unknown, county unknown, an object was seen moving across the sky and looked like it was on fire. It was cigar-shaped and silver in colour.

- 30 January 2006 at 06:00: In the town of Shrewsbury in Shropshire, a light was seen travelling rapidly due southwest.

- 7 February 2006 at 14:08: In the town of Colchester in Essex, four lights were seen in the sky, a bit like fluorescent light strips, with a yellow tinge and very bright, were floating and then disappeared.

- 10 February 2006 at 19:20: In the town of Marlborough in Wiltshire, a light was seen that was a flashing ball, changing colour from red, orange, green, and blue. It was hovering for about 30 minutes.

- 15 February 2006 at 20:40: In the town of Mitcham in Surrey, two bright lights, which were then joined by a third bright light, which then flew alongside them, were seen.

- 16 February 2006 at 21:25: In the town of Pegwell Bay/Ramsgate in Kent, a UFO was seen. It was bright blue/white in colour.

- 21 February 2006 at 19:45: Town unknown in Scotland, a blue ball of light with a tail at the end, was seen.

- 28 February 2006 at 22:00: In the town of Crewe in Cheshire, very bright lights were seen for over half an hour. They were hovering quite slowly from side to side.

- 3 March 2006, time unknown: In the town of Streatham in London, two objects were seen in the sky.

- 5 March 2006 at 17:35: In the town of Hemel Hempstead in Bedfordshire, a disc was seen flying above two aircraft.

- 18 March 2006 at 22:45: In the town of West Kilbride in Ayrshire, there were two spheres, and one was following the other. It looked like they were moving from side to side.

- 19 March 2006 at 18:35: In the town of Newquay in Cornwall, a bright disc was seen hanging in the sky. The object appeared to quiver rather than move. It moved around and then just vanished.

- 28 March 2006, time unknown: In the town of Derby in Derbyshire, a bright red light was seen in the sky. The light was moving too quickly across the sky to be an aircraft.

- 30 March 2006 at 00:40: In the town of Plymouth in Devon, there was a huge, shimmering ball of orange fire. It flew eastwards and looked like a black spot as it disappeared into the clouds.

- 14 April 2006 time unknown: Town unknown, county unknown, a UFO was seen.

- 23 April 2006 at 22:00: In the town of West Kilbride in Ayrshire, four golden spheres were seen. They drifted – south to northeast. The witness said they are definitely solid guided craft.

- 27 April 2006 at 22:30: In the town of Trestle in Stafford, an object was seen that looked like a satellite coming into the atmosphere and coming to its end, but then another object came into view and they started zig-zagging about.

- 30 April 2006, time unknown: In the town of Barlaston in Staffordshire, a witness reported seeing a mother ship and two smaller orbs that were moving around it. One of the orbs was white in colour and the other orange.

- 5 May 2006, time unknown: In the town of Barlaston in Staffordshire, the witness saw the mother ship again.

- 8 May 2006 at 13:11: In the town of St. Tudwal's Islands in Mid-Wales, an object was seen. The object looked like a black square hanging in the sky.

- 16 May 2006 at 19:4: In the town of Hastings in East Sussex, two witnesses saw an alien outside their kitchen window.

- 20 May 2006 at 22:00: In the town of East Dereham in Norfolk, orange lights were seen. They appeared to be in formation and travelling quite slowly.

- 3 June 2006 at 17:05: In the town of Maidstone in Kent, a large, round, white object with smaller, round, white objects randomly scattered surrounding it was seen. The objects started to fade.

- 5 June 2006 at 22:12: In the town of Haydock in Merseyside, a ball of light that looked like a sphere on fire was seen. It had a circular light glowing in front of it that was orange/yellow.

- 8 June 2006 at 19:00: In the town of Banbury in Oxon, an object was seen that looked like a structured object, and it glinted like metal.

- 14 June 2006 at 18:15: Town unknown in West Yorkshire, an object was seen in the sky that was glowing white.

- 17 June 2006 at 21:45: In the town of Broadstairs in Kent, five orange balls of light, going over one at a time at about 10–15 minute intervals, were seen.

- 17 June 2006 at 23:30: In the town of St Annes in Lancashire, nine bright orange objects were seen.

- 18 June 2006 at 18:45: In the town of Macclesfield in Cheshire, a spinning object which appeared to have a triangular-shaped part on either side of it was seen. It was a grey metallic colour, almost dull.

- 26 June 2006 at 23:30: In the town of Lavenham in Suffolk, a UFO was seen.

- June 2006, time unknown: In the town of Cookley in Worcestershire a shiny silver, silent triangle-shaped object was seen in the evening sky. While travelling along Lea Lane heading to the town of Cookley two people saw the object whislt heading home. The object was hovering 5 –10 metres above the floor, completely silent, and moving along the horizon.

- 4 July 2006 at 22:00: In the town of Locherbridges in Dumfries, a dome-shaped static object with lights running up and down the dome with another light swaying to and fro beneath was seen.

- 15 July 2006 at 18:00: In the town of Chorlton in Manchester, three silver dots/craft were seen very high up in the sky.

- 17 July 2006 at 02:00: In the town of Marlborough in Devon two round, stationary, slightly oval lights were seen. A third light kept arcing between the other two oval lights and lit up the sky.

- 18 July 2006 at 16:15: In the town of Stevenage in Bedfordshire, an object was seen. The object was oblong in shape and was also described as looking a bit like a scooter.

- 18 July 2006 at 21:00: In the town of Bispham in Lancashire, a row of red lights in a zig-zag shape were seen. Also, there were five to seven dim lights.

- 20 July 2006 at 23:45: In the town of Johnstone in Paisley, one pure-orange object that was spherical was seen. It was the size of a street light.

- 29 July 2006 at 22:40: In the town of Seaham in County Durham, nine balls of orange light were seen. They were following each other and were drifting northwards. They were visible for about five minutes.

- 29 July 2006 at 22:00: In the town of Seaham in County Durham, a Police Officer saw six yellow/orange lights travelling in a line/slightly staggered, from South to North.

- 5 August 2006 at 21:30: In the town of Enfield in Middlesex 13 'orb' like objects were seen in the sky. They were orange in colour. They were darting about in different directions before shooting straight up.

- 7 August 2006, time unknown: Town unknown in Derbyshire, a UFO was seen.

- 9 August 2006 at 22:15: In the town of Waterlooville, Hampshire, a strange object was seen. It was orange in colour.

- 20 August 2006, time unknown: In the town of Torquay, Devon, lights were seen in the sky.

- 21 August 2006 at 20:50: Town unknown in Shropshire, two extremely bright lights were seen.

- 27 August 2006 at 21:30: In the town of Herne Bay in Kent, eight yellow/orange spheres that looked like they had flames coming out of the back of them were seen.

- 6 September 2006, time unknown: In the town of Exeter, Devon, the witness just said a UFO was seen.

- 9 September 2006 at 22:00: In the town of Oldbury in Greater Manchester, five lights/orange fireballs were seen. They were flying in formation. They seemed to hover before one vanished.

- 9 September 2006 at 22:30: In the town of Basildon, Essex, large lights were seen static in the sky.

- 9 September 2006 at 21:00: In the town of Stamford Hill in London, there was a massive bang, and then two large fireballs were seen moving from East to West. They were very bright.

- 9 September 2006 at 21:03: In the town of Irlham in Greater Manchester, there was a circular orange ball with an aura around it. It was low in the sky, then increased in height and was very fast.

- 9 September 2006, time unknown: Town unknown in Herefordshire Borders, seven bright orange lights were seen in the sky, travelling in a straight line from South to North.

- 13 September 2006 at 21:45: In the town of Whitehaven in Cumbria, a triangular object with lights was seen. It had one green, one red, and the other two amber lights. There was a strange droning noise as it passed overhead.

- 14 September 2006 at 23:05: In the town of Kettering in Northants, a triangle-shaped object that had lights on that looked similar to a helicopter was seen. There was one white, one green, and one red light.

- 18 September 2006 at 05:00: In the town of Loch Creran in Argyll, a slim, flat object like a plate or pencil, lengthways, was seen. A circular light at either end and a bigger one in the centre was seen. It was stationary for 1–2 minutes.

- 22 September 2006 at 20:00: In the town of White Roding/Dunmow in Essex, hundreds of glowing lights were seen moving northeast in a line formation. They were moving in rows of three.

- 29 September 2006, time unknown: In the town of East Linton in East Lothian, a big, round, swirly thing in the sky was seen.

- 14 October 2006 at 17:30: In the town of Sunderland in Tyne and Wear, a silver pyramid that was rotating at a low speed and off-centre was seen.

- 31 October 2006 at 21:30: In the town of Hetton-Le-Hole in Tyne and Wear, a black triangular UFO was seen, with three lights on it.

- 1 November 2006 at 19:30: In the town of Ayr in Ayrshire, a light, way above in the sky, was seen. It moved in a zig-zag across the sky.

- 2 November 2006 at 20:10: In the town of Huntingdon in Cambridgeshire, lights that were a really dull yellow were seen. The lights looked like they were interacting with each other.

- 2 November 2006 at 20:30: In the town of Spalding in Lincolnshire, there were about ten orange lights in the sky, and they were moving around in formation.

- 3 November 2006 at 14:00: In the town of Camsham in Somerset, three silver spheres-like stars that were very shiny and shone in the sun were seen.

- 3 November 2006 at 22:30: In the town of Potters Bar in Hertfordshire, a witness saw the underside of a circular, hovering object. It had a bright light that was visible. The object was humming.

- 4 November 2006 at 21:30: In the town of Walworth, London, a line of four orange lights was seen. They were travelling at speed and quite close together.

- 5 November 2006, time unknown: In the town of Seaton in Cornwall, two unidentified flying objects were seen.

- 6 November 2006 at 11:20: In the town of Peterborough in Cambridgeshire, something like shells, with pale pink in the middle, all flying at the same speed in formation, was seen.

- 9 November 2006 time unknown: Town unknown in North Yorkshire, three spinning objects with three big lights were seen.

- 12 November 2006 at 20:20: In the town of Petworth in West Sussex, five dancing lights were seen.

- 25 November 2006 at 20:30: In the town of Newport in Shropshire, three sphere-shaped, bright yellow/white lights were seen on a clear night.

- 29 November 2006 at 00:50: In the town of Coatbridge in Glasgow, a triangular object which changed to a round shape, then became elongated was seen. It had red lights on it plus a blue circle around it.

- 10 December 2006 at 14:00: In the town of Eastleigh, Cotswolds, in Hants, a metallic spinning object that had heat sources showing green was seen.

- 11 December 2006, time unknown: In the town of Plymouth in Devon, a blue light with a white light in the middle was seen.

- 11 December 2006 at 22:50: In the town of Stratford-upon-Avon in Warwickshire, a witness saw something very unusual travelling across the sky, quite low.

- 17 December 2006 at 18:45: In the town of Cobham in Surrey, a white object moving from North to South was seen. It looked like the object was burning up; it left a trail behind it that lasted a few seconds.

- 30 December 2006, time unknown: In the town of Hunstanton in Norfolk, an object was seen. The object was silver in colour with a light underneath. It hovered in the sky and made little noises while flying. Dust came down from the sky.

- 31 December 2006 at 19:15: In the town of South Gorley in Hampshire, three orange lights were seen moving across the sky at the same speed, and then another orange light came 10 seconds later.

- 31 December 2006 at 20:55: In the town of Maidstone in Kent, many different UFOs were reported as well as strange lights.

- 31 December 2006, time unknown: Town unknown county unknown, there was a light seen darting about the sky.

- No date, no time: In the town of Bony Lake in Mid Lothian, there were five orange lights that were quite bright and moving slowly across the sky.

- No date, no time: In the town of Bony Lake in Mid Lothian, four small, bright red lights were seen moving slowly across the sky.

- No date, no time: In the town of Walsall in the West Midlands, a UFO was seen doing funny, sharp turns over a field.

- No date, no time: In the town of Oldbury in West the Midlands, a witness just said it was a UFO.

- No date, no time: Town unknown in South Yorkshire, a UFO was seen.

- No date, no time: In the town of Hunton in Hertfordshire, a witness just said a UFO was seen.

- No date, no time: In the town of Churchstoke in Powys, an object was seen. The object was disc-shaped, with four different colours: blue, green, white, and orange.

- No date at 22:15: In the town of Barton-le-Clay in Bedfordshire, four independent, bright orange lights going from South to North were seen.

- No date, no time: In the town of Rushington in West Sussex, two flying objects were seen.

- No date, no time: In the town of Hetton-Le-Hole in Tyne and Wear there were many lights seen up in the sky.

- No date, no time: In the town of Clevedon in Somerset, a globe-shaped, lighted object was seen fluttering through the sky. It looked erratic.

- No date, no time: In the town of Polgate in East Sussex, two objects were seen. The first object changed shape. The second object was red and star-shaped.

- No date, no time: In the town of Chigwell, Essex a UFO was seen.

- No date, no time: In the town of Bedford in Bedfordshire, a series of orange orbs were seen.

- No date at 20:00: In the town of Market Deeping in Lincolnshire, an orange light with no noise was seen.

- No date, no time: In the town of Stoke-on-Trent in Staffordshire, a flying object was seen.

- No date, no time: In the town of Bury St Edmunds in Suffolk, a bright white object like a white star in the sky was seen. The object had a tail.

- No date at 22:55: In the town of Dudley in the West Midlands, a white light was seen.

- No date, no time: In the town of Midlothian in Scotland, a weird light that was going in all sorts of weird directions was seen.

- No date, no time: Town unknown, county unknown, a UFO was seen.

2007

- 3 January 2007 at 22:08: Town unknown, county unknown, objects were seen in the sky heading towards the moon.

- 6 January 2007 time unknown: Town unknown, county unknown, a UFO was seen.

- 16 January 2007 at 20:45: In the town of Llanpumsaint in Carmarthenshire, a ball of light was seen that faded away then came back again. The orange ball was near the car. Three red lights were seen moving clockwise.

- 1 February 2007 at 17:25: In the town of Archway/Islington in London, twelve–fifteen orange balls of light were seen moving across the sky. They moved upward, then faded away.

- 3 February 2007, time unknown: On the M4 Motorway/Swindon in Wiltshire, an object fell from the sky. It had something like a green halo around it. It was very bright.

- 3 March 2007 at 22:29: In the town of Long Eaton in Nottinghamshire, a curved, diamond-shaped object passed over the witness's head, going North. It was travelling very fast.

- 7 March 2007, time unknown: In the town of Cold Ashby in Northamptonshire, lights were seen suddenly moving independently, erratically, and sometimes vertically.

- 14 March 2007 at 19:00: In the town of Idridgehay in Derbyshire, a very bright light was seen.

- 21 March 2007 at 19:30: In the town of Wirksworth in Derbyshire, an object was seen that looked like three small aircraft. They were totally still in the sky. They were very white.

- 29 March 2007 at 11:25: In the town of Lincoln in Lincolnshire, two objects with very bright lights were seen. They were moving too slowly to be aircraft.

- 8 April 2007 at 00:11: In the town of Southampton in Hampshire, two distinctive lights, which were reddish in colour and were moving rapidly from southwest to north were seen.

- 9 April 2007 at 21:00: In the town of Skegness in Lincolnshire, there was a dark silhouette/figure/thing quite low in the sky. It seemed quite flat, and the edges seemed to curve downward slightly.

- 12 April 2007 at 20:30: In the town of Duxford in Cambridgeshire, fifty objects, each with a single orange light, were seen. They gathered before ascending directly upward.

- 13 April 2007 at 21:46: In the town of Forress/Moray, a very bright light that was much brighter than a star was seen with rays radiating outwards. The object was stationary.

- 14 April 2007 at 06:30: In the town of Liverpool in Merseyside a red, pipe-like object was seen. It was seen for about 10–15 seconds, and it was very close to the plane. It then disappeared into the clouds.

- 17 April 2007 at 21:20: In the town of Glasgow in S'clyde, five orange/red glows were seen in the sky. They were moving quite fast. They were in formation and then parted and disappeared.

- 17 April 2007 at 02:45: In the town of Stafford, Staffordshire, a flying saucer with lights on it was seen. It changed from a saucer shape to a star shape and then disappeared.

- 20 April 2007 at 21:30: In the town of Bexley in Kent, there were over fifty lights floating in the sky. They were red/orange in colour.

- 21 April 2007 at 09:27: In the town of Bury St. Edmunds in Suffolk, four black sphere-shaped objects were seen flying through the sky.

- 23 April 2007 at 14:09: In the air near Alderney in the Channel Islands, two Pilots in different planes saw two different objects. The object was bright orange/yellow. There was a gap in the lighter or darker area. The second object was identical.

- 1 May 2007 at 15:55: In the town of Leicester in Leicestershire, a tear-shaped object that was black in colour was seen. The object was travelling fast and left what sounded like a rocket sound behind it.

- 20 May 2007 at 02:04: Town unknown in West Derbyshire, a round orange ball, which then turned into an orange speck as it moved further away, was seen.

- 21 May 2007 at 22:00: In the town of Parley Cross/Bournemouth in East Sussex, bright orange lights were seen. The lights seemed to split up and go in different directions. Then they all silently disappeared.

- 26 May 2007 at 22:30: In the town of Ewhurst in Surrey, a red light flew past the back of the witness's house and was making a pop, pop, popping sort of noise. It was brightly lit.

- 27 May 2007 at 23:27: In the town of Wandsworth in London, a red light was seen in the sky moving over the top of the witness's house.

- 29 May 2007 at 23:45: In the town of Pontrobert/Meiford in Powys, a triangular-shaped object was seen. It was 100ft high/large. It was bright green and blue. A second object appeared, and it had pink pulsating lights.

- 2 June 2007 at 10:26: In the town of Stanwell Village/Staines in Middlesex, a star-shaped object was seen that did not move for 10–15 minutes.

- 9 June 2007 at 23:00: In the town of Ilminster in Somerset, a strange object that was like an unusual star was seen. It was glowing red and then turned into a silver ball. It had a circular light around it.

- 18 June 2007 at 18:00: In the town of Southampton in Hampshire, there was an object adjacent to the moon that was seen, and it was twice the brightness. The object was stationary and looked to be 30,000 ft up.

- 21 June 2007 at 00:45: In the town of Stretton/Burton on Trent in Staffordshire, two glowing bright lights were seen moving across the sky, and then they disappeared over the horizon. They appeared to be controlled.

- 23 June 2007 at 22:45: In the town of Pilton in Devon, five lights were seen that were followed by another fifteen lights, all moving in the same direction and extinguishing in the same area.

- 28 June 2007, time unknown: In the town of Swindon in Wiltshire, a UFO was seen for a short time.

- 6 July 2007, time unknown: In the town of Huddersfield in West Yorkshire, a moon-shaped object was seen that kept reappearing every two minutes. It swerved rapidly to the left and right at different levels above the horizon.

- 7 July 2007 at 23:15: In the town of Montford Bridge/Shrewsbury in Shropshire, there was a convoy of white lights moving along the river bank. They were silent.

- 14 July 2007 at 23:00: In the town of Dollar in Clackmannanshire, four bright lights were seen moving quickly towards people that were observing them. The objects gradually came together and then moved apart.

- 21 July 2007 at 23:35: In the town of Polgate in East Sussex, strange, bright red lights were seen. They were stationary for about fifteen to twenty minutes.

- 24 July 2007 at 21:30: In the town of Lynton in North Devon, a ball of fire was seen. It had no tail and was moving from West to East.

- 30 July 2007 at 23:35: In the town of East Finchley in London, three bright lights were seen hovering and moving to the left and then to the right very fast. One was stationary and looked like a flare.

- 31 July 2007 at 23:58: In the town of Batley in, West Yorkshire, an object was seen.

- 4 August 2007 at 22:45: In the town of Sheffield in South Yorkshire, two strange objects were seen, followed by three others. They were bright and fire coloured. They were spinning and moving very fast across the sky.

- 6 August 2007 at 10:10: In the town of Hemel Hempstead in Hertfordshire, three bright orange lights were seen in the sky.

- 6 August 2007 at 21:55: Town unknown in Cornwall a UFO was seen.

- 7 August 2007 at 23:07: In the town of Wakefield in West Yorkshire, an elongated triangular-shaped object with rounded corners was seen. It had a sort of satin finish and charcoal grey colour. It was very large and moving fast.

- 7 August 2007 at 21:00: In the town of Buxted in East Sussex a fast-moving, bright object was seen, moving from south to northeast.

- 8 August 2007 at 02:00: In the town of Castleton in Derbyshire, there was an object seen moving vertically towards the ground. It had lights around it.

- 10 August 2007 at 22:45: In the town of Basingstoke in Hampshire, a single orange light as bright as Venus was seen moving at aircraft speed across the sky. The object then hovered and flickered like a flame.

- 10 August 2007, time unknown: In the town of Boreham Wood in Hertfordshire, a UFO was seen. It hovered and then shot off.

- 11 August 2007 at 22:00: In the town of Brighton in East Sussex, a bright orange sphere was seen. It shot off quite fast and then disappeared, and then reappeared a few minutes later, back to its original position.

- 11 August 2007, time unknown: In the town of Farnham, Surrey, a UFO was seen. It was going across the sky quite slowly.

- 13 August 2007 at 22:45: In the town of Houghton Le Spring in County Durham, there were two objects of the same brightness seen. They were slow, erratic, changing direction, and suddenly slowing and stopping.

- 17 August 2007 at 22:00: In the town of Blairgowrie in Perthshire, lights were seen in the sky.

- 18 August 2007, time unknown: In the town of Streatham in London, an object was seen landing in the witness's back garden. The object was round/dome shaped and metallic in colour. Doors opened, and a shadow was seen by the witness levitating towards the ground.

- 19 August 2007, time unknown: In the town of Bethnal Green in London, twenty solid red lights in the sky were seen. The lights went up and down in the sky and then just disappeared.

- 24 August 2007 at 21:20: In the town of Matlock in Derbyshire, a UFO was seen.

- 26 August 2007 at 22:53: In the town of Chelmsford in Essex, five bright orange lights in the sky were seen as they were equally spaced, forming a diagonal line. They were moving up and down and to the left and right.

- 31 August 2007 at 22:18: In the town of Dunkeld in Perthshire, orange lights were seen in the sky.

- 31 August 2007 at 22:19: In the town of Dunkeld in Perthshire, a number of orange lights were seen in the sky. They were very low and fast in the sky.

- 1 September 2007 at 21:00: In the town of Alton in Hampshire, seventeen objects were seen. They looked round, totally circular and solid, and were a bright orange colour. They were in an elongated shape.

- 1 September 2007 at 22:30: In the town of Silver Bay/Rhoscolyn on the Isle of Anglesey, an object was seen. The object looked like a brightly coloured aircraft. The object was moving quite fast.

- 1 September 2007, time unknown: In the town of Alton, Hampshire, sixty-two hundred objects were seen moving across the sky. They were moving at a steady pace.

- 1 September 2007 at 21:00: In the town of Hillmorton/Rugby in Warwickshire, six strange lights, which were yellow but had orange in the centre, were seen. They were moving in a staggered formation across the sky, below the cloud base.

- 3 September 2007 time unknown: In the town of Rotherham in South Yorkshire, a UFO was seen.

- 3 September 2007 at 22:00: In the town of Denton/Grantham in Lincolnshire, a cigar-shaped object with flashing lights was seen hovering.

- 4 September 2007 at 22:50: In the town of East Finchley in London, a UFO flared and then vanished.

- 5 September 2007 at 19:55: In the town of Wroughton/Swindon in Wiltshire, something was seen. It was a bit like re-entering orbit.

- 5 September 2007 at 19:40: In the town of Wootton Bassett in Wiltshire one object, like a small aircraft, was seen. It was arc shaped. There were also 10–12 white lights. There was constant movement from the object.

- 9 September 2007 at 01:30: In the town of Bath in Somerset, an object was seen. The object looked like a low-flying cloud, but there was a light flashing on it. The object was moving at a 100 ft above ground level and slowly across the sky.

- 12 September 2007 at 17:30: In the town of Hinckley in Leicestershire, a large object was moving fast and low over the 'perimeter road' on the outskirts of Hinckley.

- 15 September 2007 at 20:47: In the town of Stone Bay area/Broadstairs in Kent, an unusual sighting of six orange/red, glowing lights flying in a linear formation were seen. They were flying at normal helicopter height/speedx but were silent.

- 20 September 2007 at 23:45: In the town of Camden in London, there were two large pairs of lights rushing towards each other consistently over a large area in the sky over Camden.

- 22 September 2007 at 09:10: In the town of Mossley in Lancashire, a UFO was seen.

- 23 September 2007, time unknown: Town unknown in Staffordshire, a UFO was seen.

- 30 September 2007 at 21:45: In the town of Stoke-on-Trent in Staffordshire, five objects were seen travelling at speed across the sky.

- 6 October 2007 at 21:30: In the town of Uckfield in East Sussex, sixty orange glowing lights were seen going across the sky in a trail. They were moving quite slowly.

- 6 October 2007 at 22:00: In the town of Trowbridge in Wiltshire, a bright, white light was seen, like a flash and a brightness in the sky. Then 20 orange flickering lights appeared. They then faded and disappeared.

- 6 October 2007 at 21:44: In the town of Droitwich in Worcestershire, there were seven to eight spherical objects seen. They were moving in a straight line in an Easterly direction.

- 16 October 2007 at 05:45: In the town of Black Isle in Ross-shire, one object that was orb-shaped and larger than a star was seen. It was purple and green in colour and had bubbles, flames, and solar flares coming out of it.

- 20 October 2007 at 12:10: In the town of Portsmouth, Hampshire, an oval/spherical-shaped object approached an aircraft, appeared to accelerate very fast, and then wobbled from side to side. Another object appeared roughly in the same vicinity and then stayed stationary.

- 28 October 2007 at 21:45: In the town of Kiverton/Rotherham in South Yorkshire, a bright, triangular object was seen in the sky. It had one flashing strobe light and twelve fixed lights beneath it. The object was stationary at first and then moved directly above the witness.

- 3 November 2007, time unknown: In the town of Stanfields/Stoke on Trent in Staffordshire there were eight small discs moving in a formation in the sky.

- 3 November 2007, time unknown: In the town of Joyden's Wood/ Wilmington in Kent, eight flying saucers were seen flying in a line.

- 10 November 2007 at 20:20: In the town of Ladybank in Fife, one bright, red object was seen. It was quite large. It hovered for about five minutes before heading east, gaining height, and then vanishing.

- 12 November 2007 at 21:50: In the town of Shrewsbury in Shropshire, a series of lights in a circle that had an inner circle were seen. There were fifteen extra lights on the outside of the outer circle. They were moving clockwise, then anti-clockwise, through the sky, and then back again.

- 13 November 2007 at 21:40: In the town of Poulton le Fylde in Lancashire, a bright, white light was seen moving in a northeasterly direction on a slow, even course. It was about 2000ft up in the sky.

- 21 November 2007 at 19:16: In the town of Thorpe St. Andrew/Norwich in Norfolk, a ball that lit up and that lasted half a second was seen. Then a really tiny star moved rapidly, faster than any satellite or aircraft the witness had seen.

- 23 November 2007 at 08:00: In the town of Bottesford in Lincolnshire, a silver disc was seen with an orange light in the middle of it. The object was flying up and down in the sky.

- November 2007: Numerous people from the West Midlands reported sightings of a silent triangle-shaped object in the skies in the evening, which the press dubbed the "Dudley Dorito".

- 1 December 2007, time unknown: In the town of Rothwell in Northamptonshire, a circular ship with a set of white, round lights was seen.

- 1 December 2007 at 11:40: Town unknown in SW Somax, a Pilot, saw a balloon-like object.

- 8 December 2007, time unknown: In the town of Bryn in West Glamorgan, two clusters of amber/orange, and white lights in triangular formations were seen. They travelled horizontally in a NorthWesterly direction. They moved like a cork that was bobbing on water.

- 9 December 2007 at 21:30: On the M56/Altrincham/Warrington in Cheshire, at first sight, the object looked like a big, stationary flying saucer. At another angle, it then looked like two perfectly formed triangles. They had white lights with a tinge of red and green in them, like halogen lights.

- 11 December 2007 time unknown: In the town of Haywards Heath in West Sussex, there was a stationary object seen in the sky. It looked like the shape of the diagonal cross on the Scottish flag.

- 12 December 2007, time unknown: In the town of Shirley/Solihull in the West Midlands, a giant craft shone a light into the witness's back window. It shot off fast at first to the northeast and then started to move at a slow pace.

- 12 December 2007 at 18:30: In the town of Bridge of Don/Aberdeen in Aberdeenshire, there were lights seen in the sky, and then they formed into two triangle formations. They were very bright. There was a smaller light on each end of the two triangles.

- 15 December 2007 at 20:45: In the town of Sunderland in County Durham, lights were seen in the sky.

- 23 December 2007, time unknown: In the town of Bdirport, Dorset, an object hovered for a while. It was Silent. It shone a light down. It was difficult to focus on as it looked like a blurred light.

- 23 December 2007 at 17:45: Town unknown, county unknown an orange object was seen going across the sky

- 25 December 2007 at 19:20: In the town of Kettering in Northamptonshire, a brilliant yellow light was seen. There was no sound. The light was travelling faster than an aircraft but slower than a shooting star. It kept on a constant course.

- 25 December 2007, time unknown: In the town of Falmouth Bay in Cornwall, a UFO was seen.

- 25 December 2007, time unknown: In the town of Raurdean Woodside in Gloucestershire, three round things went across the sky, and then one stopped, and then the other two then stopped and waited for it.

- No date, no Time: In the town of Hull in Humberside, a round object with white lights was seen. The object also seemed to be changing colours.

- No date, no Time: In the town of Highgate in London, a flaming yellow object was seen. The yellow object was coming from the West and moving very fast.

- No date, no time: In the town of Braintree in Essex, strange orange lights that seemed to float across the sky were seen.

- No date at 23:00: In the town of Boscombe Down in Wiltshire, an exceedingly bright light, which was stationary but sometimes flew off, was seen.

- No date, no Time: In the town of Leeds in West Yorkshire, a white light was seen hovering. Two more little white lights joined the first one. They were all hovering.

- No date at 22:43: In the town of Clapham in London, a UFO was seen travelling from Clapham to Heathrow.

- No date at 23:00: In the town of Woodhall Spa in Lincolnshire, groups of lights moving through the air were seen. No less than 20, but no more than 40.

- No date at 05:45: In the town of Hastings in East Sussex, a witness saw something very strange in the sky.

- No date at 01:00: In the town of Paignton in Devon, a strange object was seen swirling about in the sky. The object was totally silent.

- No date, no time: In the town of Avonmouth/Bristol in Somerset, a ball of light was seen moving across the garden of a witness's home. It was moving slowly.

- No date, no time: Town unknown in East Sussex, ten-fifteen thousand lights were seen. Also, about seventy single lights were moving quite quickly across the sky.

- No date, no time: In the town of Mexborough in South Yorkshire, a UFO was seen.

- No date, no time: In the town of Godalming in Surrey, UFOs were seen flying very low. They were in formation. They were going quite slowly.

- No date at 22:30: In the town of Hitchin in Hertfordshire, three orange lights were seen travelling in a line formation.

- No date, no time: In the town of Newcastle upon Tyne in Tyne and Wear, an object was seen in the sky. It was as bright as a star or a satellite. It was stationary. It then moved South, then West, and then South again.

- No date, no time: In the town of Liverpool in Merseyside, six to eight glowing lights moving in a straight line across the sky were seen. They were changing patterns from diamonds to pyramids.

- No date, no time: In the town of Harrogate in North Yorkshire, eight plus, orange, unflickering lights that appeared from a Northerly direction were seen. They were the brightest on the horizon.

- No date, no time: In the town of Hastings in East Sussex, a UFO was seen.

- No date, no time: In the town of Aston on Trent in Derbyshire, orange/yellowy lights that seemed to be coming down from the sky were seen. They looked like fluorescent orange street lamps. They were gliding, then faded and disappeared.

- No date at 20:00: In the town of Epsom in Surrey, there were about 25 large, extremely bright orange lights in the sky, with one bigger light behind the rest.

- No date at 20:55: In the town of Shrewsbury in Shropshire, four orange lights were seen crossing the sky. There was a gap, and then three more lights followed. The lights were moving at quite a fast rate.

- No date, no time: In the town of Stretton/Burton-on-Trent in Staffordshire, a UFO was seen going across the sky.

- No date, no time: In the town of Shirley/Solihull in the West Midlands, a UFO was seen.

- No date, no time: In the town of West Dulwich in London, the witness just said a UFO was seen.

- No date at 17:50: In the town of Ramsgate Harbour in Kent, two UFOs were seen flying across the sky.

- No date, no time: In the town of Ramsgate in Kent, two UFOs were seen in the sky.

- No date at 05:15: In the town of Bonnyrigg in Midlothian, sixty lights were seen in the sky, moving fast. Some were red, some blue. Thirty of the lights then changed to orange. The lights were in a triangle formation.

- No date at 04:00: In the town of Choppington in Northumberland, a white pencil line of very white, bright lights was seen. They were as bright as flash bulbs. The lights exploded without noise and cut off the power in the village.

- No date, no time: In the town of Rothwell/Kettering in Northamptonshire, the object was definitely unusual and was a possible UFO sighting.

- No date, no time: In the town of Beckfoot in Cumbria, a definite UFO was seen. It was elongated and amber in colour. Then, as the object sped up, it changed to white in colour and then became very bright.

- No date, no time: In the town of Thetford, Norfolk, a UFO was seen.

- No date, no time: In the town of Pontrennau/Cardiff in West Glamorgan, a UFO was seen.

- No date at 23:00: In the town of Pontypridd in Mid-Glamorgan an object which had all these different lights was seen. When the lights flashed, they looked like they were different shapes. Then both ends of the object started to flash.

- No date, no time: In the town of Whitchurch in West Glamorgan, a UFO was seen.

- No date, no time: In the town of Cardiff in West Glamorgan, the witness saw spaceships and then said that one of them abducted his dog, car, and tent when he and some friends were out camping.

- No date, no time: In the town of Cardiff in West Glamorgan, a UFO was seen.

2008

- 8 January 2008 at 22:24: In the town of Chorley in Lancashire, a triangular shaped object was seen. It was an orange colour. The object was moving across the sky quite fast.

- 12 January 2008: A large fleet of UFOs, or "glowing red spheres," were seen over Liverpool heading East.

- 30 January 2008 at 19:15: In the town of Darley Moor in Derbyshire, two strange beams of light were seen. They were very bright. They were hovering above some trees. The lights then moved towards the borders of Staffordshire.

- 8 February 2008 at 21:00: In the town of Burntwood in Staffordshire, a dull, red object was travelling at high speed and stayed on route.

- 9 February 2008 at 18:00: In the town of Abertillery in Gwent, there was an object seen in the sky that looked like a glowing red ball. A strange substance like molten metal burst from it as it went overhead. It moved without sound.

- 9 February 2008 at 22:40: In the town of Ashton Keynes in Wiltshire, there were ten to twenty bright orange lights that were manoeuvring across the sky. They were moving quite slowly.

- 10 February 2008 at 04:00: In the town of Windermere in Cumbria, an object was seen. The object was triangular in shape, with a yellow light in each corner and a red light in the centre. The yellow lights were pulsating quickly.

- 11 February 2008 at 19:00: In the town of Walthamstow in London, eight faint orange lights were seen flying in the sky. They suddenly disappeared when a plane was in its view.

- 11 February 2008 at 20:56: In the town of Huntingdon in Cambridgeshire, a long, thick, red streak shot across the sky. There was a silver ball of light attached to the front of it. It was rather large. The ball then got bigger and burst.

- 12 February 2008, time unknown: Opposite the House of Parliament in London, there was a craft that had green, red, and white lights. It was still and static in the sky. It was seen for about an hour and a half.

- 12 February 2008, time unknown: In the town of Buxton in Derbyshire, something "very strange" was seen in the sky.

- 12 February 2008 at 18:30: In the town of Calverton in Nottinghamshire, five times more red lights were seen spreading out, and then disappearing one by one.

- 23 February 2008 at 19:30: In the town of Derby in Derbyshire, a light/object was seen hovering from left to right. The light was still hovering seven hours later. The light was moving quickly and then started zig-zagging across the sky.

- 25 February 2008 at 10:10: In the town of Euston in Leicestershire, two strange black discs were seen in the sky with orange lights on the sides of them. They were hovering and then started spinning around quite quickly.

- 27 February 2008, time unknown: In the town of Portsmouth, Hampshire, a bright orange light appeared. It was bigger than a helicopter or a plane. It zig-zagged, flashed red and blue, and moved in a circular motion. It then disappeared.

- 27 February 2008 at 22:50: In the town of Leeds in West Yorkshire, a jumbo jet-sized object was seen. The object was flat and round, with a blue rippled underside. It made no sound and then disappeared.

- 28 February 2008 time unknown: In the town of Bingley in West Yorkshire thirty UFOs were seen.

- 2 March 2008 at 23:00: In the town of Northop Hall in Flintshire, a bright circle shape was seen. It moved quickly and was quite erratic in the sky. It shot to the left, over some houses, and then disappeared.

- 3 March 2008 at 01:00: In the town of Slough in Berkshire, a triangle with lights on each corner of the craft was seen. The craft hovered at aircraft height.

- 12 March 2008 at 19:00: In the town of Portsmouth in Hampshire, bright orange lights were seen glowing brightly above trees in the distance. They were disappearing and reappearing erratically.

- 17 March 2008 at 18:30: In the town of Dundee in Tayside, there was a very bright orange sphere seen in the sky. It was acting strange and appearing and disappearing.

- 18 March 2008 at 19:30: In the town of Dundee in Tayside, there was a very bright orange sphere seen in the sky. It was acting strange and appearing and disappearing.

- 23 March 2008 at 00:15 and 01:20: In the town of Leeds in West Yorkshire, circular objects were seen over Leeds.

- 28 March 2008 at 20:20: In the town of Rainham in Kent, a huge disc-shaped object was seen. It was approximately twenty times the size of an aeroplane. It had five or six flashing lights underneath in a circular shape.

- 6 April 2008 at 22:15: In the town of Delabole in Cornwall, a bright orange light was seen. It started to move backwards, up and down, and then started to wobble to and fro very fast. It faded away, as though it was moving into the distance.

- 13 April 2008 at 21:30: In the town of Newington in Edinburgh, ten to fifteen lights in groups of twos and threes were seen moving across the sky very slowly in an Easterly direction.

- 15 April 2008, time unknown: In the town of Bisley in Gloucestershire, a UFO was seen.

- 16 April 2008 at 20:30: In the town of Haslemere in Surrey, two cylindrical objects, each with a red light, were seen. They were silent, and one was moving in front of the other. They were moving at helicopter speed.

- 29 April 2008 at 01:05: In the town of Exeter, Devon, a UFO was seen flying around and looked like it was having trouble keeping in control. It looked like it was going at about 250 miles per hour.

- 4 May 2008, time unknown: In the town of Delabole in Cornwall, lights were seen in the sky that were flying up in a straight line. They were completely silent.

- 4 May 2008 at 23:10: Town unknown, county unknown, a UFO was seen.

- 5 May 2008 at 00:02: On the M6 Motorway in West Midlands, the witness saw a fast-moving green object whilst driving on the M6 Motorway.

- 11 May 2008 at 14:00: In the town of West Wycombe/H Wycombe in Buckinghamshire, there was a black object seen in the sky. It then turned on its end and disappeared.

- 19 May 2008 at 02:30: In the town of Rhydwyn/Caergybi on the Isle of Anglesey, a round, bright white object was seen. It was moving from SW to NE and moved slowly and quietly.

- 19 May 2008 at 22:45: In the town of Delabole in Cornwall three objects were seen travelling from southeast to northwest.

- 19 May 2008 at 22:45: In the town of Delabole in Cornwall, a very bright orange light was seen that was brighter than a star. Three objects were sighted together. They accelerated over the sea.

- 31 May 2008 at 22:00: In the town of Leeds in West Yorkshire, two bright lights were seen moving fast from West to East. They were at a typical jet height. They then went behind trees and just disappeared.

- 31 May 2008 at 23:09: In the town of Stranraer in Dumfries and Galloway, a bright orange object was seen. It was heading in a South Easterly direction.

- 31 May 2008 at 23:20: In the town of Millbrook/Torpoint in Cornwall, a very bright light zig-zagged across the sky southwards until it vanished.

- 1 June 2008 at 22:30: In the town of Worthing in West Sussex, at first, there was one light like a star, which was white with a tint of orange, and then another moving light appeared. They were travelling in a slightly Westerly, slightly Southerly direction. They travelled in a perfectly straight line.

- 2 June 2008 at 20:30: In the town of Stroud in Gloucestershire, a sighting of something was reported.

- 5 June 2008 at 00:55: In the town of Tonbridge in Kent, an object was flying around in circles at aeroplane level and sounded like an industrial train. There was a strange flashing on the object.

- 6 June 2008 at 22:59: In the town of Godrer Aran/Llanuwchllyn in Gwynedd, two orange lights were seen. They were fast-moving. One moved to the east to Bala, and the other one climbed vertically.

- 7 June 2008 at 00:30: In the town of Heathrow in Middlesex, twenty-five amber lights were seen leaving the Heathrow area. They were travelling West at 45 degrees at 200–300 knots.

- 7 June 2008 at 23:00: In the town of Croydon in London, a strange object was seen in the sky. It was around for several minutes and then flew off.

- 7 June 2008 at 23:00: In the town of Westbury/Shrewsbury in Shropshire, a UFO was seen.

- 7 June 2008 at 23:00: In the town of Tern Hill Barracks in Shropshire, thirteen crafts were seen zig-zagging in the sky.

- 8 June 2008 at 00:25: In the town of Middleton/Ilkley in West Yorkshire, there were five orange objects, and then one orange 'blob' came into view.

- 8 June 2008: A number of UFO sightings took place in Wales, which involved a police helicopter following a UFO over Cardiff near MOD St Athan, the Bristol Channel, and nearby areas such as Eglwys Brewis, Barry, and Sully.

- 9 June 2008 at 01:30: In the town of Norton/Stourbridge in the West Midlands, an object that had a flat top and a rounded bottom was seen. It was roughly the width of a combined semi-detached house. There was a dim humming sound.

- 10 June 2008 at 23:30: In the town of Shortstown/Bedford in Bedfordshire, a big orange, saucer-shaped floating thing was seen in the sky. There were four flashing lights on it. It was like a light show. They then suddenly stopped flashing. This went on for over two hours.

- 15 June 2008 at 22:45: In the town of Waverton/Chester in Cheshire, a formation of eighteen lights was seen. They appeared like a 'flock of helicopters' with lights on. They gave off no sound, but there was a slight rattle.

- 17 June 2008, time unknown: In the town of New Forest in Hampshire, a UFO was seen.

- 20 June 2008 at 19:30: In the town of Thorne/Doncaster in South Yorkshire, a metallic, capsule-shaped object was seen. There was no sound. The object was moving from southeast to northwest, was going quite fast, and didn't slow down at any point.

- 20 June 2008 at 23:00: In the town of Kendal in Cumbria, there was a quite low, red, and orange light seen. A bright, phosphorus-white light fell from the orange light towards the ground before disappearing. The red light was static throughout the sighting.

- 22 June 2008 at 01:00: In the town of Stanley/Wakefield in West Yorkshire, five bright, oval-shaped orange lights were seen. Three of the lights were in a group, and the other two were also in a group, travelling behind. They were flying from East to West.

- 23 June 2008 at 17:50: In the town of Welton/Lincoln in Lincolnshire, a diamond/orb-shaped object was seen. It was white and bright. It never moved. It was a few thousand feet up in the sky.

- 23 June 2008 at 23:10: In the town of Barry in the Vale of Glamorgan, eleven objects were seen in the sky.

- 27 June 2008 at 23:45: In the town of Inverness in Inverness-shire, one brilliant orange light was seen, then five orange lights moved slowly overhead. The orange lights moved from East to West.

- 27 June 2008 at 23:55: In the town of Inverness in Inverness-shire, five orange, circular lights were seen in the sky, and a beam of light was also going up into the sky.

- 28 June 2008, time unknown: Town unknown in Kent, a UFO was seen.

- 28 June 2008, time unknown: In the town of Cobham in Surrey, something interesting was seen in the sky.

- 28 June 2008 at 23:40: In the town of Bedford/Arledsey in Bedfordshire, there were a total of seven strange lights seen moving from North to South.

- 29 June 2008, time unknown: In the town of Yeovil in Somerset, an orange ball was seen up in the sky.

- 1 July 2008 at 22:30: Town unknown in Devon, UFO activity was reported.

- 2 July 2008 at 21:30: In the town of Littlemore in Oxfordshire, sixteen square-shaped objects appeared as silhouettes. They were travelling across the sky from South to North.

- 3 July 2008 at 23:30: In the town of Coventry in the West Midlands, there were two orange balls hovering a foot in front of the witness. They hovered from left to right.

- 4 July 2008, time unknown: In the town of Barnet in London, a UFO was seen.

- 4 July 2008 at 04:00: In the town of Wroughton in Wiltshire, one white light in the shape of a triangle was seen. It was very bright. It was estimated to be about 1,000 ft up in the sky.

- 11 July 2008 at 23:30: In the town of Scarborough in North Yorkshire, a cork-shaped object that glowed like an angel flew up and over some trees.

- 12 July 2008 at 09:35: In the town of Midhurst in West Sussex, there were seven red glowing objects seen. They were moving from West to East.

- 12 July 2008 at 22:00: In the town of Davidstow in Cornwall, two lights were briefly seen before they disappeared into a huge cloud. They looked like bright orange stars.

- 12 July 2008 at 22:50: In the town of Horncastle in Lincolnshire, eight circular, large yellow, bright solid lights moving east, and southeast were seen. They were moving at high speed, low level.

- 12 July 2008 at 23:00: In the town of Amberley in Gloucestershire, a UFO was seen moving West.

- 12 July 2008 at 23:30: In the town of Oxted in Surrey, ninety orange lights were seen in a V or S-shaped pattern. They were the size of footballs. They passed over the witness's house.

- 12 July 2008 at 23:52: In the town of Scarborough in North Yorkshire, a white pea pod-shaped object flew through a blue part of the sky and then through a cloud.

- 13 July 2008 at 22:00: In the town of Davidstow in Cornwall, six lights were seen. They looked like bright orange stars, rising up into the air one after the other.

- 14 July 2008 at 02:14: In the town of Scarborough in North Yorkshire, a UFO that was shaped like a fiery star was seen. It flew through the sky and then disappeared.

- 15 July 2008, time unknown: In the town of Lowestoft in Suffolk, a UFO was seen.

- 20 July 2008 at 00:50: In the town of Chavey Down/Ascot in Berkshire, an object was seen. It resembled a white light and was travelling at a low speed. It was about two or three times bigger than Venus. It sometimes looked like a spotlight, but there was no silhouette or shadow of an aircraft. There was no noise.

- 20 July 2008 at 03:30: In the town of Redruth in Cornwall, an object moved from north to west, then disappeared after moving towards the east.

- 21 July 2008 at 22:30: On the A6 near Buxton in Derbyshire, there was a distant bright light, like a huge star seen. A wide-shaped object too, with white and coloured lights across it. It then disappeared overhead.

- 23 July 2008 at 21:00: In the town of Sutton-In-Craven/Keighley in West Yorkshire, two bright balls of light were seen. One of the balls looked like it was chasing and trying to overtake an aircraft. The other ball just burst as it was moving and disappeared.

- 24 July 2008 at 22:15: In the town of Wellington in Shropshire, a really bright, burning orange light was seen. The object was going at the speed of a helicopter.

- 25 July 2008, time unknown: In the town of Telford in Shropshire, a UFO was seen.

- 26 July 2008, time unknown: In the town of Northampton in Northamptonshire, eight strange lights were seen.

- 26 July 2008, time unknown: In the town of Bristol in Avon, a group of lights in a cluster were seen. More lights gradually joined them. Several lights were moving across the sky. More lights joined them, and both sets then disappeared.

- 26 July 2008, time unknown: In the town of Farnham in Surrey, two red round lights were seen. The objects were moving across the sky in different directions and then just disappeared.

- 26 July 2008 at 22:00: In the town of Gosport, Hampshire, a silent aircraft passed overhead. It was clearly visible, like a shooting star, but with a smooth, curving course.

- 27 July 2008, time unknown: In the town of Scunthorpe in Lincolnshire, an oval-shaped, weird light was seen in the sky. The object moved from right to left and was moving in a Westerly direction.

- 27 July 2008, time unknown: In the town of Helston in Cornwall, a mysterious light in the night sky was seen.

- 27 July 2008, time unknown: In the town of Shirley in the West Midlands, a triangle-shaped object, which had three white lights and one red light was seen. There was no noise.

- 27 July 2008 at 02:00: Town unknown, county unknown, an object moved slowly at about 2,000 ft, raised vertically, then moved slowly away.

- 27 July 2008 at 16:30: In the town of Pontypridd in Mid Glamorgan, an object was travelling at high speed. It appeared to be round, like a football. It was travelling from South East to North East. It then disappeared.

- 27 July 2008 at 23:25: In the town of Leeds in West Yorkshire, there was one lit-up circle, and then 24 appeared, all spaced. They were all in the same line of path and moving at the same speed.

- 28 July 2008 at 23:05: In the town of West Kilbride in Ayrshire, two spheres passed rapidly by, moving northward.

- 29 July 2008 at 00:00: In the town of South Croydon in Surrey, a UFO was seen.

- 30 July 2008, time unknown: On the A1/North of Darlington in Cleveland, ten orange/amber orb-shaped ships were seen. Some were in clusters, and some were scattered.

- 30 July 2008, time unknown: Town unknown county unknown, a perfect triangular-shaped, stone-looking object was seen hovering about twenty feet in the sky. It had three lights on each point, and the front nose cone was a blue light.

- 31 July 2008 time unknown: In the town of Godalming in Surrey a UFO was seen.

- 31 July 2008 at 01:15: In the town of Bodmin Moor in Cornwall, a UFO was seen.

- 1 August 2008 at 22:30: In the town of Loughborough in Leicestershire, twenty to twenty-five lights were seen moving across the sky. They were in a uniform lighting formation.

- 2 August 2008 at 22:30: In the town of Winchmore Hill in London, lights were seen in the sky.

- 2 August 2008 at 23:45: In the town of Bridgewater in Somerset a strange sighting was reported.

- 3 August 2008 at 22:00: In the town of Barry in Glamorgan, three UFOs were seen.

- 7 August 2008 at 22:25: Not stated Buckinghamshire A bright red object.

- 7 August 2008 at 22:30: In the town of Brill/Aylesbury in Buckinghamshire, a red light was seen slowly moving in the sky. The object was not terribly high up.

- 11 August 2008 at 22:05: In the town of Larkhall in Lanarkshire, a single round light was seen. It was orange/red in colour. It was moving south east. There was no sound at all.

- 15 August 2008, time unknown: In the town of Burbage/Hinckley in Leicestershire, two bright lights were seen. It looked like a spectrum of light shone through the car.

- 15 August 2008 at 21:10: In the town of Argoed in West Glamorgan, three bright orange lights/objects were seen in the sky, about a mile away. One of the objects was black and disc-shaped. It moved quickly and was silent.

- 23 August 2008 at 21:56: In the town of Darlington in County Durham, two objects that both had two lights on them were seen. Each object was moving independently from the other. There was no sound.

- 24 August 2008 at 21:00: In the town of Emsworth in Hampshire, there was a bright yellow light seen in the sky. The object was approximately 12,000 ft up.

- 24 August 2008 at 21:30: In the town of South Malling/Lewes in East Sussex, fifty-nine lights were seen in the sky that formed a 'V' shape. There were a few lights on their own. They were bright red and very big. They were silent.

- 29 August 2008 at 11:55: In the town of Westborough/Scarborough in North Yorkshire, a black rectangular object was seen wobbling in the sky. It then moved out of sight.

- 29 August 2008 at 22:41: In the town of Oakworth/Keighley in West Yorkshire, a UFO was seen. It was quite far away and too high to be a plane.

- 30 August 2008 at 17:40: In the town of Stroud in Gloucestershire, six orb-shaped objects that were red and orange in colour were seen. They initially formed a 'V' shape. They were floating around, and then the central one zoomed off like Captain Kirk Enterprise.

- 30 August 2008 at 21:41: In the town of Scholes/Holmfirth in West Yorkshire, there was a sighting of lights in the sky.

- 30 August 2008 at 22:20: In the town of Whitburn/South Tyneside in Tyne and Wear, sodium-coloured lights were seen travelling northwest. Initially, four circular bright lights were travelling in a convoy. Two of the lights made a vertical change of direction. One looked like a bright orange orb.

- 30 August 2008 at 23:00: In the town of Westborough/Scarborough in North Yorkshire, an orange circular-shaped object was seen.

- 31 August 2008 at 21:35: In the town of Littlebourne in Kent, three very low, very bright lights were seen travelling in formation, then breaking off and doing acrobatics. Then a large globe-like object appeared and was changing colours in a pulsating way.

- 1 September 2008 at 20:44: In the town of Rothwell/Leeds in West Yorkshire, an orb-shaped object with a disc shape underneath was seen in the sky for about ten to fifteen minutes.

- 3 September 2008 at 20:20: In the town of Mannamead/Plymouth in Devon, a large, bright pink light was seen. It was about a kilometre away. It was floating towards the left and then accelerated and disappeared. It looked like two small pieces came away from it.

- 3 September 2008 at 21:45: In the town of Urmston/Manchester in Greater Manchester, there were four separate lights seen. One of the lights was huge, and it had different lights on it.

- 4 September 2008 at 22:30: In the town of Guildford in Surrey, a big, red, diamond-shaped object was seen. There was no sound.

- 4 September 2008 at 22:40: In the town of Middlesbrough, in Middlesborough, the craft had bright green lights and a blue light that was moving quickly through the trees. It was very large and was moving extremely fast. It was silent.

- 6 September 2008 at 20:03: In the town of Laindon in Essex, two large orange lights were seen in the sky; they were flying east rather quickly. One light flew around the other one, then they both moved away north, at a higher speed.

- 8 September 2008 at 00:10: Near Blackpool in Lancashire, an object in the shape of a chewing gum pack that was black in colour and had three circles of lights underneath it, emitting a dull orange light, was seen. It was about 150 feet long and 50 feet wide.

- 13 September 2008 at 04:53: Town unknown, county unknown, there was quite a large flashing object, just hanging in the air, quite high up. Underneath the object was an orange/red luminating light.

- 14 September 2008 at 01:07: In the town of High Wycombe in Buckinghamshire, a UFO was seen.

- 19 September 2008 at 20:44: In the town of Stoke on Trent in Staffordshire, an orange ball which looked like it came up from the ground was seen. It then shot up vertically into the sky and disappeared.

- 20 September 2008 at 20:00: In the town of Chatteris in Cambridgeshire, multiple bright glowing objects, between 5–10,000 ft heading from south to north were seen.

- 20 September 2008 at 22:00: In the town of Calne in Wiltshire, five super bright, glowing orange/pink orbs at low altitude were seen. They had unusual flying characteristics and were totally silent in flight.

- 20 September 2008 at 22:55: In the town of Malton in North Yorkshire, there were circles of white lights with a set of fire coming from inside each of them. They were like hang gliders, totally quiet. The last circle had a red light. They were in a formation.

- 21 September 2008 at 22:15: In the town of Iver in Buckinghamshire, a stream of forty oval-roundish lights were seen. They were in separate formations, all in straight lines. They were a funny orange colour and were bright.

- 22 September 2008, time unknown: In the town of Glasgow, Glasgow, a UFO was seen.

- 27 September 2008 at 19:45: In the town of Southgate in London, a large silent squadron of red/orange-coloured flying craft was seen. There must have been in excess of thirty. Maybe more. They were flying from West to East.

- 27 September 2008, time unknown: In the town of Bletchley in Buckinghamshire, something definitely odd was reported by a witness.

- 28 September 2008, time unknown: In the town of Budleigh Salterton in Devon, there was a stationary object, too low to be a star, seen. It was orange in colour. It moved once, and then twice in a straight line in a NE – SW direction.

- 1 October 2008 at 23:00: In the town of Felixstowe in Suffolk, very fast, intense flashes were seen. Then one of the flashes formed into a ball.

- 5 October 2008 at 19:50: In the town of Wolverhampton in the West Midlands, a number of mysterious lights moving silently overhead were seen. There were three, and then another three appeared.

- 6 October 2008 at 20:55: Town unknown in Lincolnshire, a very large inverted V shape of seven dull lights – greyish almost were seen. There was no shell outline. It rotated slightly and then seemed to bounce. The lights then shot off individually at high speed.

- 8 October 2008 at 23:17: In the town of Newcastle upon Tyne in Tyne and Wear, a large, bright white object was seen moving silently at fast speed in the sky at a very high altitude, heading from northeast to southwest. The colour then changed from white to red, and then it stopped. It jumped to different parts of the sky.

- 10 October 2008 at 20:45: In the town of Cheltenham in Gloucestershire, there were five what looked like strange orange fireballs seen. They were silent.

- 11 October 2008 at 00:35: On the A12/Colchester in Essex, two bright lights were flying Northbound, in line about 500 yards apart. As they got nearer, they could only be described as two balls of fire.

- 11 October 2008 at 19:20: In the town of Portsmouth, Hampshire, a large, bright orange tube-shaped craft was seen. It was flying slowly across the sky in a NorthWesterly direction. It was stationary for a minute. It made 3–4 circles in the sky and then zoomed off to the East.

- 11 October 2008 at 23:00: In the town of Stafford, Staffordshire, there was a craft that seemed unusual. It was a shining bright orange and was moving slowly.

- 13 October 2008 at 21:00: In the town of Buxton in Derbyshire, seven orange orbs were seen. They were in a formation of three and then two sets of two. They moved generally in a straight line but with some 'dancing' in the sky.

- 13 October 2008 at 22:50: In the town of Balham in London, a UFO was seen.

- 14 October 2008, time unknown: In the town of Swansea in West Glamorgan, there was a continuous orange, strange shape in the sky. There was a very odd light, too.

- 15 October 2008, time unknown: In the town of Slough in Berkshire, there was a triangular object hovering a mile above the witness's house. It had a sort of pattern under it, like a sign. It also had three circular types of lights. There was a weird hovering sound. It then shot up into the sky and disappeared.

- 18 October 2008 at 20:05: On the A259/Brighton in East Sussex, a bright spherical light was seen hovering above a house. The object slowly departed to the east, and it spun and shifted at a rapid speed upwards in a Northerly direction before disappearing.

- 24 October 2008 at 00:10: In the town of Aylesbury in Buckinghamshire, a UFO was seen moving across the sky.

- 27 October 2008 at 00:01: In the town of Snetterton in Norfolk, a very high object came from out of space, travelling ten times the speed of sound. It was followed by a loud whooshing sound. The object was declining and was travelling far faster than any jet can go.

- 29 October 2008, time unknown: In the town of Erbistock/Wrexham in Clwyd, an unusual sighting was reported.

- 30 October 2008 at 18:30: In the town of Wakefield in West Yorkshire, there was an orange object seen in the sky, and it was the size of an aircraft. The object was about twenty miles away. It climbed into the sky very fast and then disappeared.

- 30 October 2008 at 20:35: In the town of Dumfries in Dumfriesshire, there were two lights seen moving towards each other. They then merged, disappeared, and reappeared, but were apart. The lights were seen to the southwest.

- 4 November 2008 at 17:40: In the town of Somerton in Somerset, an object was seen. The object was cigar-shaped and was 80 ft long, and 30 ft tall. It was orange in colour and looked illuminated. It had a rear, bright white light. It made a sharp right turn and then disappeared.

- 6 November 2008 at 20:10: In the town of Rainham in Kent, a UFO that looked like a yellow light was seen. The object was quite near and fairly low down in the sky. There was no sound.

- 7 November 2008 at 19:30: At Twyford train station in Berkshire, a flicker of light seemed to jump a considerable distance around the night sky. It had lights that seemed to scroll from one side to another.

- 12 November 2008 at 17:23: In the town of Carlton, nr. Rothwell/Leeds in West Yorkshire, objects were seen. The objects looked like Chinese lanterns. They were orange in colour and very bright. The objects moved very fast and were extremely manoeuvrable.

- 14 November 2008 at 16:50: In the town of Kirton/Boston in Lincolnshire, there were twelve lights seen in the sky. The lights started to fade, and then two more brighter lights came towards the first twelve. They were not in any formation.

- 15 November 2008 at 21:20: In the town of East Grinstead in West Sussex, two very bright orange lights were seen travelling from West to East. The lights were vertically spaced. Then another bright orange light came over. There was no noise.

- 16 November 2008 at 18:55: In the town of Keighley in West Yorkshire, two objects were seen.

- 21 November 2008 at 23:30: In the town of Stickford/Boston in Lincolnshire, a cloud-type dull light with no noise was seen 100 ft 200 ft from the witness's house. It was moving in an arc continuously at speed, from left to right.

- 22 November 2008, time unknown: In the town of Jersey in the Channel Islands, a UFO was seen.

- 25 November 2008 at 17:10: In the town of Shrewsbury in Shropshire a strange triangular shape was seen in the sky, with the apex to the right. It was metallic grey in colour, but the flat base end seemed to glow orange. It must have been at least fifteen feet long and ten feet wide.

- 26 November 2008, time unknown: In the town of Cheadle/Stoke on Trent in Staffordshire, a UFO was seen flying through the sky.

- 1 December 2008 at 18:50: In the town of Wettenhall/Winsford in Cheshire, a crest-shaped object was seen moving to the southeast at the rear of the witness's property.

- 1 Dec 2008 at 21:30: In the Village of Llangwm in Pembrokeshire, a very bright light, which had a long white tail was seen. It then shot across the sky, and the whole field was lit up. The light then began to break up.

- 6 December 2008 at 23:45: In the town of Stratford upon Avon in Warwickshire, an orange ball was seen. The object was stationary for about five minutes and then shot up into the sky and out of view. There was no sound.

- 10 December 2008 at 15:49: In the town of Devizes in Wiltshire, a small, bright golden-coloured orb was seen. It flew past and was very rapid and then it disappeared.

- 18 December 2008, time unknown: In the town of Halesowen in the West Midlands, a string of fifty to sixty lights was seen in the sky.

- 21 December 2008 at 17:30: In the town of Scunthorpe in Lincolnshire a bright flashing "star" was seen in the South West sky. It was too bright for a star. It looked like a little fireball. It repeatedly got bright and then died down. It looked big, but it was pretty far away.

- 24 December 2008 at 19:50: In the town of Rottingdean in East Sussex, there were fifteen UFOs/bright lights coming down from the Downs. They were travelling at very fast speeds.

- 24 December 2008 at 20:00: In the town of Felixstowe in Suffolk, an orange/red ball shot into the sky from a northeasterly direction. It travelled at terrific speed, climbing all the time, then faded and disappeared. There was no noise.

- 24 December 2008 at 21:40: In the town of High Wycombe in Buckinghamshire, there were fifteen lights seen moving across the sky about half a mile away. They were red and flickering. Then three lights formed a triangle shape. They were moving horizontally from left to right.

- 25 December 2008, time unknown: In the town of Perth in Perthshire, a UFO was seen.

- 25 December 2008 at 20:20: In the town of Glasgow in Strathclyde, six objects in two lines of three, one line above the other, were seen. They emitted a very strong yellow-orange light before disappearing in the distance to the west.

- 25 December 2008 at 22:40: In the town of Carlisle in Cumbria, four or five bright lights were seen moving across the sky north of Carlisle. They were orange in colour. They retained a constant altitude, then disappeared from view heading westward.

- 26 December 2008 at 02:30: In the town of Old Colwyn in North Wales, an object was seen that was bigger than a helicopter. It was 250 metres up in the sky, silent, with something like a bar coming off it, and then 30 seconds later it flew off over the sea, followed closely by a helicopter.

- 26 December 2008 at 18:30: In the town of Southgate in London, there was a whole procession of lights seen in the sky. Big eight orange balls with a red, flaming triangle in the centre of all of them. There was no noise.

- 26 December 2008 at 19:00: In the town of Kennington/Ashford in Kent, an orange shape was seen travelling NW to SW at a fair pace, 2000ft plus. It was bright orange. It was a similar shape to an inverted light bulb. There was no sound.

- 26 December 2008, time unknown: In the town of Ilkley, West Yorkshire, two parallel UFOs were seen.

- 26 December 2008 time unknown: In the town of Wymondham in Norfolk seven strange orange lights were seen. They were moving at great speed. They appeared one by one and remained stationary for 30 minutes before disappearing.

- 27 December 2008 at 22:10: In the town of Morecambe in Lancashire, unidentified objects were seen in the sky.

- 27 December 2008, time unknown: In the town of Kensington in London, two orbs that were quite big were seen dropping through the sky and disappearing behind some trees.

- 29 December 2008 at 19:00: In the town of Loughton/Adbridge in Essex, lights in groups of three or four but not in a line were seen. They were an orange/yellow colour. They were watched for 30 minutes. They made no sound.

- 29 December 2008, time unknown: In the town of Kettering in Northamptonshire, there were some large objects seen in the sky. There was also a constant red light heading West. The objects were bigger than a plane.

- 29 December 2008, time unknown: In the town of Farnworth in Lancashire, there was a large, bright orange light seen. There was no sound. It moved slowly initially, then there was rapid movement, and it disappeared out of sight.

- 31 December 2008 at 21:00: Town unknown, county unknown, a ball of fire was seen sitting in the sky. It changed colour from red to orange. It was diamond-shaped. It moved up and down and backwards in circles, then shot up and disappeared.

- 31 December 2008, time unknown: In the town of Brightlingsea in Essex, a police officer saw a bright orange/yellow light in the sky. It was quite large, 1500–2000 ft up. It moved very slowly in a half circle, then stopped over the water between Brightlingsea and East Mersea. It shot straight up and disappeared very fast.

- No date at 07:00: In the town of Beccles in Suffolk, a bright light was seen. While moving in a Westerly direction, it started to change shape. The light was on a constant course.

- No date, no time: In the town of Cardiff in West Glamorgan, a UFO was seen.

- No date, no time: In the town of Watchet in Somerset, an object was seen moving across the sky.

- No date at 21:00: In the town of Burgess Hill in West Sussex, fourteen orange lights came through the sky in twos and then disappeared.

- No date, no time: In the town of Chester in Cheshire, the witness just said that it was an unusual sighting of an object.

- No date at 18:00: In the town of Keynsham/Bristol in Avon and Somerset, an object was seen hovering in the sky. In one spot, there was a light running through the centre, which appeared to be going around the object.

- No date, no time: In the town of Little Hampton in West Sussex, an object was seen. The object looked like a strange light. It was quite far in the distance.

- No date, no time: In the town of Thorney Island/Emsworth in West Sussex, there were twenty to thirty bright orange lights, moving quite slowly from North to South at a 45-degree angle. They seemed to fan out as they moved.

- No date, no time: In the town of Helston in Cornwall, a UFO was seen.

- No date, no time: In the Customs House in London, a UFO was seen.

- No date, no time: In the town of Slough in Berkshire, a UFO was seen.

- No date, no time: In the town of New Romney in Kent, a UFO was seen.

- No date, no time: In the town of Worksop in Nottinghamshire, some strange, slow, low-flying lights were seen; they did not separate but were all together, as if on a craft. The lights were red, green, and yellow.

- No date, no time: In the town of East Ham in London, a UFO was seen.

- No date, no time: In the town of Bristol in Avon and Somerset, fleets of orange lights were seen moving across the sky. They had been seen for the past three weeks.

- No date, no time: In the town of Stanford le Hope in Essex a strange light was seen in the sky. At one point, it looked like a cloud that was flying around, making jerking movements.

- No date, no time: Town unknown in County Down, a UFO was seen.

- No date, no time: In the town of Newtownards in County Down, a UFO was seen.

- No date, no time: In the town of Yarm in Cleveland, a UFO was seen moving across the sky.

- No date, no time: In the town of Needham Market/Ipswich in Suffolk, a uniform of lights was seen travelling across the sky.

- No date at 21:05: In the town of Caerleon/Newport in Gwent, two balls of fire were seen hovering in the sky. They then elevated up and shot off into the distance.

- No date, no time: In the town of Rugby in Warwickshire, a UFO was seen.

- No date, no time: Town unknown, county unknown, a UFO was seen.

- No date at 01:45: In the town of Heaton/Newcastle upon Tyne in Tyne and Wear, a UFO was seen.

- No date, no time: In the town of Woodford Green in Essex, four bright orange lights were seen floating across the sky. Then, what looked like a black blob appeared.

- No date, no time: In the town of Bristol in Avon and Somerset, a big alien craft landed on the top of the witness's house. The craft then flew off over Bristol.

- No date, no time: Town unknown in London, a metallic blue UFO was seen. It was quite big. It was climbing in the sky.

- No date, no time: In the town of St Leonards-on-Sea in East Sussex, a UFO was seen.

- No date, no time: In the town of Radstock/Bath in Somerset a navy, circular, slightly off-centre UFO flew Eastwards across the sky.

- No date, no time: In the town of Linton/Swadlincote in Derbyshire, triangular lights were seen on strange objects.

- No date, no time: In the town of Carlisle in Cumbria, a UFO was seen, and there was an alien in the witness's house.

- No date, no time: In the town of New Malden in Surrey, a UFO has been stationary up in the sky for the last few days.

- No date, no time: In the town of Shirley/Solihull in the West Midlands, a UFO shot past the witness's house. It then stopped and started to hover in a southeasterly direction.

- No date, no time: In the town of Turnhill/Shrewsbury in Shropshire, a UFO was seen.

- No date, no time: In the town of Locks Heath/Southampton in Hampshire, an orange ball was seen. It hovered over the witness's car, then shot off and disappeared.

- No date, no time: In the town of Newtownards in County Down, a UFO was seen.

- No date, no time: In the town of Lambeth in London, a stationary bright, white light was seen in the sky; it was lower than the other stars with a multi-coloured pulsating light. Then three smaller, dark objects entered into the white light.

- No date, no time: In the town of Christchurch in Dorset, a large, silver metallic disc was seen. The UFO was seen over a period of two weeks ago.

- No date, no time: In the town of Bury St Edmonds in Suffolk two white lights were spotted through low clouds. The lights went backwards and forward for about forty minutes.

- No date, no time: In the town of Duns in the Borders, a UFO was seen.

- No date at 23:10: Town unknown in Cambridgeshire, flashing lights were seen. It looked like there were three hundred planes going across the sky.

- No date, no time: In the town of Bedford, Bedfordshire, balls of light were seen beaming red lights out of the sky.

- No date, no time: In the town of Aberdeen in Aberdeenshire, strange lights were seen in the sky.

- No date at 00:20: In the town of Ipswich in Suffolk, a silent orange light was seen. The light was moving faster than a helicopter from northeast to southwest.

- No date, no time: At Luton Airport/Luton in Bedfordshire, a UFO was observed for 57 minutes. It seemed to be monitoring Luton Airport air traffic.

- No date, no time: In the town of Oxford in Oxfordshire, a constant light was seen moving slowly from West to East. It was moving slowly across the sky.

- No date at 22:25: In the town of Godalming in Surrey, a light similar to a street lamp was seen. It was yellow and the size of a football. It was flying through the sky at varying speeds.

- No date at 21:21: In the town of Thorndon/Eye in Suffolk, two UFOs were seen. They were quite far away, high up, and moving quite fast. They looked like they were tracking a passenger jet.

- No date at 01:45: In the town of Newport in Gwent, a single object was seen.

- No date, no time: In the town of Gravesend in Kent, a light was seen hovering for ten minutes, showing off a very bright white light. Another object then joined it. They both went dim and disappeared.

- No date at 23:00: In the town of Northampton in Northamptonshire, an unusual sighting was reported.

- No date, no time: In the town of Chard in Somerset, a sighting was reported.

- No date, no time: In the town of Morley in West Yorkshire, lights were seen.

- No date, no time: In the town of Brill/Aylesbury in Buckinghamshire, a UFO was seen.

- No date, no time: In the town of Swansea in Glamorgan, a UFO was seen.

- No date, no time: Town unknown in the Highlands, three UFOs were seen. They looked like red, light-orb things. The UFOs were coming from the East.

- No date, no time: In the town of Cheshunt in Hertfordshire, thirty orange lights were seen moving slowly across the sky. The lights were a few hundred feet up. They were moving in a straight line, going slowly.

- No date at 23:00: In the town of Southport, Merseyside, flying objects were seen. They looked like bright lights. The objects were hovering. There was a big group of lights, and they were in a half-circle formation.

- No date at 22:10: In the town of Woodhatch/Reigate in Surrey, four UFOs in the sky were seen. They were quite near, as they flew above the witness's house.

- No date at 22:30: In the town of Little Steeping/Spilsby in Lincolnshire, an exceedingly large light was seen. It was moving back and forth across the sky. Then a group of lights appeared. They were high up above the clouds.

- No date, no time: In the town of Ramsbottom/Bury in Greater Manchester, a UFO was seen.

- No date at 23:00: In the town of Haverfordwest in Pembrokeshire, a UFO was seen.

- No date at 17:30: In the town of Rickmansworth in Hertfordshire, objects flying across the sky were seen.

- No date, no time: In the town of Enfield in Greater London, five orange balls were seen in the sky.

- No date, no time: In the town of Stoke on Trent in Staffordshire, something strange was seen in the sky.

- No date at 21:30: In the town of Isle of Dogs in London, a load of orange lights in formation were seen.

- No date, no time: In the town of Middlesbrough, Middlesborough, a UFO was seen.

- No date, no time: In the town of St. Peter in Jersey, a UFO was seen.

- No date, no time: In the town of Belfast in County Antrim ships/UFOs were seen over the witness's house various times this year. He also saw the greys.

- No date at 19:55: In the town of Sopley/Christchurch in Dorset, one hundred possible UFOs were seen in the sky.

- No date at 20:00: In the town of Buckhurst Hill in Essex, four very strange orange glow lights were seen. They were flying above the witness's house.

- No date, no time: In the town of New Malden in London, two strange objects were seen in the sky. They were together, and then they followed each other.

- No date, no time: In the town of Neath in Neath and Port Talbot, three glowing objects were seen. The objects were moving towards the witness and then moved straight up into the sky.

- No date, no time: In the town of Mumbles/Swansea in Glamorgan, a UFO was seen.

- No date, no time: In the town of Frogmore/St Albans in Hertfordshire, a UFO was seen.

- No date, no time: In the town of Redruth in Cornwall, they looked like flares or lights. They were quite far in the distance and going quite fast.

- No date at 00:00: In the town of Bedstone/Bucknell in Shropshire, there was an orange light coming over the hills. Another two approached. Then there were eight orange lights in formation. They were moving at the speed of a helicopter. There was no noise at all.

- No date at 21:20: In the town of Brandiston/Norwich in Norfolk, three bright single lights were seen. They hovered for a short while. There was no sound.

- No date, no time: In the town of Burnham on Sea in Somerset, a UFO was seen.

- No date, no time: In the town of Folkestone in Kent, there were lights seen in the sky that were circling in front of the witness's house. They were in a half-moon shape.

- No date at 19:15: In the town of Dover in Kent, there were half a dozen glowing lights seen. They were an orange-fire colour and were globular. They were silent. They were moving across the sky at the speed of a helicopter.

- No date at 20:18: In the town of East Stoke/Wareham in Dorset, a pretty unusual sighting was reported.

- No date, no time: In the town of Wellingborough in Northamptonshire, a UFO was seen.

- No date, no time: In the town of Redditch in Worcestershire, something that looked like a helicopter spotlight was 500/600 ft high in the sky. It looked like there was a fire beneath the craft. There was no engine noise at all. It was moving about 60–80 miles per hour.

- No date, no time: In the town of Poole in Dorset, a UFO flew across the sky.

- No date, no time: In the town of Ladbroke Grove in London, eight UFOs shaped like arrowheads were seen in the sky. They were orange/reddish in colour. There was no sound. They were quite high up in the sky.

- No date, no time: In the town of Todmorden in West Yorkshire, one very round, yellowy light moving across the sky was seen. It seemed to be moving vertically from the valley floor. It then moved across the sky. It was totally silent.

- No date at 23:20: In the town of Middlewich in Cheshire, an object was travelling through the sky, inside the atmosphere.

- No date, no time: Town unknown in Buckinghamshire, ten unidentified flying objects were seen in the sky.

- No date at 21:00: In the town of Coulsdon in Surrey, two very strong, clear white lights were seen.

- No date, no time: In the town of Chesterfield in Derbyshire, a UFO was seen.

- No date, no time: In the town of Kettering in Northamptonshire, a UFO was seen.

- No date at 19:00: In the town of Hainault in Essex, groups of three lights, like an orange street light colour, were seen. 30 or more in total. They came from the direction of Loughton/Adbridge. The last group of five came over to the house and disappeared at 19:30.

- No date, no time: In the town of Littlehampton in West Sussex, an orange globe/light was coming along the coastline. It was very vivid. It moved along at five hundred to a thousand ft in height.

- No date, no time: In the town of Newtownhamilton in County Down, one circle of bright light was seen. It was as high up as a telegraph pole. It was seen for thirty minutes. The object was moving towards and away from the vehicle.

- No date at 18:20: In the town of Redruth in Cornwall, an object was seen.

2009

- January 2009, time unknown: In the town of Warwick in Warwickshire, an Air Traffic Control employee saw an orange glowing object with a red light on the right-hand side.

- January 2009, time unknown: Town unknown in North Yorkshire, a very curious object was seen. It was very bright, four times that of a star.

- January 2009, time unknown: In the town of Carterton in Oxfordshire, an Air Traffic Control employee saw a very bright, constant red light.

- January 2009, time unknown: In the town of High Wycombe in Buckinghamshire, the object has been outside the individual's house for some nights and then one night.

- January 2009, time unknown: In the town of Sawtry in Cambridgeshire, a UFO was seen.

- January 2009, time unknown: In the town of Porthcawl in Mid Glamorgan, a diamond-shaped red light came towards him from the sea. The rear end of the diamond was blue. It was incredibly hot as it passed overhead. It made no sound.

- January 2009, time unknown: In the town of Halifax in West Yorkshire, a silver disc-shaped light was seen for two minutes. The witness was in his lounge.

- January 2009, time unknown: In the town of High Wycombe in Buckinghamshire, a bright object travelling very fast overhead was seen. Not a plane.

- January 2009, time unknown: In the town of St Albans in Hertfordshire, something lit up the sky. There was smoke in the sky afterwards.

- January 2009, time unknown: In the town of Colington in Edinburgh, lights were seen in the sky.

- January 2009, time unknown: In the town of Llandudno in Clwyd, a bright orange light was seen.

- 1 January 2009, time unknown: In the town of Chippenham in Wiltshire, a UFO was seen.

- 1 January 2009, time unknown: In the town of Streatham Hill in London, two bright lights/objects were seen moving through the sky.

- 1 January 2009 at 00:10: In the town of Blairgowrie in Perthshire, four bright orange lights in a group were seen.

- 1 January 2009 at 01:30: Town unknown, county unknown, an object was seen over my house. It was massive. Unbelievable. The noise was incredible. I thought we were under nuclear attack.

- 2 January 2009 at 17:00: In the town of Nuneaton in Warwickshire, five yellow/orange objects in formation were seen. Moving east to west. Slow but straight flight.

- 3–4 January 2009, time unknown: In the town of Sandbach in Cheshire, a UFO was seen. It gave off an orange/yellow light.

- 4 January 2009, time unknown: In the town of Haslingdale/Rossendale in Lancashire, four or more moving, bright, solid orange lights were seen. Followed by a further eight identical objects. They rose vertically over the side of the valley. They made no sound.

- 5 January 2009 at 19:00: In the town of Malvern in Worcestershire, a V shaped formation similar to how birds fly of seven lights. They moved rapidly across the sky, rotated slightly, then the lights split up and vanished. The lights were the size and brightness of stars. They made no noise and left no visible trails in the sky.

- 6 January 2009, time unknown: In the town of Cardigan, in Cardiganshire, five rather big orange things flew over the witness. He was terrified.

- 6 January 2009 at 21:00: In the town of Northampton in Northamptonshire, strange lights. Eleven in total were seen.

- 8 January 2009 at 04:40: In the town of Blackpool in Lancashire, a green light with a white light on the outer rim was seen. It flew over the hills and disappeared once it passed the motorway.

- 9 January 2009, time unknown: In the town of Exeter, Devon, an object in the sky over Exeter was seen.

- 11 January 2009 at 00:10: On the W9 in Greater London, a strange white light got smaller and turned green. Pulsated in brightness.

- 12 January 2009, time unknown: In the town of Old Coulson in Surrey, a witness saw a large shape in the sky. It didn't look like a helicopter but sounded like one and was very loud. It hovered for an hour. Then headed towards Caterham.

- 13 January 2009, time unknown: In the town of Leyton in London, an object that moved quickly through the sky was seen.

- 13 January 2009 at 20:15: In the town of High Wycombe in Buckinghamshire, strange burning objects were seen in the sky.

- 14 January 2009, time unknown: In the town of Leyton in London, an object that moved quickly through the sky was seen.

- 18 January 2009, time unknown: In the town of Leyton in London, an object that moved quickly through the sky was seen.

- 18 January 2009 at 19:44: In the town of Lichfield, Staffordshire, an Air Traffic Control employee saw a bright yellow light. It vanished for a few seconds, then reappeared.

- 19 January 2009, time unknown: In the town of Tarland in Aberdeenshire, a bright steady light was seen in the sky. It then just moved and disappeared.

- 23 January 2009 at 20:40: In the town of Anlaby in Hull, a very large ball (looked like a fireball). The object was small but rather far away.

- 23 January 2009 at 20:58: In the town of Undy in Newport, an object had a large light on the front and a smaller red and green light on either side, as if on the ends of a plane's wings. The base was a perfect square and black in colour. It made a quiet humming sound.

- 23 January 2009 at 21:40: In the town of West Cross in Swansea, a large ball of light was seen. The light did not diminish. Very strange. Made no sound. Very strange.

- 24 January 2009 at 23:05: In the town of Henleaze in Bristol, a large spherical object, bright orange in colour, was seen. It was much bigger than any plane or helicopter. Glowed brightly all over. It was completely soundless.

- 25 January 2009 at 18:00: In the town of Perton in the West Midlands, a star-shaped and very bright, brilliant white object was seen. Changing shape. No noise.

- 25 January 2009 at 19:00: In the town of Livingston in West Lothian, an extremely bright blue circular light was seen. After diving down at a steep angle, rising, then diving again, it vanished.

- 25 January 2009 at 23:25: In the town of Sittingbourne in Kent, a strange ball of bright orange light was seen. Light faded out.

- 26 January 2009 at 17:15: In the town of Northholt in Middlesex, a bright oval orange was seen in the sky. Thought at first it was an aircraft on fire. After five minutes, the bright glow petered out and then became totally black. Lived in the area all her life but had never seen anything like it before.

- 26 January 2009 at 18:15: In the town of Bromley in Kent, three orange lights in horizontal lines above the opposite side of the hill were seen. Stopped car but saw only four lights, two separate at the top and two close together at the bottom. The top two rose and disappeared. The second two moved higher, then also vanished.

- 26 January 2009 at 21:45: In the town of Tarring in West Sussex, four orange lights were seen. At first, mistook them for stars. Faded one by one.

- 28 January 2009 at 22:10: In the town of Grimsby in Lincolnshire, a light was seen in the sky. Other lights falling or dripping from it to the ground. At first, thought it was fireworks. Made no noise and was the size of a helicopter.

- 29 January 2009, time unknown: In the town of Colchester, Essex, we keep getting flown over by aliens galore. They are dropping germs, and we keep getting colds. Please send the RAF or USAF to stop them.

- February 2009, time unknown: In the town of Swadlincote in Derbyshire, 15 fireballs were seen in the sky. Not aircraft.

- February 2009, date unknown: In the town of East Kilbride in Lanarkshire, five orange lights were seen high in the sky over the house. Disappeared into the atmosphere.

- 3 February 2009 at 01:00: Town unknown in the Thames Estuary, same as the UFO seen over the House of Commons in February 2008. Matches description The Sun gave.

- 3 February 2009 at 10:10: In the town of West Row in Suffolk, a bright, clear light shooting across the sky was seen. There were blue lights almost in line with the clear light. They were evenly spaced.

- 4 February 2009 at 18:32: In the town of Chesterton in Newcastle under Lyme, a dullish orange light low was seen in the sky. Circular in shape with no defined edge. Surface had the texture of the Sun's surface but not as bright. It reduced in size as it backed away from the witness. An aircraft flew in its direction whilst giving it a wide berth.

- 5 February 2009, time unknown: In the town of Portslade in Sussex, six red or orange lights in a large oval shape moving slowly towards Brighton were seen. They made no noise.

- 5 February 2009 at 06:30: In the town of Cropwell Bishop in Nottinghamshire, a series of UFO Sightings were reported. Three orange lights arranged vertically in the sky. No way they could be aircraft. Four sets of them.

- 6 February 2009, time unknown: In the town of Rossendale, in Lancashire a blue and purple flashing light over the moors for 30 minutes.

- 6 February 2009 at 17:30: Between Mealrigg and Langrigg, Cumbria, a clearly defined, shiny silvery metallic cylinder with rounded ends was seen. Estimated 50 ft in length. Small protrusion on the upper rear body. The Object made no sound or visible emissions.

- 6 February 2009 at 20:10: Near Edinburgh Airport, Edinburgh, an object was seen that had white on the outer edges. 7–800 ft long. It was moving very fast from North to South.

- 7 February 2009, time unknown: In the town of Gorseinon in Swansea, a strange object was seen when he developed photographs he had taken.

- 7 February 2009 at 19:30: Between Norwich and Lenwade, Norfolk, ten orange orbs were seen. Orbs had slightly pulsating orange lights. Not like navigation lights. Made no noise.

- 7 February 2009 at 20:05: Town unknown, county unknown; six lights, some red, some orange, and some white, all travelling in the same direction, were seen. It was either one big object or six single objects. All travelling in the same direction.

- 7 February 2009 at 23:10: In the town of Basingstoke in Hampshire, a bright orange light travelling very fast from North to southeast was seen. Too large and bright to be a plane. In view for one minute, then disappeared behind a cloud. Noticed no noise or tail.

- 7 February 2009 at 22:05: In the town of Fowey in Cornwall, a strange object was seen in the sky. It was bright orange in colour with the intensity of fire. Like a huge hanglider.

- 8 February 2009 at 20:00: In the town of Ashingdon in Essex, lights were seen in the sky. Definitely not a plane. Very strange.

- 8 February 2009 at 21:00: In the town of Sutton in Surrey, five UFOs were seen. They were bright, round orange lights. They made no noise, and they disappeared in the direction of London.

- 9 February 2009, time unknown: In the town of Romsley in Shropshire, a peculiar bright light was seen. The object was spherically shaped like a satellite. It moved west to east very quickly. It was definitely not a satellite, a helicopter, or a light aircraft.

- 10 February 2009 at 21:00: Town unknown in Somerset, bright orange lights were seen continuously going up and down on the horizon. They were heading East in the direction of Frome or Wiltshire.

- 10 February 2009 at 22:45: In the town of Western-superMare in Somerset, an orange/yellow object was seen moving NW to SE. It was followed by three more objects. It had no navigation lights, and they made no sound. They were not that high up, and they disappeared into the distance quicker than they arrived.

- 13 February 2009 at 23:12: In the town of Bradford-on-Avon in Wiltshire, a brightly glowing orange ball was seen. It seemed to be a controlled craft. It hovered for a couple of minutes, then the light seemed to deliberately fade. It was a few hundred feet up and a quarter of a mile from the house.

- 14 February 2009 at 20:10: In the town of Roxwell in Essex, a bright orange object was seen. The top was rounded like the top of a balloon and was brighter orange towards the bottom. It appeared to be stationary.

- 15 February 2009, time unknown: In the town of Aberford in Leeds, a witness saw a long light flashing like a laser. Sometimes there were two lights crossing over. This is the third time they have been seen in six weeks.

- 15 February 2009 at 00:15: In the town of Winwick, in Warrington, a Police Officer saw two orange lights in the sky that hovered over the old hospital site. The lights were not together but were stationary. They made no noise. They then moved off in a southerly direction.

- 15 February 2009 at 06:30: In the town of Bennech in Anglesey, strange lights were seen over the bay.

- 16 February 2009 at 19:00: In the town of Colchester in Essex, a bright light was seen that went straight up in the sky above the A12 near Colchester.

- 16 February 2009 at 19:19: In the town of Leigh in Greater Manchester, a dome-shaped orange ball of light was seen. It suddenly took off from a field. It was organic, like a jellyfish. Transparent, and you could see its internal workings. It departed, swaying left to right, and made a droning noise. 150–200ft in the air.

- 19 February 2009 at 19:50: In the town of Gravesend, Kent, a ball of light with a few lights inside was seen. It hovered over Gravesend for some 30 minutes. Too static for a helicopter.

- 20 February 2009 at 21:45: In the town of Bradford in West Yorkshire, two strange lights were seen behind the clouds that appeared to be playing with each other, pretending to crash into each other. Then they were joined by a third light that hovered underneath them, going back and forth.

- 21 February 2009 at 22:45: In the town of Arundel in West Sussex, five bright orange lights were seen in the sky. One was in the lead, the other four in a loose rectangular formation. Disappeared behind trees, then were seen in a line with long gaps between them. Heard no engine noise. Headed south for two miles before vanishing.

- 22 February 2009 time unknown: In South East London an object with white and alternating red lights at an angle was seen. It came from South East London towards Canary Wharf. It stopped in mid-air, and an alternating sequence of red lights flashed at 180 degrees. The lights switched sides instantly.

- 22 February 2009 at 01:10: In the town of Chepstow in Gwent, a single object the size of a large car was seen. It was silver, with flames flickering from the underside. It then moved up and away.

- 22 February 2009 at 19:00: In the town of Oxted in Surrey, an object came in trajectory into the back garden. It was like the upper part of an egg, glowing bright orange like hot steel. On the bottom, it had something like a root structure. It looked like it was having some trouble but righted itself and gently flew off.

- 22 February 2009 at 19:30: In the town of Swindon in Wiltshire, 80 bright lights were seen over the top of Queen's Hill in Swindon.

- 22 February 2009 at 19:30: In the town of Bedford in Bedfordshire, a sizable, silent, flickering orange light was seen. Difficult to judge height and speed but much slower than any meteorite and much faster than the prevailing wind, which was negligible.

- 23 February 2009 at 19:17: In the town of New Ash Green in Kent, a ball of light in the clouds, moving slowly and falling apart, was seen. Had other white lights coming off it. Made no sound.

- 23 February 2009 at 22:52: In South East London, there was the flashing of a huge object with one normal and two green lights. It was flying low. Only saw it for four seconds, then it vanished from sight.

- 24 February 2009 at 18:45: In the town of Hartlepool in Cleveland, a witness saw four spaceships that flew over the house into the sky. They had a bright light that faded and was then gone. They returned to the same spot they had come from.

- 25 February 2009 at 18:30: In the town of Oldham in Manchester, a very bright object that glows red and bright was seen.

- 26 February 2009 at 19:15: In the town of Malmesbury in Wiltshire, two lights above the cloud with beams of light coming out from them horizontally were seen. Dotting about like two fireflies. The beams are coming from the lights, not the ground. Seen to the north. The lights are very round and flying in a small area.

- 27 February 2009 at 18:15: In Central London, one white light to the southeast that flashes red, green, and an off yellow at about 8–10000 ft was seen. Another across central London at 10–15000 ft with the same colours was seen. The objects are identical and 3–4 miles apart on the approach path to Heathrow or London City.

- 27 February 2009 at 21:00: In the town of Lelant in Cornwall, two orange lights were seen over Hayle Estuary moving at the speed of a helicopter but had no aircraft navigation lights.

- 27 February 2009 at 23:00: In the town of Newquay in Cornwall, a bright orange object was seen travelling west to east across the sky.

- 28 February 2009 at 04:30: In the town of Portlethen in Aberdeenshire, a big yellow glow was seen in the sky to the south of Aberdeen. About 2500 ft high, but not aircraft landing lights.

- 28 February 2009 at 21:50: In the town of Mary Tavy/Dartmoor in Devon, orange lights were seen in the sky. Like fairy lights. Made no sound.

- 1 March 2009 at 18:45: In the town of Bishopsmill in Morayshire, lights like little stars in a half moon shape were seen. A bright light at the centre was moving very slightly.

- 1 March 2009 at 19:00: In the town of Warlingham in Surrey, three very bright orange lights in triangular formation were seen. They were circular, with no tails. Travelling at speed towards the east. Made no sound. Could not tell height. Visible for 4–5 minutes before fading away one by one.

- 1 March 2009 at 20:15: In the town of West Bridgford in Nottingham, a swarm of about 100 flashing white lights, high in the sky and moving from the NE to SE, were seen. Very quick and keeping equidistant and of equal speed. Disappeared about 45 degrees above the horizon. The swarm moved in an arc of 40 degrees in about 10 seconds.

- 4 March 2009 at 22:50: In the town of Swindon in Wiltshire, various different lights were seen in a star shape.

- 5 March 2009, time unknown: In the town of Selby in North Yorkshire, two sphere-like objects, orange/red in colour, were seen. The first object ran parallel to the witness, dropped, then disappeared. The second object moved straight across the skyline then disappeared.

- 7 March 2009 at 05:00: In the town of Cottingham in Humberside, an object was seen in the sky changing colour.

- 8 March 2009 at 01:30: In the town of Bolton in Lancashire, a large fireball but with an oblong shape was seen. Thought it was a crashing aeroplane, but it stopped and hovered. It then came towards Dascar, stopped, and headed in a SE direction towards Bury. It hovered in the distance for a minute before disappearing.

- 9 March 2009 at 21:15: In the town of Hayes in Middlesex, an object was seen hovering in the sky. The object had bright lights.

- 9 March 2009 at 23:10: In the town of Holland-on-Sea in Essex an emerald green object that was like a torchlight or a large grapefruit was seen. It flitted up, down, and around outside the landing window. The beam of light narrowed, and it came back as a ball shape. It was still for 90 seconds, then vanished.

- 10 March 2009 at 18:15: On the A3 South of M25, a long cylinder of gold light was seen. It looked like a very bright shooting star. Observed it for 3 seconds.

- 10 March 2009 at 18:50: In the town of Barrow-in-Furness in Cumbria, the whole object was glowing like hot metal, and there was no sound. It was travelling at the speed of a fighter or a satellite, from NW to SE. It looked to be flying quite low.

- 10 March 2009 at 22:10: In the town of Spalding in Lincolnshire, strange orange lights were seen in the sky.

- 14 March 2009 at 18:50: In the town of Bugbrooke in Northamptonshire, a big, bright red ball of fire was seen travelling at a terrific speed.

- 14 March 2009 at 20:15: In the town of Flitwick in Bedfordshire, two UFOs were seen. Orange globes that moved in together then separated and very gradually disappeared.

- 14 March 2009 at 20:30: In the town of Harlyn Bay in Cornwall, five strange orange lights were seen in formation, moving very quickly.

- 14 March 2009 at 20:40: In the town of King's Lynn in Norfolk, an object was seen travelling east/southeast. An extremely bright, constant red/orange light shining down. The shape of the object was obscured by the light. It made no sound. Cannot determine speed but was visible for two minutes. May have speeded up.

- 17 March 2009, time unknown: In the town of Croydon in London, a bright orange light the size of a helicopter was seen. It looked like a flame or a flare but made no sound. It was moving very slowly.

- 17 March 2009 at 00:35: Town unknown, county unknown, the shape of a rectangle was seen. It had a dull green glow with no other lights showing.

- 17 March 2009 at 05:35: Portsmouth, Hampshire, MoD Guard Service A wide, pear drop-shaped, translucent green light with a small tail of light. Moved in the NW direction. Made no noise and vanished after a few seconds.

- 17 March 2009 at 20:30: In the town of Heywood in Lancashire, three orange lights, evenly spaced and moving at the same speed, were seen. Gradually, they disappeared after five minutes. Heading from SE to NW.

- 17 March 2009 at 21:02: In the town of Bromsgrove in Worcestershire, a red fireball travelling at extreme speed was seen. It made no sound. Heading from Coventry to Leominster.

- 18 March 2009 at 22:00: In the town of Milton Keynes in Buckinghamshire, two very bright, glowing orange lights were seen moving at very high speed.

- 19 March 2009, time unknown: Town unknown in West Sussex, a constant light was seen travelling West to East. Very erratic, wobbling off course, then just disappeared.

- 20 March 2009 at 18:50: In the town of Exton in Rutland a large bright light was seen to the east of Exton, moving south to north at high speed – at first mistaken for a planet.

- 22 March 2009 at 19:55: In the town of Newtimber in West Sussex, a bright diamond-shaped light was seen. Definitely not an aircraft. Faster than an aircraft. Headed east for one minute before moving upward and disappearing.

- 22 March 2009 at 20:00: In the town of Adfa in Powys, what looked like a satellite crashing or a star was seen. It was fairly pacey and then slowed to a halt. It moved off after 20 seconds and gathered speed. It became a dot and vanished.

- 24 March 2009 at 05:17: In the town of Bridgend in Glamorgan, four UFOs flying beneath two aircraft were seen. They moved much faster than the aircraft. Greyish in colour with a dome on top and bottom. Flew over the Waterton Industrial Estate.

- 25 March 2009 at 20:25: In the town of Godalming in Surrey, a very bright spherical object was seen. Size of a full moon. Yellow/orange in colour. Object seemed wrapped in a bright, glowing cloud of light. It made no noise. It moved towards Hascombe. Performed a series of erratic moves.

- 27 March 2009 at 16:10: In the town of Walthamstow in London, three objects were seen in the sky. They were circling and dipping in and out of the clouds. They could have been light sources or just reflecting light.

A possible tail of light at a slight angle away from the direction of travel on each of the objects.

- 28 March 2009 at 08:45: In the town of Torquay in Devon, a group of very bright orange objects were seen heading NW to SE at a consistent speed and low altitude. There was a group of 15, followed by groups of 2–3 and 3–4 over a five-minute period. They made no noise.

- 29 March 2009 at 20:45: In the town of Preston in Lancashire, three bright lights were seen heading in the same direction some 2 minutes apart. The third light disintegrated and split up.

- 4 April 2009, time unknown: In the town of Swindon, Wiltshire, a massive orange thing was seen. Going so fast, it passed a plane going towards RAF Lyneham.

- 4 April 2009 at 00:30: In the town of Saddleworth in Lancashire, a bright orange ball of fire was seen. It was quite high up in the sky over the house. It was changing colour and disappeared straight into the sky.

- 4 April 2009 at 10:30: In the town of Harrogate in North Yorkshire, it was a square with orange lights.

- 4 April 2009 at 21:02: In the town of Abergavenny in Gwent, two UFOs were seen.

- 4 April 2009 at 23:15: In the town of Leyland in Lancashire, an object was seen for 6–7 minutes.

- 5 April 2009 at 09:00: In the town of Swindon in Wiltshire, something peculiar was seen.

- 6 April 2009, time unknown: In the town of Hessel in Humberside, a very bright white light was seen. Its trail followed it for half an hour, heading towards Brough.

- 8 April 2009, time unknown: In the town of Leeds in West Yorkshire, a ball of fire was seen.

- 8 April 2009 at 01:00: In the town of Brighton in Sussex, what looked like a squashed balloon and had no wings was seen. Rounder at the front and pointed at the back. It had no lights at the front but 2–3 at the back: one red, one red and flashing, and one white/green. Witness heard the noise first, which grew louder.

- 9 April 2009 at 21:26: Town unknown in Liverpool, two parallel lights were seen. Red or orange lights in the sky.

- 11 April 2009 at 21:35: In the town of Ellon in Aberdeenshire, a very bright orange glow was seen. Moved about the speed of an airliner, heading south to north.

- 11 April 2009 at 20:30: In the town of Bromley in Kent, a UFO was seen.

- 11 April 2009 at 21:05: In the town of Harrow in London, a big ball of fire, like a star, was seen. It decreased in size over the next two minutes.

- 11 April 2009 at 21:20: In the town of Chesterfield in Derbyshire, several orange lights, the same colour and brightness of street lights, were seen. Three were close together, and the others were in a horizontal line.

- 11 April 2009 at 21:40: In the town of Goole in Humberside, a light was seen. It moved past very slowly, then shot off at phenomenal speed. It was round, but twice it changed into a cone shape. 300–400 ft up.

- 12 April 2009, time unknown: In the town of Swindon in Wiltshire, four glowing objects came from the southwest and then turned north. They were glowing duller and brighter, then disappeared.

- 12 April 2009 at 23:10: In the town of Linlithgow in West Lothian, a UFO was seen.

- 13 April 2009, time unknown: In the town of Farnborough in Hampshire, a ball of glowing red light was seen. After 30 seconds, the light dimmed slightly and then just disappeared.

- 13 April 2009 at 21:00: In the town of Moelfre in Angelsey, what looked like a Chinese lantern was seen.

- 13 April 2009 at 21:30: In the town of Derby in Derbyshire, two orange lights in the sky moving towards each other were seen. Then a ball of light approached the other lights. All three were stationary for a while before disappearing into the distance. Another light then hovered where the others had been.

- 14 April 2009 at 21:45: In the town of Strathspey in Invernesshire, a bright orange light approached at low level and then remained stationary for 10 minutes. Then it turned red.

- 14 April 2009 at 22:00: In the town of Smalley in Derbyshire, a round yellow ball was seen. It looked like it had a parachute on top, in the shape of a helmet.

- 14 April 2009 at 22:45: In the town of Wallington in Surrey, nine green lights were seen in the sky.

- 15 April 2009 at 20:30: In the town of Dover in Kent, two objects, five minutes apart, heading east to west were seen. They looked like orange fiery balls but made no sound. They travelled at the speed of a plane. They had no tail.

- 18 April 2009 at 22:22: In the town of Brandon in Suffolk, two yellow objects like giant sparklers heading North to South were seen.

- 18 April 2009, time unknown: In the town of Oswestry in Shropshire, a UFO was seen.

- 19 April 2009 at 10:00: In the town of Maghull in Merseyside, an orange ball was seen in the sky, travelling very quickly, then stopped and faded away.

- 19 April 2009 at 20:40: In the town of Snodlands in Kent, an oval shaped glowing red object in two dimensions was seen. It spun in one direction, then reversed and swung in the other.

- 19 April 2009 at 21:23: Town unknown in Liverpool, a UFO Southwest of Liverpool was seen.

- 21 April 2009 at 21:34: In the town of Maidstone in Kent, lights rising from the ground into the sky, much like debris from a fire, were seen. However, lights were too intense to be a fire. Seen in the direction of the North Downs from Maidstone.

- 21 April 2009 at 22:03: In the town of Pendleton in Manchester, a bright orange object was seen moving at a steady pace.

- 21 April 2009 at 22:55: In the town of Brighton in Sussex, a bright flaming object about a quarter the size of the moon was seen. It was like a special effect. It was silent and went from horizon to horizon, starting in the North.

- 22 April 2009 at 15:10: In the town of Basingstoke in Hampshire, a large black parachute with nothing suspended from it was seen. It changed shape and gradually got smaller as it went into the distance. Observed for 10–20 minutes.

- 24 April 2009 at 01:22: In the town of Harrow in London, a long shaped vehicle with a red light at the front and two gold lights either side was seen. It hovered above the house and then moved off to the right at tremendous speed before returning. It then drifted slowly away. It was louder than a plane or helicopter.

- 25 April 2009 at 10:15: In the town of Croydon in London, a bright red light was seen over the house.

- 25 April 2009 at 20:30: In the town of Bury St Edmunds in Suffolk, a former Air Traffic Controller saw a large black ball with a light underneath. Travelling South over western Bury St Edmunds at 3000ft at 200 miles an hour.

- 26 April 2009, time unknown: In the town of Holmefirth/Huddersfield in West Yorkshire, a black spherical object 12m in diameter was seen. It was 500ft up and travelling at 500 mph. It made no sound. It had a light on but switched it off when the witness shone a torch at it.

- 26 April 2009 at 00:50: In the town of Hackney in London, two bright lights heading towards the city were seen. Like a white octopus-shaped kite. It was like they were propelled, but travelling on their own.

- 26 April 2009 at 18:15: In Regents Park in London, a spherical object with a red flashing light underneath was seen. It was stationary in the sky for 10 minutes and then just faded away. It had made no movement at all.

- 26 April 2009 at 18:30: In Central London, a single small white orb, shortly joined by two others, was seen. Changed into a dull, flat, circular shape. They were hovering over Central London at 15–20,000 ft but not being blown by the wind. Objects disappeared, but one reappeared for five minutes.

- 26 April 2009 at 22:05: In the town of Grimsby in Lincolnshire, what looked like a star or satellite was seen. The witness saw three within 20 minutes. Came from the south. Its speed increased and then slowed down. Finally headed east over the North Sea.

- 28 April 2009, time unknown: In the town of Tywyn in Gwynedd, a big, bright orange light was seen. It turned white and then disappeared very quickly. It made no noise.

- 28 April 2009 at 21:48: In the town of Ferrers in Essex, a sighting occurred.

- 29 April 2009 at 23:10: In the town of Nottingham in Nottinghamshire, two orange lights flying in a parallel formation in an arc were seen. One slowed and went behind the other, then they both gradually faded away. Far too fast to be an aircraft. They had no flashing lights and made no sound.

- 29 April 2009 at 23:44: In the town of Caterham in Surrey, a very small white light with no flashing lights or smoke trail was seen. Headed north, then did a sharp turn to the east, and then was just gone.

- 30 April 2009 at 20:30: In the town of Sutton in Surrey, a bright green light whizzed about the sky for an hour. It was very fast, and a few planes got in its way.

- 2 May 2009 at 21:36: In the town of Chorley in Lancashire, the witness saw orange lights that looked like flames. They were heading South to North towards Preston. Police said it was the open rear of an aircraft undertaking parachute training.

- 2 May 2009 at 21:50: In Upper Norwood, London, six very bright orange lights were seen flying in formation and passed by in 15 minutes. Heading from Upper Norwood towards Crystal Palace.

- 2 May 2009 at 22:00: In the town of Burbage in Wiltshire, initially one, then five pitch-black hot air balloon-shaped objects with continual flames underneath were seen.

- 2 May 2009 at 23:00: In the town of Long Eaton in Nottinghamshire, a large, bright yellow object was seen hovering in the sky. Too bright to be an aircraft and the wrong colour. It didn't move for ages and then disappeared in the blink of an eye.

- 2 May 2009 at 23:30: In the town of Buckhurst Hill in Essex, a slow moving, silent, orangey/red light was seen. The witness does not think it was a helicopter or aircraft. Flew at the same height as a helicopter.

- 2 May 2009 at 23:55: In the town of Southampton in Hampshire, six bright white and orange lights, two single and two in two-object formations, were seen. Lower and faster than a satellite. The witness contacted local police, who had no other reports.

- 3 May 2009, time unknown: In the town of Darlington in County Durham, two bright orangey/red lights were seen moving towards Durham/Tees Valley Airport. The objects flew steady, level, and straight.

- 3 May 2009 at 15:50: In the town of Otmoor in Oxfordshire, a Pilot saw a shiny black flying cylinder, 20–30 ft long at about 4700 ft, which was 200 ft above the pilot's aircraft. Although the pilot sighted the object. Air Traffic Control forwarded the details to the UFO Desk.

- 3 May 2009 at 21:30: In the town of Ammanford in Dyfed, a Pilot saw seven orange orbs that suddenly disappeared. They were on a North-South trajectory. The witness contacted Cardiff Air Traffic Control, who had nothing on radar.

- 4 May 2009 at 00:20: In the town of Barton near the A6 in Lancashire, nine bright orange lights were seen moving at slow speed and at 2000ft. They made no sound.

- 5 May 2009 at 22:10: In the town of Roade in Northampton, an orange flash and a loud bang were witnessed.

- 7 May 2009 at 22:25: In the town of High Peak in Derbyshire, three bright small lights very close together travelling in a straight line were seen. They were flashing rapidly but made no noise and looked like they were on fire but clearly were not. Speed of 100–150 mph at 1000 ft. Came back eight minutes later.

- 9 May 2009 at 17:55: In the town of St Helens in Merseyside, a UFO was seen over the witness's house. It was at 30,000ft and he had seen it before.

- 9 May 2009 at 22:00: In the town of Harlow in Essex, a diamond shaped orange light was seen. If you held out your hand, it would have been the size of a 20p coin. It was totally silent. The object carried on in the distance, and then another one appeared and followed the same path.

- 9 May 2009 at 22:10: In the town of Northwich in Cheshire, four big lights in a line formation were seen. Two dropped down, and the other two moved off quickly into the distance.

- 9 May 2009 at 22:50: In Central London, twenty orange balls were seen heading north.

- 11 May 2009, time unknown: In the town of Tomintoul in Banffshire, what looked like a star but was jumping all over the sky was seen. It was 70 degrees above the horizon. It was a blue/white colour and occasionally red and left a light trail.

- 11 May 2009 at 21:38: In the town of Southampton, Hampshire, a very bright light was seen. It made no sound but was very low.

- 14 May 2009 at 22:00: In the town of Nenthead in Cumbria, a bright orange light was seen. Too bright for a Chinese lantern. The light looked electrical, not a flame. Travelled in a straight line at a steady speed. Travelled east to west with the wind. Made no noise. It was about the size of a quarter moon.

- 16 May 2009, time unknown: In the town of Brandon in Suffolk, four flaming balloons that disappeared over the horizon fairly quickly were seen. Was not very high.

- 16 May 2009 at 00:20: In the town of Bedford in Bedfordshire, a strange blue light near the Cardington Hangers was seen. Flew straight past the witness.

- 16 May 2009 at 21:50: In the town of Petts Wood in Kent, 8–10 bright red lights were seen. They were hovering. They moved independently into the distance and disappeared when a light aircraft appeared.

- 16 May 2009 at 22:00: In the town of Deeside in Flintshire, seven bright orange lights were seen in the sky. Silent. Travelling towards the Wirral.

- 19 May 2009 at 10:00: In the town of Redruth in Cornwall, a big, bright light was seen. Came from west Cornwall towards Plymouth.

- 19 May 2009 at 21:30: In the town of Bexhill-on-Sea in East Sussex, a series of orange balls of fire were seen.

- 19 May 2009 at 22:15: In the town of Long Eaton in Nottingham, an ellipse-shaped object the size of a commercial plane was seen. It was on fire. It glowed bright orange. It moved from south east to north, and then returned and hovered for at least a minute. Moved further away at supersonic speed.

- 21 May 2009, time unknown: Town unknown, county unknown, a very bright blue light flew behind the house.

- 21 May 2009 at 23:40: In the town of King's Lynn in Norfolk, very strange circular objects without a definite shape were seen. They stayed around for about five minutes. There were 8–9 of them.

- 23 May 2009 at 22:00: In the town of Penzance in Cornwall, ten orange lights in a line with intermittent gaps were seen. They made no sound and flew at helicopter height.

- 23 May 2009 at 22:10: In the town of Dudley in the West Midlands, a big, bright light was seen. Thought it was a helicopter at first. Within seconds, followed by three others, and then a further three. Flew low but made no sound.

- 23 May 2009 at 22:10: In the town of Bodium in East Sussex, a strange sighting occurred.

- 23 May 2009 at 23:00: In the town of Hove in East Sussex, a very big red light was seen moving slowly. It then faded away.

- 23 May 2009 at 23:00: In the town of Winsford in Cheshire, an orange light travelling from the south was seen. It was followed by two more orange lights on the same path, then five more, and then two more. They made no noise but were at the height of a helicopter.

- 24 May 2009 at 00:00: In the town of Llandaff City in Cardiff, seven bright red lights were seen.

- 24 May 2009 at 13:42: In the town of Wakefield in West Yorkshire, a white object with a silver beam coming from it over Pugneys Country Park was seen. It looked square but changed shape as it moved about. The witness saw it through binoculars. An aircraft flew very close to it.

- 24 May 2009 at 22:15: In the town of Solihull in the West Midlands, three objects like fireballs falling to earth were seen. They were glowing and orange. There was one large object and two smaller ones, which converged together and rose into the atmosphere until they faded away.

- 25 May 2009 at 12:00: In the town of Swansea in West Glamorgan, three small yellow orbs were seen travelling quite slowly.

- 25 May 2009 at 23:00: In the town of Bracknell in Berkshire, a UFO was seen. It was a "glowing ball of something or other". Definitely not a plane.

- 30 May 2009, time unknown: In the town of Spilsby in Lincolnshire, a sighting was reported.

- 30 May 2009 at 02:47: In the town of Folkestone in Kent, a bright circular amber light the size of a 2p coin was seen. It was moving very slowly in a straight line, but once it flew over the witness's house, it accelerated away very very quickly into the distance. It made no noise and left no vapour trail.

- 30 May 2009 at 22:30: Tunstall to Butley Road in Suffolk, two clusters of bright lights were seen. They were stationary for a while, then the first group of 15 headed towards Woodbridge, followed by the second cluster of 6–7 lights. They were very high up. They made no sound.

- 30 May 2009 at 23:30: In the town of Ballynahinch in County Down, three distinct sets of green, orange, and white lights were seen. Don't match any constellation and are in the wrong place. Static to the eye, but with binoculars are moving at speed and at random.

- 31 May 2009 at 00:30: In the town of Chapel-en-le-Frith in Derbyshire, the witness was watching shooting stars when the witness saw two bright, luminous orange objects like birds or swans. The witness does not think they were birds, as they moved too fast.

- June 2009 at 22:00: In the town of Eltham in London, a black shaped square object was seen.

- June 2009, time unknown: In the town of Baswich in Stafford, two objects were seen. Photograph taken in June, a week after the mystery hot air balloon search.

- June 2009 at 16:00: In the town of Rowley Regis in the West Midlands, a witness saw a long greyish tube in the sky, when driving home along the A4031.

- 2 June 2009 at 22:50: In the town of Chesterfield in Derbyshire, a sighting was reported.

- 6 June 2009, time unknown: In the town of Lewes in East Sussex, eleven bright star-like objects were seen heading northeast.

- 7 June 2009 at 00:15: In the town of Ripon in North Yorkshire, an Air Traffic Controller saw bright orange lights. A single light, followed by a group of three, and then another single light. On a northeast to southwest track.

- 9 June 2009, time unknown: In the town of Bradford in West Yorkshire, different coloured pulsating lights were seen. The Police checked with Air Traffic Control, who said they had nothing. Police suspect Chinese lanterns.

- 12 June 2009 at 23:10: In the town of Shoreham in Kent, initially two UFOs increased to six were seen. Bright orange. The last four were bigger and brighter than the first two.

- 13 June 2009, time unknown: In the town of Porthcawl in Mid Glamorgan, a very bright orange circular shape was seen. Got smaller as it moved away. Moving from southwest to south.

- 14 June 2009, time unknown: In the town of Cardiff in South Glamorgon, a UFO was seen.

- 14 June 2009 at 19:30: In the town of Wroughton in Wiltshire, black disc-shaped objects were seen hovering over crop circles near Barbury Castle. They cast shadows on the ground.

- 18 June 2009 at 23:20: In the town of Stevenage in Hertfordshire, two huge lights chasing each other like cat and mouse were seen. It was a broken cloud, and the lights would never leave the clouds, just go to the edge. It looked like a strong light was coming from above the clouds. They both shot off to the North.

- 20 June 2009, time unknown: In the town of Angmering in West Sussex, a large orange glowing ball was seen in the sky. It was stationary and not very high up.

- 20 June 2009, time unknown: In the town of Abingdon in Oxfordshire, a UFO was seen.

- 20 June 2009 at 22:00: In the town of Chelmsford in Essex, two objects the size of light aircraft but perfectly spherical and glowing bright orange were seen. They were solid and made no sound. They headed NW to SE.

- 20 June 2009 at 22:45: Town unknown in Norfolk, 11–12 objects were seen in the sky. The witness thinks they may be Chinese lanterns.

- 20 June 2009 at 23:30: In the town of Angmering in West Sussex, ten orange lights moving at a sedate pace from west to east were seen. Went from horizon to horizon in two minutes.

- 21 June 2009 at 21:45: On the A3, 50–100 objects were seen moving together in the same direction. They were helicopter-sized but made no noise.

- 23 June 2009 at 19:06: In the town of Hull in Humberside, a light at about 1000 ft was seen. It split in two and flew away.

- 23 June 2009 at 19:09: In the town of Rotherham in South Yorkshire, a circular object, metallic in colour, was seen. It was following a plane. It shot downward several times and then back up again to the same level as the plane.

- 24 June 2009 at 22:05: In Swansea Bay, West Glamorgan, a bright circle of fire was seen travelling southwesterly. It was only a few hundred feet up, moving silently across the sky at 30mph, and then, after four minutes, vanished.

- 25 June 2009 at 01:00: In the town of Minehead in Somerset, what looked like a highly lit aeroplane with wings was seen. It was heading NNW to SSE. It was visible for 20 seconds, then changed direction quickly and dropped out of the sky or disappeared.

- 25 June 2009 at 16:22: In the town of Milnathort in Fife, a witness was watching two helicopters (one a Chinook) coming from the Edinburgh area when she saw an orb-shaped object through her binoculars glistening in the sun. The orb was quite high above the helicopters.

- 25 June 2009 at 23:00: In the town of Bridport in Dorset, three orange lights south of Bridport were seen from the east. They were the size of a two-thirds moon. They moved away to the West, rapidly diminishing.

- 26 June 2009: British singer Kim Wilde reported having seen a "huge bright light behind a cloud" above her Hertfordshire garden. She described the light as "brighter than the moon but similar to the light from the moon". Upon further inspection, Wilde reported to have witnessed the light moving very quickly, from about 11:00 to 1:00. Then it just did that, back and forth for several minutes. Whenever it moved, something shifted in the air, but it was absolutely silent. A second report of this UFO was subsequently made by a fellow local Hertfordshire resident who had managed to obtain photographic evidence to support the apparent sighting.

- 26 June 2009 at 22:20: In the town of Chesterfield in Derbyshire, twelve bright lights were seen in the sky. Moving slowly.

- 26 June 2009 at 22:25: In the town of Rotherham in South Yorkshire, an object approached from the direction of Doncaster. It was a bright orange ball in the sky. It kept a level flight path, then stopped. It then zigzagged a few times before shooting off at tremendous speed, vanishing in a few seconds.

- 26 June 2009 at 22:35: In the town of Moreton-in-Marsh in Gloucestershire, six round brilliant objects in pairs, apart from the last two, which were in line, were seen. Travelling from south to east.

- 26 June 2009 at 22:45: In the town of Welwyn Garden City in Hertfordshire, a UFO was seen.

- 27 June 2009 at 22:45: In the town of Swindon in Wiltshire, an orange light/lights travelled in formation like a mis-shaped diamond. There were 12–13 of them. They travelled from left to right.

- 27 June 2009, time unknown: In the town of Hope Valley in Derbyshire, red objects were seen moving slowly. They were not high and were silent. Might have been going over Bakewell.

- 27 June 2009 at 00:05: In the town of Bow in London, nine objects like golden globes were seen. They hovered for a bit and were joined by three others before shooting off.

- 27 June 2009 at 22:30: In the town of Looe in Cornwall, two orange balls of light were seen travelling North in parallel to each other. Then a further ball of light was seen, heading North. The lights made no noise. They faded and then disappeared.

- 27 June 2009 at 22:45: In the town of Redruth in Cornwall, two brown objects, like balls of fire, were seen. Appeared to be in convoy heading towards Portreath.

- 27 June 2009 at 23:20: In the town of Stafford, Staffordshire, four UFOs were seen flying North. They were silent. A plane was flying in the opposite direction.

- 27 June 2009 at 23:59: In the town of Pulborough in West Sussex, up to 20 orange and red glowing lights were seen. They appeared to be in formation and under some form of control. They came from the Eastern horizon. They moved upwards, were then stationary, moved side to side, and then disappeared upwards. Seen for 20 minutes.

- 30 June 2009 at 02:41: In the town of Hayes in Middlesex, a roundish glowing shape was seen. Flying at a steady speed with no noise. It was a clear night. Filmed it, but the camera died.

- July 2009 time unknown: In the town of Sheffield in South Yorkshire something strange was seen and reported.

- 1 July 2009 at 18:45: In the town of Swansea in West Glamorgan, what seemed like a rather large disc or round in appearance was seen. It was dark in colour but bounced sunlight off its surface. It was floating or bobbing up and down. Other aircraft were at the same altitude and could be heard, but the object made no noise.

- 2 July 2009 at 00:30: In Queens Park in London, two UFOs were seen.

- 2 July 2009 at 16:00: In the town of Harlow in Essex, several sightings were seen. A bright orb that travelled in a straight line. As a helicopter approached it, the orb slowed down and vanished. The helicopter reacted as if the pilot was startled. Saw several other orbs, but the main one was half the size.

- 2 July 2009 at 22:20: In the town of Blackwood in Gwent, an Ex-test engineer for Hawker Siddley saw a bright orange light seen through the tree line. It turned and cleared the tree line. The other side of the object appeared to be a large rectangle shape of fire red/orange. It was silent. The object slowly climbed in the direction of Gloucester.

- 3 July 2009 at 11:15: In the town of Cawood in Yorkshire, two very bright orange lights that appeared to get closer to the car then just hung in the sky were seen. Five minutes later, a second bright orange light with a red glow seen then disappeared. A third light then hung in the sky and disappeared after five minutes.

- 3 July 2009 at 22:45: In the town of Sheffield in South Yorkshire, six bright orange/red lights in formation were seen. They climbed like balloons and made no sound. A sphere like a balloon appeared at the side, and then another.

- 4 July 2009 at 22:30: In the town of Bideford-on-Avon in Warwickshire, a round orange light was seen.

- 4 July 2009 at 23:00: In the town of Teignmouth in Devon, a bright yellowy-orange object travelling SE to NW in a straight line was seen. It made no noise. At a 50-degree angle of elevation.

- 4 July 2009 at 23:30: In the town of Lichfield in Staffordshire, eight alien aircraft were seen just above helicopter height travelling SW to NE. There was a humming sound. They looked like they were "eyeing the place up".

- 4 July 2009, time unknown: In West Grinstead, West Sussex, a Part-Time Pilot saw 12–15 objects. Not like normal fixed-wing aircraft, more like bright orange lights. Moving West at an indeterminate height. Objects entered the cloud and then turned around.

- 4 July 2009 at 00:15: In the town of Brighton in Sussex, a red light followed by seven others was seen. They came from the West, flew overhead, and disappeared. Definitely not aircraft.

- 4 July 2009 at 23:30: In the town of Marston Green in Birmingham, some 30 orange lights heading from Birmingham Airport towards Coleshill were seen.

- 5 July 2009, time unknown: Town unknown county unknown, three very bright orange lights were seen. Fairly large and moving much faster than an aircraft. They disappeared. Then two lights appeared from the South. The lights appeared coordinated. They were not aircraft.

- 5 July 2009 at 01:35: In the town of Stratford-upon-Avon in Warwickshire, a dormant blue light which changed colour many times over the hour it was witnessed was seen. At first, it was moving steadily, and then it stopped in midair. Then started moving from left to right. A white beam could be seen shining down from it. It had red lights.

- 5 July 2009 at 02:00: In the town of Peterborough in Cambridgeshire, two objects, one with a brighter light, were seen. The second one was behind it and had a dimmer light. No navigation lights. Not normal. Reluctant to say it was a UFO – perhaps it is a plane.

- 5 July 2009 at 14:32: In the town of Bedford, Bedfordshire, a UFO was seen. A witness photographed it.

- 7 July 2009 at 22:25: In the town of Pagham in West Sussex, five orange bright lights were seen. Half a mile distance between each one. Took photos.

- 10 July 2009 at 00:20: In the town of Northampton in Northamptonshire, fast, shiny discs were seen. Lower and faster than a plane, not a plane or helicopter. Sphere, brilliant light.

- 10 July 2009 at 00:30: In the town of Glasgow in Strathclyde, two sightings were reported. First at 12:30 (bright light), second at 01:30 (flashing green).

- 10 July 2009 at 12:15: In the town of Finaghy in Belfast, a witness observed fifty golden balls moving slowly SSE.

- 11 July 2009 at 20:00: In the town of Palmers Green in London, the witness was having a BBQ with some friends when saw an orange fireball about to crash two gardens away, but on checking, it was now high in the sky about half a mile away. 3–5 minutes later, another object appeared, then a third spherical object with a leg protruding.

- 12 July 2009, time unknown: In the town of Oswestry in Shropshire, a UFO was seen.

- 12 July 2009 at 01:07: In the town of Perivale in Middlesex, a ball of light was seen. No noise. A bright light, rising behind a fence, went up into the sky.

- 12 July 2009 at 01:39: In the town of Stoke on Trent in Staffordshire, a huge red light was seen moving through the sky.

- 12 July 2009 at 10:30: In the town of London in Greater London, a UFO was seen.

- 12 July 2009 at 23:16: In the town of Shrewsbury in Shropshire, no description provided by the witness.

- 13 July 2009 at 23:01: In the town of Worthing in West Sussex, a large bright silver/white ball/sphere was seen. Moving slowly from W to E. The object was much bigger and brighter than an aircraft. It appeared to stop still several times as it went into the distance. The light did not dim as it moved further away.

- 14 July 2009 at 00:20: On the W1 in London, a very bright, very big object was seen. It was not a satellite, not a plane, stationary. Light disappeared.

- 14 July 2009 at 01:00: In the town of Taunton in Somerset, a bright star went from bright yellow to bright red. Did not look like a shooting star or plane. Moved no more than 2–3 feet.

- 14 July 2009 at 23:39: In the town of Woking in Surrey, a UFO was seen.

- 15 July 2009 at 22:40: Town unknown, county unknown, a round white object was seen. Not like a ball. Very bright, but not casting a beam of light. It was rising vertically. The higher it went, the smaller it became. It started at the size of a pound coin and ended as a pinhead. The witness observed the object for two minutes.

- 15 July 2009 at 23:30: In the town of Trimley St Mary in Suffolk, a very bright white light like a star was seen. It moved south, then double-backed on itself and was joined by another light. The lights danced around each other, then split and moved off in different directions. The light suddenly disappeared.

- 16 July 2009 at 00:15: In the town of Weston Super Mare in Somerset, a UFO was seen.

- 17 July 2009 at 22:00: In the town of Westonbirt in Gloucestershire, a ball of light the size of a small car, 26 metres above the ground, was seen. It pulsated every 5–8 seconds but then shot off. Definitely not an aircraft or a Chinese Lantern.

- 18 July 2009 at 01:50: In the town of Cheshunt in Herts, a bright orange light, which hovered in one place, was seen. It became more pink than red, and then it disappeared.

- 18 July 2009 at 02:35: In the town of Weston Super Mare in Somerset, a metallic aircraft shaped like a missile was seen. One quarter was white, another green/blue, and another red. Was circling. It had no wings and was moving diagonally. It made a sound like a motorbike.

- 18 July 2009 at 09:45: Town unknown in Lincolnshire, the witness saw an object like a ball of fire.

- 18 July 2009 at 22:00: In the town of Rotherham in Yorkshire, the witness has a video of a UFO on his mobile phone.

- 18 July 2009 at 22:23: In the town of Littleborough in Lancashire, the witness has a pilot's licence and saw an orb-like object at 120 degrees from the north. Orange in colour, moving in a NE direction. Visible for 10 minutes. It had no aircraft type navigation lights.

- 18 July 2009 at 22:30: In the town of Ruislip in Middlesex, three bright orange lights, not flashing, were seen. Very big, high up, set equally apart. Reported it to RAF Northolt. Never saw anything like this before.

- 18 July 2009 at 22:35: In the town of River Severn in Gloucestershire, a UFO of orangey/red colour was seen. It hovered and moved slightly in the direction of Stroud, then suddenly dropped downward.

- 19 July 2009, time unknown: In the town of London in Greater London, 10–15 circular objects were seen.

- 19 July 2009 at 01:22: In the town of Newport in Gwent, a bright, reddish light travelling W to E, below cloud level, was seen. It made no sound. It was moving in a straight line but too slow to be a meteorite. It had no navigation-type lights.

- 19 July 2009 at 09:01: Town unknown, county unknown, 10–12 bright orange objects that were silent were seen. Has a photo of them saved on his mobile?

- 19 July 2009 at 14:58: In the town of Leigh in Lancashire, a UFO was seen.

- 19 July 2009 at 22:30: In the town of Sheffield, Yorkshire, six yellow lights were seen stationary at first, then moved off.

- 19 July 2009 at 22:55: In the town of Nottingham in Nottinghamshire, an ex-police officer saw four-five orange lights, fluctuating lights. Lights under the flight path of Donnington Airfield. Objects moved in a line. Lights faded. Returned 10 minutes later.

- 19 July 2009 at 23:00: Town unknown in Cornwall: Video footage in Cornwall near an Air Station (possibly Culdrose) was taken. Five-minute sighting.

- 23 July 2009 at 12:48: In the town of Hitchin in Hertfordshire, a large round object was seen. Two planes flew around it. Could be something natural, such as an eclipse.

- 24 July 2009, time unknown: In the town of Ashburton in Devon, a light was seen in the sky. Also above this was a large round shape which looked rocky and was blue and pink in colour.

- 24 July 2009 at 10:03: In the town of Newmarket in Suffolk, 15 to 20 orange and red lights looked as though they were coming down to land but then went overhead and 'went out'.

- 24 July 2009 at 11:00: In the town of Edinburgh, Scotland, a witness saw through the clouds flashing pale blue lights of odd shapes but mostly circles. Movement continued for 25 minutes. A small red light was on the outside parameter of blue lights, which disappeared/amalgamated into one large blue light, which speedily disappeared.

- 24 July 2009 at 23:20: In the town of Barking in Essex, a bright, oval shaped object with red and green lights was seen. No noise.

- 24 July 2009 at 23:57: In the town of Bradford in Yorkshire, a large balloon shape with 'shimmer fire' effect underneath it was seen.

- 25 July 2009, time unknown: In the town of Downham Market in Norfolk, a UFO was seen with another one circling it. There was one main light and no sound.

- 25 July 2009 at 09:57: In the town of Kettering in Northamptonshire, a big and very bright red/yellow/orange ball was seen flying past the backend of the garden, just under cloud cover. Then went through cloud cover and lit cloud cover up.

- 25 July 2009 at 10:22: In the town of Twyford in Berkshire, an orange light with 'some sort of flame' in the sky was seen. Moved from the driveway to over the front of the house. Then changed direction towards Wallgrave, direction changed again towards reading then back in the direction of Wallgrave.

- 25 July 2009 at 10:45: In the town of Bury St Edmunds in Suffolk, fifteen red/orangey lights were seen in the sky, which gradually started fading out and then disappearing.

- 25 July 2009 at 10:45: In the town of Henley on Thames in Oxfordshire, six orange lights with fire around them were seen. The UFOs were in formation (One behind the other across horizon to horizon).

- 25 July 2009 at 11:00: In the town of Plymouth in Devon, a Professional Photographer saw six orange/white lights lying astern. Thought they were aircraft navigation lights but were evenly spaced out. No noise but moved with the speed of a passing helicopter. Changed into a 'hammer head' shape.

- 25 July 2009 at 11:00: In the town of Dumfries in Scotland, six or seven bright lights which were seen in the sky for approximately 10 minutes. They were spaced out, and one by one, flew away and disappeared very quickly.

- 25 July 2009 at 11:25: In the town of Goring by Sea in West Sussex, three orange lights were seen high in the sky over the sea. There was an explosion, and the centre light then dropped into the sea. No sound heard from the lights.

- 25 July 2009 at 11:30: In the town of Doncaster in Yorkshire, seven bright orange lights were seen in a straight line. Only two lights were in view at any time. As the last two came, a white moonball flew over at double the speed of the orange lights. Thirty minutes later, six white balls in a triangle formation were seen.

- 25 July 2009 at 12:10: In the town of Newquay in Cornwall, a triangular-shaped object was seen.

- 25 July 2009 at 22:30: In the town of Coningsby in Lincolnshire, three huge orange lights were seen. First and second objects moving at the speed of an aircraft. Third object moves much faster, as if trying to catch up.

- 25 July 2009 at 22:45: In the town of Barnsley in South Yorkshire, two bright orange lights, three to four minutes apart, and no sound heard, were seen. The lights then went into the clouds.

- 25 July 2009 at 23:39: In the town of Rochdale in Lancashire, five really bright orange flame ball-type objects were seen flying across the sky, moving irregularly. One moving faster than a plane, and one zig-zagged down towards the ground, then reappeared after the other four had moved across the sky and had gone.

- 26 July 2009 at 00:20: In the town of Hoddesdon in Hertfordshire, the witness first saw three orange objects. Forty minutes later, looking north, saw an orange-glowing object travelling slowly from SW to NE. It was at an angle to the ground of about 30–40 deg.

- 26 July 2009 at 21:30: In the town of Brighton in East Sussex, a bright orange light was seen travelling in a straight line from Brighton Centre. Which then passed over the house.

- 28 July 2009 at 09:30: In the town of Bromley in Kent, a witness saw an orange, yellow object in the sky with a shape similar to a hot air balloon.

- 31 July 2009, time unknown: Town unknown in Jersey, an Air Traffic Control saw a UFO.

- 31 July 2009, time unknown: In the town of Peterborough in Cambridgeshire, three bright orange lights and one dimmer one were seen. Faded after being static.

- 31 July 2009 at 00:50: Town unknown, county unknown, a witness saw a UFO.

- 31 July 2009 at 21:30: In the town of Bedford, Bedfordshire, the witness said they went to get the cat off the wall and then saw a UFO higher than eye level. It was a bright orange object, not plane-shaped, no engine noise.

- 1 August 2009 at 00:00: In the town of Chigwell in Essex, just reported a sighting. No other details.

- 1 August 2009 at 03:42: In the town of Preston in Lancashire, a Police officer saw a bright object in the sky, very large.

- 1 August 2009 at 10:00: In the town of Croydon in Greater London, 60–70 lights were seen suddenly disappearing.

- 1 August 2009 at 10:30: In the town of New Mills/High Peak in Derbyshire, nine bright orange circular shapes gliding across the sky were seen. The sighting lasted a couple of minutes.

- 1 August 2009 at 12:13: In the town of Upminster, Essex, clusters of UFOs were seen with orange lights in the distance. Zoomed off when they got closer, big and round.

- 1 August 2009 at 21:58: In the town of South Glenrothes in Fife, a large orange ball of flame was seen. Lasted 20 seconds.

- 1 August 2009 at 22:30: In the town of Elgin in Moray, lights were seen moving slowly. One light leads a group of five, with one light acting as tail-ender.

- 1 August 2009 at 22:57: In the town of Michell in Coldon, a Police officer saw 17 UFOs above the village. Red and green lights, no sound.

- 1 August 2009 at 23:20: In the town of York in Yorkshire, orange lights were seen in the sky.

- 2 August 2009, time unknown: Town unknown in Nottinghamshire, what looked like an aeroplane on fire was seen.

- 2 August 2009, time unknown: Town unknown county unknown, a scary sighting was reported.

- 2 August 2009 at 00:22: In the town of Shirley in Croydon, an orange point of light was seen in the sky. No haze or smoke visible around the object. The object was flickering slightly. Lasted about 60 secs.

- 2 August 2009 at 04:00: In the town of Preston in Lancashire, a bright light was seen.

- 2 August 2009 at 14:00: In the town of Hauxton in Cambridgeshire, a retired merchant seaman saw glider-like objects in the sky. Flying around in an anti-clockwise direction.

- 2 August 2009 at 21:30: Town unknown, county unknown, a red object that looked like a cloud was seen. It went over the roof and vanished. No noise/engine. Big orange colour, lower than a plane. Gliding straight.

- 2 August 2009 at 21:45: In the town of Aylesford in Kent, a large orange glow was seen in the sky, moving slowly and then disappearing. Reappeared after five minutes. The witness knows a bit about astronomy.

- 2 August 2009 at 21:45: In the town of Kingsbridge in Devon, a low, bright light was seen.

- 4 August 2009 at 00:15: In the town of Woburn Sands in Buckinghamshire, a witness saw an orange ball in the distance, no flashing lights, no engine noise. Left suddenly.

- 4 August 2009 at 04:01: In the town of Formby in Merseyside, a large oval craft was seen, very low, and could not make out any distinguishing features. It had on it a number of red, orange, and green lights. The sighting lasted only 5–10 seconds.

- 4 August 2009 at 09:50: In the town of Poole in Dorset, a bright white fireball the size of a football flew into the kitchen and landed in a plastic carrier bag on the table. It immediately disappeared but seemed to cause an almost blinding white sheet of lightning.

- 4 August 2009 at 10:00: In the town of Brighton in East Sussex, a witness saw an orange light rising from the SE – looked like the tail from a rocket launch, like when the shuttle goes up. The object then moved north before disappearing behind clouds. Happened three times over a period of 30 minutes. Third-time bright flash.

- 4 August 2009 at 22:30: In the town of Seaford in East Sussex, a large, bright light was seen. Looked like a ball of fire or a hot air balloon.

- 5 August 2009, time unknown: In the town of Mitcham in Surrey, a witness saw four strange orange lights in the sky following each other. The lights then just disappeared. Lights are then seen again moving across the night sky. Went inside and saw the same lights in a three-prong triangle.

- 6 August 2009 at 00:30: In the town of Hassocks in East Sussex, a witness saw six moving orange balls glowing. They were following each other. One minute between them. There was no noise.

- 6 August 2009 at 21:25: In the town of Chester in Cheshire, an orb shape, glowing on the underside only, was seen. Orange colour. Orange faded, and the object looked like a black shadow.

- 6 August 2009 at 22:00: In the town of Eastcote in Middlesex, big circular orange lights were seen.

- 7 August 2009 at 10:00: In the town of Cardiff in Wales, unusual lights above Cardiff were seen travelling silently.

- 7 August 2009 at 22:00: In the Ullswater Lake District, six balloons of fire were seen over Ullswater. These UFOs moved at different speeds from each other and in different directions before burning out.

- 7 August 2009 at 22:00: In the town of Cardiff in South Glamorgon, unusual lights were seen travelling silently from West to East.

- 7 August 2009 at 22:00: In the town of Barnston in Merseyside, six to seven bright orange lights were seen moving down the Wirral peninsula from Birkenhead to Ellesmere Port. No noise. Saw a second UFO five minutes later.

- 7 August 2009 at 22:09: In the town of Wirral in Merseyside, eight orange, non-flashing lights made no sound. Round shapes.

- 7 August 2009 at 22:18: In the town of Coningsby in Lincolnshire, four wavering lights were seen hovering, taken on a video camera, and photographed.

- 7 August 2009 at 23:24: In the town of Nuneaton in Staffs, five to six objects were seen.

- 7 August 2009 at 22:45: In the town of Newport in Shropshire, a retired RAF saw two yellow lights, one above the other, in the sky. On arriving home five minutes later watched the lights disappear behind a narrow cloud bank.

- 8 August 2009, time unknown: Town unknown county unknown, two sightings were observed. Single bright yellow/white light moving fast. Second sighting in daylight: single bright yellow/white moving fast.

- 8 August 2009 at 00:05: In the town of East Kilbride in Lanarkshire, a bright orange bulb was seen. Stayed for 10 minutes, came towards him like a tornado, then disappeared.

- 8 August 2009 at 09:40: In the town of Saltcoats in Ayrshire, a very large bright, light was seen, and it made no sound.

- 8 August 2009 at 09:45: In the town of Stockport in Cheshire, a bright orange object which looked as though it was on fire was seen. Moving at a steady pace, slowed then gained altitude slowly, and disappeared into the clouds. The sighting lasted 2–3 minutes. The object was similar to a hot air balloon but had no outline or shape.

- 8 August 2009 at 20:45: Town unknown, county unknown, a bright light was seen from the northwest – lights went out, and turned towards the south.

- 8 August 2009 at 22:00: In the town of Bradford in Yorkshire, a witness saw a very bright orange ball-shaped object in the sky. No noise from objects. Went to get mobiles to take pictures and videos, but the object had just vanished.

- 8 August 2009 at 22:50: In the town of Northampton in Northamptonshire, lights coming towards me. 40–50 lights.

- 9 August 2009 at 13:30: In the town of Huddersfield in Yorkshire, one object was seen in the sky in the daytime.

- 9 August 2009 at 17:16: Town unknown, county unknown, report received from "Psychic Control Centre".

- 10 August 2009 at 17:15: In London report on behalf of her sister, who said she saw a UFO at Holborn Station.

- 10 August 2009 at 22:13: In the town of Northampton in Northamptonshire, a bright red and orange ball was seen making no

322

sound, moving faster than an aircraft. Could not find a camera in time to take photos.

- 11 August 2009 at 10:46: In the town of Rayleigh in Essex, a UFO visible for 6–7 seconds was seen. Changed direction by approx. 60 degrees downward towards the horizon before disappearing. The object was a dull brown colour with a magnitude of 3.5 to 5 and resembled a slightly luminous brown paper bag. No sound was heard.

- 11 August 2009 at 23:00: In the town of Thorpe-le-Soken in Essex, an amateur astronomer saw a meteor shower which contained something he could not explain.

- 12 August 2009 at 23:03: In the town of Morfa Nefyn in Pwllheli, a bright light shone through the window. The witness saw three lights the size of a basketball moving up/down and rotating on their own axis. Seemed to lose power after 30 seconds and vanished.

- 13 August 2009 at 16:30: In the town of Preston in Lancashire, a dog wanted to go out, went out, and I saw a UFO.

- 15 August 2009 at 20:00: In the town of Billericay in Essex, no flashing lights, an orange-looking object was seen. Looked like it was hovering, flew towards the observer's car, and faded slowly into the distance.

- 15 August 2009 at 23:50: In the town of Wimborne in Dorset, a pair of "lanterns" directly overhead, slightly faster than a plane, faster than a satellite, and slower than a meteor, were seen.

- 16 August 2009 at 23:00: In the town of Westmuir in Moray, one light, joined by another, hovering over the village was seen. No noise. One light no longer there; the other disappeared. Like a lightbulb with an orange top.

- 17 August 2009 at 03:30: In the town of Langport in Somerset, a very bright light stops and spins slowly, moves right and left, as if looking for something or taking photos, long beams of light. No sound.

- 17 August 2009 at 21:19: In the town of Newport in Gwent, a bright orange light, definitely not a plane, was seen.

- 17 August 2009 at 21:25: In the town of Altrincham in Lancashire, two bright orange lights were seen. Witnessed for about five minutes.

- 17 August 2009 at 23:00: In the town of Wythall in Birmingham emitting a large, bright orange light, much larger than normal lights on a plane/helicopter, travelling in an arc with no sound. After 10 mins light became dimmer and appeared to gain height; the light now size as normal aircraft light and disappeared.

- 19 August 2009, time unknown: In the town of Exmouth, Devon, a bright orange object was seen. Above cloud level. Travelling at a high rate of knots. Came inland from the coast over Exmouth and headed off towards Woodbury and Taunton.

- 19 August 2009 at 21:00: In the town of Northampton in Northamptonshire, a witness was carrying a camera, as is her usual practice, saw a pinpoint, a silver dot that was clearly a UFO.

- 19 August 2009 at 23:44: In the town of Withington in Lancashire, three red lights in the shape of a triangle with the nose moving forward, not a usual aircraft, suspect it was a UFO.

- 20 August 2009 at 11:45: In the town of Cliftonville in Kent, three orange orbs and two red orbs were seen.

- 20 August 2009 at 14:00: In the town of Herne Bay in Kent, a witness reported a UFO.

- 20 August 2009 at 23:00: In the town of Shebbear in Devon, a circular shape with a mixture of stars, one was getting brighter and then dimmer and disappearing for a short number of minutes. Another red light hovered around the object. The camera on the phone would not pick anything up.

- 22 August 2009, time unknown: In the town of Chesterfield in Derbyshire, lights were seen in the sky.

- 22 August 2009 time unknown: In the town of Mansfield in Nottinghamshire, a witness saw a UFO.

- 22 August 2009, time unknown: Town unknown county unknown a witness saw something strange.

- 22 August 2009 at 13:40: Town unknown, county unknown, five orange globe balls were seen.

- 22 August 2009 at 16:56: Town unknown, county unknown, a UFO was seen at the back of the sky.

- 22 August 2009 at 20:35: In the town of Harpenden in Hertfordshire, a tall and thin, like a pencil, square, blue-black object was seen.

- 22 August 2009 at 20:55: In the town of Northampton in Northamptonshire, a witness saw 40 flickering orange lights from the kitchen window. They made no noise, moved around to the side window of the house, and disappeared behind a cloud. The witness watched them for 5–10 minutes.

- 22 August 2009 at 22:00: In the town of Stevenage in Hertfordshire, two orbs/lights were seen flickering and sliding across the sky.

- 22 August 2009 at 22:20: In the town of Gerrards Cross in Buckinghamshire, around eight yellow balls of light were seen floating slowly in the night sky, slowly disappearing. Then one or two more would appear at 500 to 800 ft and follow the same line of flight. This happened for around two minutes.

- 23 August 2009 at 21:00: In the town of Skegness in Lincolnshire, a large orange light with no noise was seen.

- 24 August 2009, time unknown: In the town of Derby in Derbyshire, a witness saw a UFO.

- 24 August 2009 at 00:00: In the town of Tunbridge Wells in Kent, bright orange lights lasted for two minutes, went out, then four more. Could have been a meteorological balloon. A very bright light.

- 24 August 2009 at 03:30: In the town of Swindon in Wiltshire, three lights in formation, forming an isosceles triangle, were seen. Two lights visible at first, then joined by a third. The light lasted for 2–3 minutes. No sound.

- 24 August 2009 at 05:30: In the town of Lewes in East Sussex, a witness reported seeing a UFO.

- 24 August 2009 at 21:45: In the town of Hersham in Surrey, a large orange fireball burning for 35 seconds was seen. No noise from objects which reduced in size until nothing over the duration of their flight.

- 24 August 2009 at 23:30: In the town of Glasgow in Strathclyde, strange lights over G62 0TD were seen. Two big white lights.

- 25 August 2009 at 21:45: In the town of Derby in Derbyshire, seven aircraft over Derby were seen.

- 25 August 2009 at 23:00: In the town of Shebbear in Devon, an object was seen to get brighter and dimmer.

- 27 August 2009 at 20:15: Town unknown in East Anglia, an object came over the top of the field – red – flew very quickly like a shooting star.

- 27 August 2009 at 20:30: In the town of Dronfield in Derbyshire, a round shape was seen lightening and darkening with a dark shape behind it. No engine noise.

- 27 August 2009 at 21:29: In Manor Park in London, a witness saw a bright light heading towards Essex – bright light standing still.

- 28 August 2009 at 21:30: Town unknown county unknown, an orange ball going in a straight line was seen. No visible trail. No smoke or noise. Appeared to be getting smaller and burning itself up.

- 29 August 2009, time unknown: In the town of Sark in Guernsey, a witness saw what looked like a flying log, blue with a white edge.

- 29 August 2009, time unknown: In the town of Kings Lynn in Norfolk, extraterrestrials were seen coming from King's Lynn towards Swaffham, Norfolk.

- 29 August 2009 at 05:20: In the town of Gloucester in Gloucestershire, a witness saw a sighting in Gloucester.

- 29 August 2009 at 05:20: In the town of Gloucester, Gloucestershire, two UFOs were seen flying overhead.

- 29 August 2009 at 06:40: In the town of Bearsdsen in Glasgow, the witness has a video of a UFO with no sound.

- 29 August 2009 at 21:00: In the town of Kettering in Northamptonshire, two glowing sphere/domed-shaped objects followed each other in the southeast direction. Completely silent and not flashing at all, as you would expect from an aircraft.

- 29 August 2009 at 21:09: In the town of Plymouth in Devon, one object rising in the sky was seen. Semi-circle outline. Flames glowing orange/red. Flickering around the edge. At first, I thought it was fireworks, but then it disappeared.

- 29 August 2009 at 21:35: In the town of Yeovil in Somerset, seven lights over Yeovil were seen. No noise.

- 29 August 2009 at 21:40: In the town of Lyneham in Wiltshire, orange lights following each other in the same direction were seen. No noise, no flashing lights, same trajectory. In the vicinity of Lyneham radar. Some lights disappeared.

- 29 August 2009 at 21:47: In the town of Stratford-upon-Avon in Warwickshire, a witness saw lights, moved into view from right to left, then stopped and formed a pattern before pulsing and fading out their bright orange lights.

- 29 August 2009 at 22:05: In the town of Telford in Shropshire, twenty-two lights were seen. No noise, same speed.

- 29 August 2009 at 22:05: In the town of Smethwick in the West Midlands, a witness saw strange lights in the sky, in threes then one, then twos, then threes – Fifteen in all.

- 30 August 2009 at 09:14: In the town of Blakeney in Norfolk a red fire-like ball was seen. The glow was constant. It was travelling at a constant speed from west to east. Also watched it through binoculars and it appeared as a red circle with dots around the circle. In the 10 o'clock position and watched it for 4–5 mins.

- 30 August 2009 at 12:10: In the town of Petts Wood in Kent, a witness saw eight orange single lights in the sky. Lights were very clear, single bright orange spots which travelled at constant speed slowly higher into the eastern atmosphere. At first, four lights, in close proximity, followed by four more within approx. one minute.

- 31 August 2009 time unknown: In the town of Ashingdon Heights in Essex, approx. 10 orange lights were seen flying over. The first eight were going at a steady, slow rate, three of which merged into a triangle formation, separated, and then disappeared. Two others appeared about a minute or so travelling faster and disappeared in the same area of the sky.

- 31 August 2009 at 17:00: Town unknown in the Thames Estuary, a witness saw a vertical cylinder, silvery colour, and underneath was a great bright yellow, fiery glow. Watched the object for about 20 minutes.

- 31 August 2009 at 21:45: In the town of Twickenham in Middlesex, a ball of fire was seen in the sky.

- September 2009, time unknown: In the town of Penarth in South Wales, a very bright object was seen above the sun.

- September 2009, time unknown: In the town of Catford in London, six bright orange lights – not flashing – silent. After a few minutes, there was another one.

- September 2009 at 21:00: In the town of Sherborne in Dorset, a witness saw a very bright light – looking south to the right of the moon. It was very large. There were four or five bright lights.

- 1 September 2009 at 11:00: In the town of Inverness in Scotland, an object was seen moving very fast from SE to North and watched the object for about 10 seconds. Thought at first it was a star or a plane.

- 2 September 2009 at 00:46: In the town of Filey in Yorkshire, a brilliant and dazzling pure white horizontal ring of light was seen. It appeared to be perfectly still in the sky above the houses and was totally silent. The object was hovering over the Belle Vue Crescent area.

- 2 September 2009 at 11:00: In the town of Leeds in Yorkshire, a low-flying object was seen. Nine orange lights, no sound.

- 4 September 2009 at 23:15: In the town of Ashton Under Lyne in Greater Manchester, eight orange UFOs shone brightly, travelling at speed, low in the sky. Objects came across one by one with approx. 20 seconds between them. They stopped over the reservoir and changed direction at approx. 90-degree angle towards Holmfirth. No noise.

- 5 September 2009 at 21:40: Town unknown in Kent, a semi-circle of light, golden orange, moved off towards the east. No noise heard.

- 5 September 2009 at 21:45: In the town of Oakwood in Essex, a witness saw 25 to 30 bright orange lights in the sky – Flying in a triangular shape.

- 5 September 2009 at 22:00: In the town of Frome in Somerset fifteen to twenty bright vertical lines going slowly – no noise.

- 6 September 2009 at 22:35: In the town of East Kilbride in South Lanarkshire, a witness saw three UFOs which appeared to be composed of fiery orange light and a symmetrical vertical diamond shape. No sound.

- 8 September 2009, time unknown: In the town of Diss in Norfolk, a pink and red dome with a bright yellow light underneath was seen. For about 30 seconds.

- 8 September 2009 at 20:00: At the RAF Valley in Anglesey, two round balls were seen in the sky chasing each other.

- 9 September 2009 at 20:30: In the town of Epsom in Surrey, thirty orange globes, in four waves, travelling at a constant speed, were seen. May have been lanterns of some kind, but they would have been 1–2 metres in diameter.

- 9 September 2009 at 21:15: In the town of Old Bilsthorpe in Nottinghamshire, a witness saw orange flamed lights, in formation, slowly and silently across the night sky.

- 9 September 2009 at 21:20: In the town of Tooting in London, a black sphere was seen. Bobbing about half a mile away. Covered with a phosphorus chemical cloud. It goes light grey. A flash of lightning then reappears. Some of the clouds light up. Various sightings at 20:30 and 12:15.

- 10 September 2009 at 21:00: In the town of South Hinksey in Oxford, a witness saw a UFO. It was not a plane; it disappeared very quickly.

- 10 September 2009 at 21:05: In the town of Godalming in Surrey, an intense, bright white light was seen between the flight path of Gatwick and Heathrow.

- 10 September 2009, at 22:50: In the town of Norwich, Norfolk, a sighting was reported.

- 10 September 2009: In Glen Road near Lennoxtown, three people in a car were reportedly struck by a colourful beam of light; the event reportedly lasted for over two minutes.

- 11 September 2009 at 11:30: In the town of Charles Barn in Kent, a white fixed-wing object was seen. Flying over a field, East Street, Charles Barn. It was squared off with something behind it – no cockpit – silent not a glider.

- 11 September 2009 at 20:45: Town unknown, county unknown, a witness saw over the roof of their house an orange/gold round circle about the size of a beach ball moving from behind the house going sideways across the roof and down the road. As it moved down the road, it changed to a smaller light with no fiery glow.

- 12 September 2009 at 00:15: In the town of Cockbrook in Ashton-under-Lyme, twelve circles were seen.

- 12 September 2009 at 11:23: In the town of Belfast in Northern Ireland, three blazing gold orbs in a diagonal line in the sky were seen. No sound. Remaining static for approx. one minute before moving slowly together to form a shape like Orion's Belt and then into a small triangle. Two lights further out faded and disappeared, then the third too.

- 13 September 2009 at 20:25: In the town of Shepton Mallet in Somerset, RN Air Traffic Control saw seven silent objects emitting a bright orange light. One group of three, and then singles. Travelled at about 100 knots, then turned right.

- 12 September 2009 at 20:40: In the town of Grantham in Lincolnshire, seven objects were seen. One group of three, followed by one group of four. Orange, large, no distinct shape. Bright, no noise.

- 12 September 2009 at 20:45: In the town of St Ives in Cornwall, a witness saw a bright orange-red light in the sky. The light took several minutes before it began to dim. Its path was straight and steady, indicating perhaps powered flight.

- 12 September 2009 at 20:50: In the town of Mansfield in Nottingham, a strange red and orange object was seen in the sky.

- 17 September 2009 at 21:40: In the town of Findon Valley in West Sussex, an Ex-pilot saw an extremely bright star-like light in the sky. Continued flying then started to climb vertically with no change in speed, dimmed, and disappeared into a faint light.

- 19 September 2009 at 19:40: In the town of Bromley in Kent, a bright orange light was seen moving across the sky, made no noise.

- 19 September 2009 at 22:00: In the town of New Forest in Hampshire, a witness saw an object in the sky like a fireball. It burned pretty brightly, then would burn out a little, then appear to burn brightly again before extinguishing about thirty seconds later.

- 19 September 2009 at 22:00: In the town of Sheepridge in Huddersfield, six to eight red lights were seen moving across the skyline. Red spheres with a white centre. Eventually passed over the house from back to front.

- 19 September 2009 at 21:45: In the town of Carluke in Lanarkshire, a witness saw an orange light in the distance. It came nearer and eventually disappeared into the cloud overhead, but before it did, I saw other similar lights appearing in the distance. They were travelling at regular intervals.

- 19 September 2009 at 20:15: In the town of Watford in Hertfordshire, a witness saw three consecutive passes of single, bright yellowish lights. Moving approximately three minutes apart on the same orbit.

- 19 September 2009 at 20:15: In the town of Betws in Dyfed, a Journalist saw three objects, like bright orange tennis balls stuck together, flying across the sky.

- 19 September 2009 at 20:19: In the town of Anglesey in North Wales, an object was seen similar to an egg shape, was amber in colour, and appeared to be hovering over fields before disappearing. Five minutes later, two objects appeared in the same area, then disappeared and reappeared over the Meni Straits.

- 19 September 2009 at 20:20: In the town of Burnley in Lancashire, an orange light was seen in the sky.

- 19 September 2009 at 21:01: In the town of West Wickham in Kent, a Pilot saw a series of 30 or more orange lights, which then disappeared after moving at speed.

- 19 September 2009 at 21:35: In the town of Arbroath in Angus, a witness saw four lights travelling together. One veered off, heading East. Three remained in a triangle formation. Two disappeared into the horizon, and one light went overhead. Looked like a red fireball with no sound.

- 19 September 2009 at 22:02: Town unknown in Lanarkshire, a witness saw eight to ten lights in the sky. First, they appeared like very bright fireworks which were fired vertically into the sky. In no particular pattern stayed at the same flight level, with no engine sound. Picked up speed and disappeared. Lasted about five minutes.

- 19 September 2009 at 23:30: In the town of Letchlade in Gloucestershire, forty to fifty orange lights following the same trajectory with more lights coming over were seen.

- 20 September 2009 at 18:45: In the town of Mulbarton in Norfolk, two orbs were seen in the sky. Lead aircraft stopped dead in mid-air then backtracked for a second or two before rising directly vertically, approx. 200–500m then stopping. As the lead craft came within 50m of the other craft, both headed off into the distance.

- 20 September 2009 at 19:45: In the town of Harpley in Norfolk, two orange lights were seen travelling over Harpley village and did not flicker or flash. The distance between the lights was approx. 10m and 60 ft above ground, and there was no sound. Turned the car around, but it had disappeared.

- 20 September 2009 at 20:00: In Bristol, a red/orange light passed overhead. What looked like a gaseous golf ball with a red rotating light rotating clockwise inside it.

- 20 September 2009 at 21:00: In the town of Moreton-in-Marsh in Gloucestershire, six strange lights flew low with no sound of engines with orange, red, and other colours.

- 20 September 2009 at 23:30: In the town of Clydebank in West Dunbartonshire, a witness saw five orange lights in the sky in a line.

- 21 September 2009 at 20:55: In the town of Kenilworth in Warwickshire, a very unusual object was seen flying across the sky. The object was a cone shape with a circular top. It had an orangey/red light in the middle and an outer, see-through red/pink layer.

- 22 September 2009 at 22:30: In the town of Earlsdon in Coventry, six orange orbs floating in an arc in the sky were seen. All following the same trajectory and faded at similar points in the sky.

- 24 September 2009 at 02:12: In the town of Bradford in Yorkshire, a witness saw an object which was round and yellowish colour. Had a clear view of the sighting for about two–three minutes.

- 24 September 2009 at 21:55: Town unknown, county unknown, an Ex-RAF saw fifteen to twenty very bright orange lights travelling about a mile apart and in a perfectly straight line.

- 24 September 2009 at 23:40: In the town of Hednesford in Staffordshire, a large orange light was seen. It stopped for several minutes and then disappeared.

- 25 September 2009 at 20:45: In the town of Long Melford in Suffolk, a pulsating/shimmering object was seen flashing red, blue, and green.

- 26 September 2009 at 12:00: In the town of High Peak in Derbyshire, eight orange lights were seen over the top of a house.

- 26 September 2009 at 19:22: In the town of Chatham in Kent, two orange balls of light were seen. One ball of light was leading, with the other two behind it. No sound of any engines.

- 26 September 2009 at 20:00: In the town of Tattershall in Lincolnshire, three separate orange lights with no sound hovered for approx. 40 minutes, then blanked out of sight.

- 26 September 2009 at 20:50: In the town of Ditton in Kent, three bright orange/red lights were seen, followed by another three.

- 26 September 2009 at 21:22: In the town of Peterborough, loads of lights coming over the village were seen gaining height very quickly.

- 26 September 2009 at 21:30: In the town of Cradley Heath in the West Midlands, seven lights were seen.

- 26 September 2009 at 21:50: In the town of Formby in Lancashire, a large luminous, pulsating object was seen changing colour and shape.

- 26 September 2009 at 22:00: In the town of Grangemouth in Stirlingshire, two bright orange objects were seen. One from the south at ferocious speed, then dead halt with others. Not man-made; no sound.

- 26 September 2009 at 22:15: At Gatwick Airport in Sussex, five UFOs, two miles to the northeast of Gatwick, were seen. They all shot up in the sky and disappeared one by one.

- 26 September 2009 at 22:30: In the town of Letchworth in Hertfordshire, an orange object in the sky was seen getting higher and higher; it looked like a plastic bag with a flame in the middle. Round and glowing. Stopped in the middle of the sky and disappeared.

- 26 September 2009 at 22:30: In the town of Farncombe in Surrey, two orange/red dots were seen in the sky. Seemed to be still but slowly moved adjacent to one another. One then disappeared, followed about a minute later by the other.

- 26 September 2009 at 22:32: In the town of Matlock in Derbyshire, a witness saw three orange lights, then as they rounded a corner, saw five in formation. No noise.

- 27 September 2009 at 11:15: In the town of Deal in Kent, a silver object was seen in the sky over Deal.

- 27 September 2009 at 19:40: In the town of Lincoln in Lincolnshire, the witness could not see a defined shape, but no noise, and no rear, port, or starboard lights were seen. Two coned lights (yellow and white) flickering randomly. Finally disappeared into the clouds.

- 27 September 2009 at 20: In the town of Northolt in Middlesex, a RAF saw two UFOs. They looked like balls of fire. As they approached RAF

Northolt, the fireball went out. However, the craft was still visible and was in the shape of a jellyfish dome.

- 27 September 2009 at 21:15: In the town of Maghull in Liverpool, a perfect rectangle the length of a car but 3 ft wide. It started swaying and then swooped like a bird. The witness followed it through the town.

- 29 September 2009 at 20:10: In the town of Connah's Quay in Flintshire, a bright orange light was seen 1 cm deep, joined by a second light, no sound.

- 1 October 2009, time unknown: In the town of Chippenham in Wiltshire, lights not sure what number were seen.

- 1 October 2009, time unknown: On the M1 South, a very sharp turn in the jet stream, very sharp for an aircraft, and very high up, like a usual airliner height, was seen.

- 2 October 2009 at 20:45: In the town of Hastings in East Sussex, a witness saw eight orange lights on an oblong-shaped object, but no noise.

- 3 October 2009, time unknown: In the town of Woking in Surrey, eight lights at intervals were seen slowly flying.

- 3 October 2009, time unknown: Town unknown in Kent, a little moon thing was seen.

- 3 October 2009 at 21:50: In the town of Hove in East Sussex, two bright objects were seen. Disk-shaped with a red light that goes orange and then back. On one of them, the light went on and off, and then they both went out. It looked like there was only one light on the ship.

- 4 October 2009, time unknown: Town unknown in the South Pennines, bright orange lights were seen in the sky.

- 4 October 2009, time unknown: In the town of Stonehaven in Aberdeenshire, white and red lights were seen moving around.

- 4 October 2009, time unknown: In the town of Chipping Sodbury in Bristol, a ball of fire shot across the sky over her house.

- 4 October 2009 at 19:25: In the town of Halesowen in the West Midlands, two orange glows were seen travelling quite fast, one in front of the other. Turned sharply and formed what appeared to be a triangular or arrow shape.

- 4 October 2009 at 19:45: In the town of Tiptree in Essex, fire was seen in the sky, orange, moving slowly, hovered, the flames went out, and it was 45 degrees from the ground.

- 4 October 2009 at 20:30: In the town of Pudsey in Leeds, an incredibly bright light was seen in the sky. At first light was white but changed to a bright orange. Appeared to be big and pulsating and followed him. Light shot across the sky and then disappeared.

- 5 October 2009 time unknown: In the town of Cardiff in South Glamorgon, two objects were seen in the sky.

- 5 October 2009, time unknown: Town unknown in Sussex, two bright lights hovered, then turned north and headed inland.

- 8 October 2009 at 01:55: In the town of Luton in Bedfordshire, red and green lights were seen in the sky with twinkles underneath. 3–4 minutes hovering, shot up and came back down, and hovered then shot off. Strange noises recorded on the witness's mobile phone.

- 8 October 2009 at 23:00: In the town of Southgate in London, three red/orange lights in the shape of a triangle were seen. Moved silently with an exhaust-type, object coming from it.

- 9 October 2009 at 21:45: In the town of Edinburgh in Midlothian, no details were given.

- 10 October 2009 at 12:20: In the town of Widnes in Cheshire, fourteen objects were seen, one every minute, no sound.

- 10 October 2009 at 18:00: In the town of Willsbridge in Bristol, a witness observed three objects in the sky for about 10 minutes. Appeared stationary and then disappeared behind clouds. Changed shape from cigar to round. Were red or white in colour.

- 10 October 2009 at 18:00: In the town of Glasgow in Pollock, four lights were seen moving around the sky, moving in a formation for over an hour.

- 10 October 2009 at 19:10: In the town of Huddersfield in West Yorkshire, a bright orange light was seen travelling slowly.

- 10 October 2009 at 20:12: In the town of Kirkcaldy in Fife, a bright orange glow was seen at the top of Rabbie Brae; it hovered near Victoria Hospital and went up to the sky.

- 10 October 2009 at 20:45: In the town of Edinburgh in Midlothian, two objects were seen making no sound. One object three weeks ago.

- 10 October 2009 at 23:10: In the town of Beaumaris in Anglesey, two triangular orange lights were seen about 10 seconds apart.

- 10 October 2009 at 23:15: In the town of Aberdeen in Aberdeenshire, nine red lights over the North Sea in a V formation were seen, then they disappeared, then came back and were there for some time.

- 11 October 2009 at 14:39: In the town of Crosby in Liverpool, a triangle shape was seen with an orange ball in the middle, no noise.

- 11 October 2009 at 19:45: In the town of Gilberdyke in East Yorkshire, 14 balls of light, no formation, no noise.

- 11 October 2009 at 22:00: Town unknown in Wigan White, an arrow shape was seen with green lights, moving slowly.

- 12 October 2009, time unknown: In the Reservoir in London, objects were seen to land in the reservoir.

- 12 October 2009 at 20:35: In the town of Plymouth in Dorset, an orange light that was a round shape, solid in the middle, and straight was seen.

- 13 October 2009 at 10:00: In the town of Birchington in Kent, bright lights were seen moving closer.

- 16 October 2009 at 00:25: In the town of Kirkaldy in Fife, orange lights were seen front and back, with white lights chasing what sounded like fireworks but no flashes.

- 16 October 2009 at 15:00: In the town of Saffron Walden in Essex, a strange cluster of objects was seen at high altitude flying close together towards London.

- 16 October 2009 at 19:00: In the town of Gargrave in Skipton, three red and orange lights were seen making no noise.

- 16 October 2009 at 19:25: In the town of Shah Delf near Oldham, a slow-pulsing orange light with three lots of lights was seen moving slowly and silently.

- 16 October 2009 at 20:20: In the town of March in Cambridgeshire, seven orange and red lights were seen not moving; they had no shape and disappeared one after another.

- 16 October 2009 at 22:30: In the town of West Drayton in Middlesex, a light the size of a star made erratic movements and looped, then went out of sight, reappeared, and did a further loop.

- 17 October 2009 at 18:45: In the town of Leith in Edinburgh, fourteen objects that were a yellowy-orange colour were seen. Then the witness saw another 8–9 objects. No sound. Not on the same flight trajectory.

- 17 October 2009 at 19:15: Town unknown, county unknown, the witness saw approx. 24 objects.

- 17 October 2009 at 21:00: In the town of Stockton-on-Tees in Cleveland, a large orange burning object was seen.

- 17 October 2009 at 22:45: In the town of Orpington in Kent, twenty-five lights, red and orange with a vapour trail, disappearing into blue-green colours, spinning, were seen.

- 17 October 2009 at 23:35: In the town of Enfield in London, no details were given.

- 17 October 2009 at 23:50: In the town of Warburton in Cheshire, two orange glowing lights were seen in the sky high above Warburton Toll Bridge – strange shapes like a no. 7, fuzzy, and close together. No sound.

- 18 October 2009, time unknown: On the A81 to Strathblane, three orange lights appeared, and then disappeared behind clouds. Further orange light disappeared again.

- 18 October 2009 at 19:00: In the town of Gee Cross in Cheshire, an orange/yellow bright light travelled fast across the sky, followed by another within 30 secs and repeated around ten times. Three balls of light – one on top, two on either side. No sound.

- 18 October 2009 at 20:25: In the town of West Ealing in London, an orange object was seen moving across the sky, flickering.

- 18 October 2009 at 22:30: Town unknown in Merseyside, two orange lights were seen making no noise, one disappeared; one static hovered, then went away, came back, and went away again.
- 18 October 2009 at 22:34: Town unknown, county unknown, an object was seen; it wasn't flashing; it moved across below cloud, then dropped down to the ground, then disappeared.

- 19 October 2009 at 21:00: In the town of Alton in Staffordshire, strange light activity was seen and lots of helicopters, unusual for the area.

- 21 October 2009 at 12:12: In the town of Flookburgh in Cumbria, a strange object was seen in the sky over the sea, far away so difficult to define.

- 22 October 2009 at 19:35: In the town of Whitehaven in Cumbria, two orange balls were seen. No sound. No strobe lights.

- 23 October 2009 at 19:04: In the town of Rotherham in South Yorkshire, a glowing object-like an aircraft on fire from low down over the town centre rising fast and straight up in a straight line across town was seen.

- 23 October 2009 at 21:30: In the town of Leverton in Boston, two to four dancing lights with no density to them were seen.

- 23 October 2009 at 22:06: In the town of Yeovil in Somerset, a metallic ball was seen in the sky, chased by a fast jet and then a helicopter from Yeovilton.

- 23 October 2009 at 23:38: In the town of Brigstock in Northamptonshire, a bright orangey-red light lit from one end to the other was seen making no noise, approx. 40–50 feet long.

- 26 October 2009 at 17:15: In the town of Eastbourne in Brighton, what looked like a flying bonfire, or similar to a plane on fire, too dark for a balloon was seen.

- 26 October 2009 at 17:35: In the town of Kirkby in Liverpool, three bright orange objects hovered for five minutes before ascending straight up into the sky. Strangely shaped.

- 26 October 2009 at 17:46: In the town of Bolton in Lancashire, red and orange lights were seen high in the sky moving slowly; numerous sightings over several weeks.

- 26 October 2009 at 20:30: In the town of Malton in Yorkshire, strange lights were seen in the sky.

- 27 October 2009 at 19:40: In the town of Hamilton in Lanarkshire, two fiery red flame-like objects hovered about and then disappeared.

- 27 October 2009 at 21:10: In the town of Chesterfield in Derbyshire, bright orange spheres were seen; they got smaller the further away they went.

- 27 October 2009 at 23:10: In the town of Barlborough in Derbyshire, lights were seen in the sky, no object. Orbs with trails following, moving in a circular direction. Four orbs, two following the other two, reaching a point, then repeating the sequence.

- 28 October 2009, time unknown: In the town of Alvaston in Derbyshire, two glowing crosses 50 metres apart were silent. More 5 to 6 minutes later, intelligent craft.

- 28 October 2009, time unknown: In the town of Derby in Derbyshire, a Journalist reported seeing a UFO; no description was provided.

- 28 October 2009 at 17:50: In the town of Evesham in Worcestershire, an airborne craft with non-conform lighting was seen. It was a steady strong orange colour.

- 28 October 2009 at 19:20: In the town of Warbleton in East Sussex, 10–12 orange lights were seen in a row with no sound.

- 28 October 2009 at 19:30: In the town of Bensford in Staffordshire, one orange light not flashing and three in a triangle formation were seen.

- 28 October 2009 at 20:00: In the town of Charnock Richard in Lancashire ten flaming balls of fire were seen.

- 28 October 2009 at 21:10: In the town of Salcombe in Devon, three to four silent aircraft, three leading and one trailing, with bright red lights.

- 28 October 2009 at 21:18: In the town of Hampton Court, SW of London, a bright orange glow arched over him appeared for 15 seconds, then went upwards.

- 29 October 2009, time unknown: In the town of Norwich, Norfolk, a large orange ball was seen making no noise or flashing.

- 30 October 2009 at 17:47: In the town of Great Barr in Birmingham, a really bright light, jellyfish-shaped object was seen.

- 31 October 2009, time unknown: In the town of Maesteg in Bridgend, an orange-red sphere giving off light moved up into the clouds without making any noise.

- 31 October 2009 at 17:35: In the town of Netherton in Liverpool, a large spherical ball looked like it was on fire; small objects dropped from it, then flew away.

- 31 October 2009 at 18:25: In the town of Leicester in Leicestershire, a bright orange, glowing triangular shape was seen. It was very bright; it flew up into the sky, and it was silent.

- 31 October 2009 at 19:30: In the town of Huddersfield in West Yorkshire, a bright burning white light continued at a steady pace, glowing bright orange and visible in the distance. It could have been fireworks, but possibly not.

- 31 October 2009 at 19:49: In the town of Diss in Norfolk, a witness saw a UFO but left no description.

- 31 October 2009 at 20:00: In the town of Birmingham in the West Midlands, a strange orange shape was seen in the sky, pulsating top half less bright and silent.

- 31 October 2009 at 20:20: In the town of Llynfi Valley in Mid-Glamorgan, an orange oval UFO was seen passing by.

- 31 October 2009 at 20:30: In the town of Winchburgh in West Lothian, a cylindrical shape, flying low, silent, with two large red navigation lights on its body, flashing red strobe lights, then disappeared from view.

- 31 October 2009 at 20:52: In the town of Derby in Derbyshire, a circle with yellow and white lights was seen.

- 31 October 2009 at 22:00: In the town of Westbury in Wiltshire, a circular bright light was seen. It was definitely not a helicopter.

- 31 October 2009 at 22:45: In the town of Norton Canes in Cannock, six objects, five large red balls, no lights moving steadily one behind the other, for 10–15 minutes. Sixth, twice as big.

- 31 October 2009 at 23:15: In the town of Hove in Sussex, five large round orange balls of lights in a formation were seen. Two fronts, one middle, two at the back, no sound.

- 31 October 2009 at 23:15: In the town of Bosham in Chichester, three UFOs that were sun bright and orange, looked like flames, and had sort of wings were seen. The first two were 2–3 miles apart; later one was 10 miles to the rear all going to the right with no sound.

- 31 October 2009 at 23:15: Town unknown, county unknown, an orange light was seen; it made no noise and appeared for around 8 minutes.

- 31 October 2009 at 23:58: In the town of Gravesend in Kent, a yellow assortment of lights that were much brighter than an average star were seen.

- 1 November 2009 at 01:46: In the town of Glasgow in Strathclyde, a large orange object was seen.

- 1 November 2009 at 12:31: In the town of Humberston, NE of Lincs six lights, in a S shape were seen. They were misty in the sky, and the ground was clear; they gradually disappeared.

- 1 November 2009 at 17:44: In the town of Beckenham in Greater London, three orange objects were seen, and then four more joined them.

- 1 November 2009 at 19:35: In the town of Leeds, orange circular lights were seen going very fast towards the west to Leeds centre.

- 1 November 2009 at 19:40: In the town of Matlock in Derbyshire, a very bright light was seen in the sky changing to green, no noise.

- 2 November 2009 at 23:20: In the town of Kensal Green in London, a Police Sergeant saw a UFO but provided no description.

- 3 November 2009 at 16:15: In the town of Bristol in Avon, a clear and bright object long, bluish-white light with a narrow tail and a fast, gradual descent.

- 3 November 2009 at 19:20: In the town of Clacton in Essex, a single object full of lights approximately the same size as 10 planes, the object made no noise. Lights were seen to dim and change colour, with some turning off. The object was described as a straight line of lights with a "U" shape attached underneath.

- 3 November 2009 at 19:10: In the town of Pontefract in West Yorkshire, what looked like a balloon or lantern was seen. It was hollow, with bright orange light inside.

- 3 November 2009 at 21:03: In the town of Tipton in the West Midlands, a bright red light with no engine noise was seen glowing brightly and then faded.

- 4 November 2009 at 18:45: In the town of Cannock in Staffordshire, a bright white light was seen blinking on and off every 2–3 seconds, stayed for 2–4 minutes, and then disappeared.

- 5 November 2009, time unknown: Town unknown county unknown, a UFO was reported; it was definitely not a firework; it was the third time he has seen a UFO but the first time he has reported it.

- 5 November 2009, time unknown: In the town of Peterlee, NE of England, 12 orange lights are silent but seen moving fast.

- 5 November 2009, time unknown: In the town of Featherstone in West Yorkshire, a ball of fire was seen moving across the sky, white hot at one end, moving for too long to be a firework.

- 5 November 2009, time unknown: In the town of Bolton in Lancashire, a bright orange light was seen moving fast across the sky, appeared lots of times and moved in directions that cannot be explained.

- 5 November 2009 at 19:00: In the town of Bolton in Manchester, a UFO appeared several times during the night.

- 5 November 2009 at 19:34: In the town of Pontarddulais in Swansea, silent, off-red, blood-orange colour, and the entire sphere emitted light. No spotlights. The light remained constant and didn't flicker. The witness saw this for four minutes.

- 5 November 2009 at 19:45: In the town of Newton Grange in Mid-Lothian, 21–22 high-flying objects shining red at even intervals for around 15 minutes were seen.

- 5 November 2009 at 23:55: In the town of Burwarton in Bridgnorth, a big orange ball was seen moving slowly.

- 5 November 2009 at 18:30: In the town of Stockport, an amber glowing ball quarter the size of the moon's diameter dimmed to nothing and then vanished was seen.

- 5 November 2009 at 18:35: In the town of Bourne in Lincolnshire, four UFOs, three close together and one behind, with a bright red glow around a light with a glow on the bottom. No noise was close.

- 5 November 2009 at 20:10: In the town of Leigh in Lancashire, a large triangle structure with red light in each corner, red with fire in the middle was seen.

- 6 November 2009, time unknown: In the town of Crawley in East Sussex orange lights were seen in the sky moving slowly and then fading away.

- 6 November 2009 at 18:00: In the town of Ironbridge in Shropshire, eight sightings, not Chinese lanterns; the witness saw one more a week later.

- 6 November 2009 at 23:00: In the town of Heckmondwike in West Yorkshire, a formation of six bright orange lights was seen in the sky. One minute behind were two more, then one more, and the last was much bigger and brighter.

- 7 November 2009, time unknown: Town unknown, county unknown, two bright orange lights were seen.

- 7 November 2009, time unknown: Town unknown in South Africa, a flat object was seen in the sky moving at a rate of knots, looked strange.

- 7 November 2009 at 08:45: In Central London, the witness saw several very bright lights flying and drifting quickly and silently up in the sky. They were bright, flickering, tiny white, green, and light red lights. I counted at least 10–15; some seemed to be drifting in groups and others separately.

- 7 November 2009 at 18:50: In the town of South Birmingham in the West Midlands, two orange glowing orbs silently travelling in a straight line, not travelling fast and in tandem. Disappeared over the Moseley area. Not fireworks.

- 7 November 2009 at 19:20: In the town of Colchester in Essex, four slow-moving round orange lights, completely silent, seemed to turn white and were pulsing.

- 7 November 2009 at 20:00: Town unknown, county unknown, six orange lights not fireworks were seen.

- 7 November 2009 at 20:30: In the town of Tring in Hertfordshire, a reddish-amber bright object was seen flying across the sky.

- 7 November 2009 at 21:00: In the town of Cusworth in Doncaster, a witness saw a UFO. It was definitely not a Chinese lantern.

- 7 November 2009 at 21:35: In the town of Hemel Hempstead in Hertfordshire, two red bright lights, but not glowing, were seen.

- 7 November 2009 at 21:59: In the town of Peterborough in Cambridgeshire, an Ex-RN Cdr saw an orange sphere 30 degrees above the eastern horizon. The speed was substantial, no noise, no normal navigation lights, just an eerie orange glow.

- 7 November 2009 at 22:00: In the town of Peterborough in Cambridgeshire, a UFO was reported, but no details/description were given.

- 7 November 2009 at 22:00: In the town of Callander in Perthshire, up to 20 individual orange lights were static for 15 seconds before tilting and then moved off.

- 7 November 2009 at 23:30: In the town of Gillingham in Kent, two UFOs, bright orange lights appeared from nowhere, faster than a plane.

- 8 November 2009 at 00:10: In the town of Oswestry in Shropshire, an orange light was seen. It was not a firework.

- 8 November 2009 at 18:10: In the town of Porthcawl in Mid-Glamorgan, a UFO was reported but no description was provided.

- 8 November 2009 at 19:00: In the town of Ipswich, Suffolk, a UFO was reported, but no description was provided.

- 8 November 2009 at 19:12: In the town of Telford in Shropshire, two orange lights were seen moving slowly south. No sound, not jet afterburners, not helicopters, as they did not flash. Wrong colour for distress rockets.

- 8 November 2009 at 19:15: In the town of Maidenhead in Berkshire, a fiery ball, with no flashing lights and variable speeds, disappeared into a star and was red and burning.

- 8 November 2009 at 20:00: In the town of Leicester in Leicestershire, three lights were seen in the sky in 5 x 3 groups of disc shapes in a triangle formation.

- 9 November 2009 at 15:55: In the town of Port Talbot in Bryn Valley, an orange-yellow UFO was seen with no contrails, and no hazard lights flashing.

- 9 November 2009 at 17:10: In the town of Whitley Bay in Tyne and Wear, an orange ball shape going across the sky on a flight path was seen. Silent. The witness was so concerned they called 999.

- 9 November 2009 at 19:23: In the town of Plympton in Devon, a red and orange sphere half the size of the moon, no noise, but bits were falling off it, tracked it for 20 seconds, and saw a plane four minutes later which might have seen it.

- 10 November 2009 at 17:00: In the town of Nottingham in West Bridgford, seven orangish orbs were seen floating over houses in formation.

- 10 November 2009 at 18:00: In the town of Glasgow in Pollock, four lights were seen moving around in a circle over and over again for more than an hour.

- 11 November 2009 at 17:30: In Glasgow, a kaleidoscope effect of lights was seen above the building.

- 11 November 2009 at 20:45: In the town of Edenbridge in Kent, a very bright yellow in the centre surrounded by an orange outer edge, and a fat boomerang on its side with a fire glow inside. Totally silent and 30–40 ft across.

- 12 November 2009 at 20:30: In Northumberland, two very bright, large lights, one higher than the other. The lower one then disappeared and reappeared above the higher one; they swapped sides and then evened out to the same level. They disappeared when a plane came into view.

- 14 November 2009 at 06:55: In the town of Haddenham in Cambridgeshire, a large bright white light, no trailing light rays groundward, so not a police helicopter or aircraft heading for Mildenhall. And no sound or vibration.

- 14 November 2009 at 18:05: In the town of Shrewsbury in Shropshire, a bright light was seen hovering in the sky. Three parts, one of which was red, appeared for 45 minutes before it disappeared.

- 14 November 2009 at 23:30: In the town of Ellesmere Port in Wirral, seven to eight bright orange flame lights were seen in the sky, not planes or helicopters, with no noise, moved fast, then disappeared.

- 15 November 2009 at 02:00: In the town of Milford-On-Sea in Hampshire, a tiny speck of light over Southampton direction, was seen. It was seen twice by binoculars. The N/NE explosion and bang, but not thunder, lightning, or fireworks, lasted 30 seconds.

- 16 November 2009 at 20:00: Town unknown in North Yorkshire, two small red lights were seen moving across the sky like fighter jets, but not a fighter jet, reappeared again an hour later.

- 19 November 2009, time unknown: In the town of Rumney in Cardiff, four lights whirling about above the nature reserve were seen.

- 19 November 2009 at 22:20: In the town of Hollerton in Bradford, a small ball of fire was seen.

- 20 November 2009 at 23:20: In the town of Castleford in Yorkshire, a mushroom-shaped light was seen (like a balloon blowing in the wind) being tracked by three brightly lit aircraft, saw approx. 6–7 mushroom shapes and four aircraft. Couldn't hear any engines.

- 22 November 2009 at 00:00: In the town of Farnham in Surrey, a witness saw a bright red and orange object. There was no noise or boom. Believe it was probably a meteor.

- 25 November 2009 at 19:15: In the town of Long Marston in Yorkshire, ten unidentified lights were seen in the sky. They appeared for five minutes, one after the other.

- 25 November at 09 21:20: In the town of Doncaster in Yorkshire, a witness saw a very large, bright orange ball of fire travelling over woodland. There was no sound. Its size would have been 20 to 30 times bigger than a jumbo jet.

- 26 November 2009 at 21:50: In the town of Wymondham in Norfolk, two large orange circular objects were seen crossing the sky at an equal distance apart, uniform speed, not shimmering, larger than a plane, and half a metre in diameter.

- 28 November 2009 at 01:55: In the town of Blackline Hill in Northamptonshire, lights were seen in the sky going up and down for the last half hour.

- 28 November 2009 at 21:00: In the town of Witney in Oxfordshire, a very bright orange light was seen in the sky around 9 pm. It has appeared four times recently, not a plane, and no other explanation other than UFO.

- 29 November 2009 at 00:25: In the town of Hill Green in Cheshire, two orange lights were seen moving slowly over Wilmslow, veering off in a different direction. No noise and flashing flights, not aircraft.

- 30 November 2009 at 19:40: In the town of Wilnecote in Staffordshire, a strange orange light was seen coming from the North, clear night, no port and starboard indicators, translucent halo, lasted 1 min 20 secs, constant speed, straight line.

2013

- 13 July 2013: An Airbus A320 pilot encounters an object closing in on his passenger plane, which passes extremely close to the cockpit whilst flying at 34,000 ft above Berkshire. With no time to make an evasive manoeuvre, the captain instinctively ducked as he believed a collision was imminent.

Conclusion

I believe in extra-terrestrial life, but the question is, after reading these witness statements, do you believe no matter your answer to this question, always remember that…the truth is out there.

Echoes of Revolution

Listen
Can you hear the beating of the drums
Can you hear the firing of the distant guns
Can you smell the blood thick in the air
Can you smell their discontent and their despair

Listen
Can you hear the symphony of their sorrow souls
Can you hear the crunching of their withered bones
Can you see the blackened boots marching through the streets
Can you see that there will be no peace

Listen
Can you hear the cries of your fellow man
Can you feel the warmth of his heart pounding in your hand
Can you see the streets filled with rage
Can you see the people breaking free from this cage

Listen
Can you hear the raging of the storm
Can you see we unite as one a hero born
Can you feel the fire spreading
Can you see where we are heading

Listen
Can you see the barricades rise
Can you see we have no fear in our eyes
Can you feel the masses waking from their slumber
Can you hear our voices increasing in number

Listen
Can you see our banners raised
Can you see we are not fazed
Can you hear our voices now
Can you see how we avow

Listen
Can you see your order crumble
Can you see your tyranny crumple
Can you hear the dust settling on a new dawn now emerging
Can you hear the revolution inspiring justice now converging

I listened to the beating of those drums
I listened to the firing of those distant guns
I saw the revolution begin
It's embedded deep within me underneath my very skin

by Joshua Whittaker